IN HER OWN WORDS . . .

"It all started when I was told that I had a gift.
The gods are Yankee traders. There are no gifts.
Everything has a price, and in bitter moments I
have been tempted to cry 'Usury!'

"It is true that I have lived with nerves
exposed. My pulse has raced in endless crisis.
My gullibility has begged for treachery. But
there is the positive side to the story. . . ."

Bette Davis

THE LONELY LIFE

THE LONELY LIFE

AN AUTOBIOGRAPHY

BETTE DAVIS

BERKLEY BOOKS, NEW YORK

"Tears and Laughter Abound as Industry Remembers Bette Davis" is reprinted courtesy of *The Hollywood Reporter* © The Hollywood Reporter.

"I Wish You Love"
French words and music by Charles Trenet.
English lyrics by Albert A. Beach.
Copyright © 1946, 1955, 1956, 1973 by Editions Salabert, France. Sole selling agent MCA Music Publishing, a division of MCA, Inc., New York, New York 10019 for U.S.A. and Canada. Used by Permission.
All rights reserved.

THE LONELY LIFE

A Berkley Book / published by arrangement with
the author

PRINTING HISTORY
G. P. Putnam's Sons edition published 1962
Published simultaneously in the Dominion of Canada by Longmans, Canada Limited, Toronto
Berkley edition / November 1990

ISBN: 0-425-12350-2

A BERKLEY BOOK ® TM 757,375
Berkley Books are published by The Berkley Publishing Group, 200 Madison Avenue, New York, New York 10016.
The name "Berkley" and the "B" logo are trademarks belonging to Berkley Publishing Corporation.

PRINTED IN THE UNITED STATES OF AMERICA

10 9 8 7 6 5 4 3 2 1

My darling Ruthie,

This book I dedicate to you, my mother. Without your belief in me, this story would have been a different one.

I am so sad you are not alive to read what I have written. Were you, once and for all you would know, even though I told you so many times, that without you this famed and often "de-famed" creature known as Bette Davis, would never have materialized.

You will always be in the front row.

Pinky

New York City
April 25, 1962

I attribute the enormous research, the persistence of putting together the pieces of this very "crossed"-word puzzle which comprises my life, to Sandford Dody.

Without him this book could never have been! His understanding of my reluctance to face the past was his most valuable contribution. We were collaborators in every sense of the word.

—BETTE DAVIS

March 8, 1962

CHAPTER

1

I have always been driven by some distant music—a battle hymn no doubt—for I have been at war from the beginning. I rode into the field with sword gleaming and standard flying. I was going to conquer the world.

When the war was won, I knew the triumph of standing victorious over my own dead body, for there among the vanquished, I found a woman lying at my feet. A gold band and a silver thimble on her left hand. Against my full regalia, she had been defenseless.

With my passion for order, I tidied up the battlefield and buried her with full military honors. I even wrote her epitaph. It is the most honorable I know. HERE LIES RUTH ELIZABETH DAVIS . . . 1908–1961 . . . SHE DID IT THE HARD WAY.

I've never looked back before. I've never had the time and it has always seemed so dangerous. To look back is to relax one's vigil.

Any vogue has always bored me. I find no exception in the now stylish trip to the inner world of the psyche where Mama and Papa are the villains of one's life. I could never afford this kind of vacation into self-pity and the transference of one's mistakes to another. This is Pass-the-Buck-Land and it is a desert.

As I piece things together and see my life up to now, I refuse to yield to that vogue. Whatever I did, I did. My mistakes are mine. I, alone, am responsible.

If you hate your parents for willing you buck teeth, have them fixed or become a comic—only keep quiet about it.

My father's cavalier disappearance from our home when I was a small child certainly has significance. Consider my quartette of marriages. But his hypothetical perfection as a father might have bound me to him and spoiled other men for me.

I only know that when Mother told me that Father was gone, I said, "Now we can go on a picnic and have a baby."

But why waste time hating your father when he had a father who had a father? The die was cast when Daddy left us. My sister Bobby's world went up in smoke. Mine shifted on its axis. It's as simple as that.

At thirty I learned what it means to be responsible for the outcome of the show. You must set the tempo, chart the course. You are a star.

If you aim high, the pygmies will jump on your back and tug at your skirts. The people who call you a driving female will come along for the ride. If they weigh you down, you will fight them off. It is then that you are called a bitch.

I do not regret one professional enemy I have made. Any actor who doesn't dare to make an enemy should get out of the business. I worked for my career and I'll protect it as I would my children—every inch of the way. I do not regret the dust I've kicked up. I always fought people my own size and more often than not they were bigger.

My father is not the star of my drama—nor my mother, my sister, those brothers Warner or my husbands four. They helped and they hindered, but the spark that was Bette Davis was there from the beginning. It emerged in Lowell, Massachusetts, during a thunderstorm. It is true that the spark was fanned by events into something else—but it could never have been snuffed out.

How strange it is, writing this book and going back. Rushing past a cavalcade of Bettes, each younger, each surer of herself, each purer . . . simpler . . . a mist of blond puritanism . . . smaller . . . shyer . . . tinier.

It was true about the thunderstorm. Ruthie said the gods were going mad and the earth was holding its head in a panic.

The offstage noises were deafening. Thank God, I didn't have a line at my entrance.

I happened between a clap of thunder and a streak of lightning. It almost hit the house and destroyed a tree out front. As a child I fancied that the Finger of God was directing the attention of the world to me. Further and divine proof—from the stump of that tree—that one should never point.

My Episcopal Minister Uncle Paul detected a note of blasphemy in this conceit and my Baptist grandfather took to his bed; but I was undisturbed by the unanimous rejection of my fantasy. I always felt special—part of a wonderful secret. I was always going to be somebody. I didn't know exactly what at first—perhaps the beautiful nurse in the Red Cross posters immaculately extending her hand of mercy to the world—but when my dream became clear, I followed it.

A woman has to fly high and fight to reach the top. She tires and needs a resting place. She should travel light—unburdened—but I've always done things the hard way. If I fell in love, I married. Had I been a European, I would have managed things differently. The deflowering of New England was unthinkable to this passionate Pilgrim.

I wanted to be married. I wanted a home. Ruthie, Bobby and I hadn't had one since I was seven years old. We were on the move for years—gypsies. Small wonder that when I could, I acquired houses as other women acquire jewels.

A nest was always being improvised. My dressing rooms in the theatre were immediately decorated. Pictures were hung and familiar sentimental objects were strewn about to give an air of continuity. My bungalow at Warners was a mansion. It had everything but a ghost and a six-hundred-year-old lawn.

Even on one-night stands, the pattern remains unchanged. Bits of fabric that "may brighten the place up" . . . dog-eared volumes I couldn't possibly have time to read again . . . choice pieces of china and brass which only crowd the tiny rooms. Favorite cigarette boxes and ashtrays have followed me around the world. I am a nester—and I've always found myself out on a limb.

It all started when I was told that I had a gift. The gods are Yankee traders. There are no gifts. Everything has a price, and in bitter moments I have been tempted to cry "Usury!"

It is true that I have lived with nerves exposed. My pulse

has raced in endless crisis. My gullibility has begged for treachery. But there is the positive side to the story. I have also marveled at life and exulted in struggle. I have never lost my initial wonder. To be aware that you're part of the flow—part of the whole miracle—is overwhelming.

Obviously, I have lived in a permanent state of rapture. I was never able to share it with a mate. It exhausted them. I evidently drove them mad; but I was as helpless as they. Once you've heard the sound of that distant music, you're deaf to everything else.

The Yankee in me is still appalled by my repeated attempts at marriage. Knowing that I failed at the impossible doesn't help. My mistake was the repeated trying.

What can you do when newspapers call your husband "Mr. Davis"? How helpless and yielding can a woman be when her weekly salary exceeds his annual income? What Mrs. could I have been to avoid this?

It is true that I never should have married, but I didn't want to live without a man. Brought up to respect the conventions, love had to end in marriage. I'm afraid it did.

Morality to me is honesty, integrity, character. Old-fashioned words straight from Emerson, Thoreau, my grandmother. There are new words now that excuse everyone. Give me the good old days of heroes and villains. The people you can bravo or hiss. There was a truth to them that all the slick credulity of today cannot touch. People love their mavericks in the grand manner. The blacks and the whites. How wonderful it would be to know again where we stand and which side we're on.

The cornerstone of my career in films was the power for action with which all women identified. When I portrayed evil on the screen, the women of the world were purged of suppressed violence and sheer boredom. In Spain, I've always been known as *La Lupe*, the she-wolf. Evidently, I rivaled bullfighting as the national cathartic.

The newspapers of the Middle West voted me the Queen of films. I had the strangest consorts. One year, Mickey Rooney shared my throne. Immensely talented as he is, we were a strange couple. But my morganatic marriages were no less odd. Elizabeth Tudor was right. She ruled alone.

I'm afraid I am a Queen—with all the prerogatives of that

station. All except one. With it, heads would have rolled.

It is fortunate for some that the laws of our land stayed my hand. Yes! A Queen I was. Ask any of my husbands. There wasn't one who didn't end up calling me one. Or was it Queenie? I'm not quite sure.

I suppose I'm larger than life. That's my problem. Created in a fury, I'm at home in a tempest.

When I opened on Broadway in *The World of Carl Sandburg*, Walter Kerr asked when "someone would write Davis a piece of beefsteak she can dig her teeth into." If no one ever had, I would always have managed to cook up something. At least three men would happily testify that I am difficult to live with. But the Four Horsemen didn't kill me. I'm too ornery to die.

If I have survived the last ten years, I can survive anything. Mother Goddam—that's me. I had the book thrown at me. Illness and defeat come hard to someone who has rarely known either. La Lupe only stopped to lick her wounds.

It is the end of a black chapter.

I am living alone for the first time. Alone without the love of a man I always wanted. I knew I would end up this way. I have always said I would end up a lonely old woman on a hill.

I've gone solo. Read your programs. Bette Davis in her no-man show!

At this point I wouldn't change a thing if I could—even the death of that girl who wanted to be the wife. The cards were stacked against her anyway. She was naïve, sentimental, altogether too vulnerable. She was a Patsy.

She made the mistake of fighting like a lady.

CHAPTER

2

The Davises of Marlborough, Wiltshire, bore arms with a golden stag on a red shield—the seal of an ancient Welsh tribe. We derived our name from St. David, patron saint of Wales, and first appeared in England in 1276.

The Pilgrim, James Davis, of Marlborough, came to America and was made a freeman of Newbury, Massachusetts, on March 4, 1634. He and eleven others cleared the forest at the Indian village of Pentucket and founded the present city of Haverhill, Mass. A selectman and representative of the general court, he was a Puritan and accused one John Godfrey of witchcraft. He would have dropped dead had he foreseen "La Lupe" lurking in his loins.

No doubt he would disassociate himself from any responsibility. It is true that there is, as usual, another side to my story. The Keyes family, which arrived in New England the same year from England, intermarried eventually with the Favors, Huguenots who settled here in 1688 and helped found New Rochelle. They then moved on to the shores of the Merrimac River, first at Bristol Hill and then, permanently, in Lowell, Mass. The Favors (Le Fievre) were French and perhaps more than titularly feverish. They were collaterally descended from Jean Jacques Le Fievre, who was court chaplain to Margaret of Navarre and an arch enemy of the Conservative Catholics. Through the Queen's agency he was a friend of Martin Luther, who gave him asylum in Strasbourg.

The historic drive that propelled both Davises and Keyeses to establish churches and industries, administer colleges, captain clipper ships and fight both Indians and English was blended with the more sensual and esthetic impulsions of the Favors, who have also sprinkled France with actors and musicians. This mixture created the power-house I knew as my grandmother, Eugenia Favor.

She was five feet of T.N.T. Handsome, imperious, she ruled her house by divine right. Blood-proud and deeply religious, she saw herself as a bridge between two generations of a royal line—dedicated to the Victorian concept of decorous accomplishment. There were daily lessons of Industry, Obedience and Enterprise. There were never idle hands or brains in her manse. She was going to equip her children for a life of personal fulfillment and public service. She did.

Her love of music chained her children to the piano from the age of seven through high school; but through the miracle of her happy tyranny they came—after a cowed apprenticeship—to love it. Discipline and habit became voluntary and enthusiastic practice. So with their studies, their household duties, and their required reading of Emerson, Whittier, Wordsworth and, of course, the Bible. Grandmother Favor believed in example, not preachment. Her unfailing attendance and involvement in the work of Lowell's First Baptist Church made piety unnecessary in the home. Not at all strangely, the disciplines proved—according to Ruthie and Uncle Paul—not austere but warming in their rewards in achievement and approval. Her refinement of nature and spiritual elegance were not difficult to take. Evidently, her force was, in all ways, irresistible.

Her penchant for china painting has enriched our cupboard with exquisite heirlooms. Her worship of nature was bequeathed to us along with her will and her complexion. I feel her presence in my home today at the sight of any flower.

Straitlaced and florid, she buried her own grandmother, Harriet Keyes Thompson, in Lowell, and had carved on the headstone—BEARING THE WHITE LILY OF AN UNSULLIED LIFE. Harriet's mother, in turn, had been a Hamlin and first cousin to Lincoln's Vice-President, Hannibal Hamlin. Each woman had used her drive and talents to enrich her children. Ladies were still using their power exclusively in their own domain. But these ladies ruled. Their homes were truly their castles.

Grandmother Favor's house on Chester Street in Lowell was a maple-shaded palace. Her motto was "kind hearts are more than coronets and simple faith than Norman blood." This was more an admonition against pride than it was a directive against ambition. Grandmother Favor had no objection to that. She was a Yankee Sovereign. The matriarch to end them all.

My mother, Ruthie, didn't tumble far from the tree. She inherited Eugenia's energy and taste plus talents she relinquished in favor of her firstborn. At the age of eleven, Ruthie was a sensitive tomboy who, on summer vacations, wore Uncle Paul's clothes and insisted on being called "Fred"; but she starred in school theatricals, edited her high school magazine, painted and sketched with great delicacy. She exploded in all directions. She was Miss Alcott's Jo.

Mother studied elocution and dramatics with Miss Porter in Lowell. From the record, she astonished her audience at the Temple, Chautauqua's auditorium in Ocean Park, Maine, with a reading of Lew Wallace's "Tamerlane" from his *Prince of India*. Yes, Ruthie was always an actress. Till the day of her death at seventy-six, she still was the star of the family.

Ruthie first met my father in Ocean Park, when she was seven. They came to know each other well in the succession of summer vacations both families enjoyed at the popular resort. In 1905, Mother was a beautiful young girl—accomplished, gay, graceful and filled with the joy of life. She was a painting by Mr. Sargent. With an appropriate stroke of humor, nature gave her one blue eye and one hazel.

Harlow Morrell Davis was a brooding, Roualt clown. Tall, gaunt, with a bulging forehead, rimless glasses and a Phi Beta key straight from Bates College. He was four times president of his class, champion debater, and head of the Athletic Association. He had been accepted at Oxford, but declined when he discovered that he had to give up cigarettes. He was soon to enter Harvard Law School where he could smoke his brilliant head off. He was already considered a young man of remarkable intellectual gifts. Although his father was Deacon of the Baptist Church in Augusta, Maine, Father was a nonbeliever. He approached life as if it were a soluble problem in geometry. His logic was glacial; his snobbery solely intellectual. His grand-father, the Reverend A. H. Morrell, was one of the founders of Storer College in Harpers Ferry, the first Southern school for the advancement of colored people after the Civil War. Of extremely serious mien, Father had—early in life—an apparent hankering for fast horses and the beauty of Ruthie.

Father courted Mother with a flattering persistence that aroused interest if not love. But Grandmother Favor, after a discreet investigation of the Davis exchequer, wielded her scepter and decreed that it was a good match. Mother was friendly with Mrs. Davis, who frankly confided to Ruthie that her son was brilliant and utterly disagreeable. She warned Mother that the alliance would destroy her spirit—"He will make your life miserable, my dear"—but as usual, things were decided in Grandmother Favor's favor.

On their wedding day, immediately after the ceremony, some happy things in white eyelet and wasp waists happily threw confetti at the bride and groom, laughed gaily and in time-honored custom threw fistfuls of rice. Harlow Morrell Davis turned to them in high dudgeon and said, "God damn you, I'll get you for this!" A rather startling reaction for a bridegroom. The new Mrs. Davis' heart sank.

After their honeymoon, they moved into Grandmother Favor's house on Chester Street in Lowell. Daddy attended Harvard Law School. They had been married on July 1st and, much to Father's distress, I was born the following April 5th. Interestingly enough, Ruthie died on July 1st on her 53rd wedding anniversary.

I understand to some degree my father's distress. He was a student whose preoccupation with the laws of the land and the universe made him impatient with Ruthie's lesser gifts as a homemaker. Efficient and esthetically developed, Ruthie—on the face of it—was the perfect wife. She ran the house beautifully. She aimed to please. Father would mull over an unbelievably prophetic paper on China's eventual place on the international scene and Ruthie would excitedly decide to have his study chair reupholstered in green leather.

This counterpoint might have strengthened his own image of the Olympian intellect dallying with a lovely mortal. It might not have displeased him for the first months of the marriage. But with parenthood, this was changed.

They had not planned a family so quickly and Ruthie's "inefficiency" was a demerit. The first of many. Her inability to share his intellectual life became a source of irritation. Ruthie's naïve enthusiasm for life in general and the baby in particular was beyond his ken. Father's wit was a knife. He sharpened it on Mother.

Surprisingly, I was an ingratiating infant. I toiled not, spun not—but neither did I cry. I was a minimum of trouble. I was trying. Wreathed in smiles, a picture of amiability, I looked around my world in constant wonder. I discovered my feet on the 12th of August, laughed out loud—according to my baby book—and immediately decided to go places. I learned I had to crawl first and got around like mad, harming absolutely no one. Whenever I disappeared, I could be found on Father's leather couch in his study.

My first word was "Papa." I called to him. He was studying for an examination. My first sentence was, "Papa forgot his rompers—he catch cold." A manager already.

We moved to Winchester, Mass., and Mother compounded her felony by giving birth to my sister, Barbara. I was eighteen months old and stayed, it seems, with Grandmother Favor. On my return I was ecstatic with my new "doll" for a day. I then, incredibly, removed Bobby from my crib and placed her face down on a chair nearby. When Mother and our nurse, Rose Worthington, discovered Bobby, I explained, "I don't want Dolly *here*." A few years later I cut her hair in scallops. Even though we are different as night and day, Bobby and I have always been great friends.

Daddy believed that children should not sit at the dining room table with grownups until they were able to conduct an intelligent conversation. We were allowed to have dinner on Sundays, however, with the family. We were always banished in tears for some impropriety or lack of wit. Bobby and I were treated by Daddy as a necessary evil. Daddy's mind was original and his only descent into banality was his sampler, "Children should be seen and not heard." If it had been up to my father, I could only have made my name in silent pictures.

Since it was impossible to reach Daddy, I had to furnish my own bridge. Once, when Mr. and Mrs. Brown—neighbors— were having Sunday breakfast with Mother and Daddy, I brought a dead rat to the table. (I planned no such entertainment after that, believe me!)

Bobby spent every waking moment trying to please Daddy. I somehow knew it would never work. I simply kept out of his way.

In a supreme effort to make up for Daddy's boredom with us, Ruthie showered us with love. Mother was sunlit—Daddy the dark cloud. I cannot recall one moment of affection between my parents in our home.

Daddy, however, had another dimension. He was very generous with gifts to Ruthie. When Grandmother's fortunes ebbed, he put Mother's brother Richard through Harvard and invited him to live with us. He helped to support others as well. Daddy cared nothing for the opinions of others—was solely prompted by his own code of ethics, which was very high. Preoccupied and unamiable, Daddy lived in his own world. Yet it is so difficult to label people. Christmas should have exacted a loud "bah humbug" from Harlow M. Davis. It was Daddy's favorite holiday.

He personally decorated the tree every year. Christmas Eve was his night. He was our Santa Claus. What a thrill those Christmas mornings were. One would have thought the Magi had visited us from the shower of gifts that spilled into the hallway. There was an *entente cordiale* in the family—peace on earth, good will toward children. Christmas! With Daddy towering over everyone—all 6 feet 2 of him—the happy inventor of the happiest day.

I remember receiving one skate from Uncle Myron and bravely hiding my disappointment. How could I wait a whole year for the other? I smiled bravely—and then the other skate was retrieved from its hiding place in the closet. How everyone roared! Christmas was the only time I remember the whole family's laughing together.

My impression of my early childhood is a happy one—due completely to the efforts of my mother. There is a quick succession of bright moments. Aunt Mildred's wedding at our house on Cambridge Street in Winchester. Bobby and I were flower girls and Ruthie the matron of honor—Japanese lanterns hung from the maple trees transforming our lawn into a fairyland. Those biting, cold, white days when Bobby and I would slide down the hill behind the house on our backsides, without our sleds. The swing near the kitchen which I strained to help me touch the sky. It got even by tripping me up and knocking the wind out of me. The kitchen, shiny and busy and expectant with custards and fruit pies. The flowers in the woods nearby and our vegetable garden in the summer. The fresh colors and tastes of that garden! The first Cadillac Daddy brought home. The family outings on Sundays. Grandmother Favor would hang out of the car and shriek, "Harlow, stop!"

The brakes would screech.

"What's the matter?"

"Children—look at those apple blossoms. Ruthie, we simply have to take home some apple blossoms."

The Cadillac would look like a hearse on our return.

I was always happiest when I was outdoors and wandering through the woods. One day a pack of dogs chased me and I started running. One of them caught hold of my long, yellow hair streaming behind me. What a horror it must have been as a spectacle and what a terror it was for me; but I kept running as I screamed and my endurance proved greater than his and he let go. I still am terrified of police dogs.

Life was a constant source of excitement to me. I remember when I discovered a summer night. I sat in a reverie staring at the stars. The sky was silver with them. I was bewitched. Daddy was sitting with me. He broke the spell.

"Do you see all those stars up there?"

My heart beat expectantly. The riddle would be solved. After all Daddy did know everything.

He continued, "There are millions and millions of them. Remember that always and you'll know how unimportant you are."

Daddy in his infinite knowledge always saw the roots and not the flowers. He took all the watches of the world apart and never knew what time it was. I never heard Daddy enthuse about anything or anybody except the singing of Mme. Schumann-Heink, the great contralto. In Hollywood many years later I was introduced to Schumann-Heink and was photographed with her. Had Daddy been alive to know, he would have believed I had finally "arrived."

If I could never win my father, I completely conquered Ruthie. I became an absolute despot at the age of two. Partly to compensate for Father but mostly through sheer terror,

Ruthie surrendered. I sensed her weaknesses early and pounced on them. The tantrum got me what I wanted. My demands were frightening and unusual. My passion for order and perfection were unheard of in a child so young. An untied lace on a shoe, a wrinkle on a dress, drove me into a fury.

One Sunday when I was dressed to visit Grandmother Favor, I turned blue with rage. Father raised his eyes to heaven and hands to ears. Mother looked for open safety pins. Nothing would quiet me until Ruthie, remembering, tried an experiment. She removed my dress, which had a deep wrinkle down the front, and slipped a freshly starched one over my head. I was not only pacified but smiled—displaying my first tooth. I should have been whipped until I stood in firm peaks.

Daddy spanked me only once and at Mother's request. Bobby and I—at my instigation—had eaten some unripe grapes forbidden to us in our arbor. We had a Roman feast which ended classically. Ruthie said: "Harlow, I gave them castor oil. You can give them a spanking." He did!

Daddy did try. He took us to the circus once and it was a marvel to me until I noticed the long, green carpet that was placed in the ring to accommodate the parade of animals. The seam down the middle was crooked and it drove me mad. I was so disturbed by it that I sat amongst all the laughing children—brooding—like a Charles Addams monster. To this day, I would walk over burning coals to straighten a picture, to adjust a blind; but Daddy simply decided I was an ungrateful brat. He only knew that he had sacrificed an afternoon for nothing.

Daddy was by now graduated from Harvard Law School and was a patent attorney with the United Shoe Machinery Company of Boston. He was on his way to becoming one of the most respected specialists in the patent field and he was ambitious. His three women were strangling him. The more yielding Mother was, the more suffocating the marriage became. He was barely conscious of us.

When I was seven years old, our family went to dinner at the Copley Plaza in Boston. Mother and Bobby and I were going to Florida for a vacation and Father was seeing us off. It was festive with a string orchestra, hot rolls on a silver wagon and lemon sherbet.

The scene is still vivid to me. Mother and Daddy picked at

their food and looked pale. Daddy was attentive and kind.
Ruthie was quiet. Even the grownups at the other tables seemed
to speak in whispers and move in slow motion. It was a shadow
play that ended when Daddy took us to the railway station. I
remember he kissed Mother good-bye.

We all looked out the window and waved good-bye. Daddy
looked sad as he waved back. I can still see him—standing
alone, tall and thin, as the train began to move. He stood on
the platform like a statue, receding and then disappearing in a
cloud of smoke.

Ruthie put her arms around us and watched the outskirts of
Boston rush by. After we arrived in Florida she told us that
Daddy wouldn't live with us anymore. Bobby cried her eyes
out. I started planning our life without him, but I still cry when
I hear a string orchestra.

Once a decision has been made, I go on from there. Daddy
didn't want us anymore.

When we returned from Florida, we lived in Newton. Daddy's monthly alimony check wouldn't go far. Mother decided
she would have to go to work to give us a proper education.
Bobby and I would have to be sent to a boarding school, since
Mother would be working all the time.

Grandmother, who took the *Atlantic Monthly* and swore by
it, found an ad for a school that met the necessary requirements.
Crestalban, a farm school in the Berkshire Hills. Miss Marjorie
Whiting was the principal. Miss Whiting was the niece of
Abbott Thayer, the painter. It was a fine family. The school
was singular, small, healthful and in the country which delighted both Mother and Grandmother.

Mother took a deep breath, put us in school and left her
world for the jungle. Sheltered as she had been, this took
courage. She faced facts and resolved to give her children a
good life. She started looking for a job. Through Grace Hospital
in New York City she found a job as governess for three little
boys on 78th Street (the same street I live on now). Thus began
her years of struggle to raise her children. Being separated from
us was hard; but there was no other way.

If Ruthie was impressed with Crestalban so—later—were
we. It was high up in the Great Divide between the Hoosac
and Housatonic rivers. Huge red barns surrounded the long,
white farmhouse. It looked modeled in snow—part of winter.

A brown-shingled school-house was across the way. All distances were covered by sleigh. Along with our studies, we were taught sewing, cooking and house-cleaning. Crestalban was a farm with pigs, cows, horses and chickens. The food was good and plentiful and, at lunch, French was spoken exclusively. Eighteen hours of every day were spent out of doors. We had school out of doors and we slept outdoors on a sleeping porch. I believe my basic great health came from my years at Crestalban. My greatest delight was the naked snowbaths I used to take every morning. We had a Spartan routine and Mr. Emerson's Self-Reliance was the order of each day. I adored it. In the evenings, we would sit around the fire and Miss Whiting would read aloud to us while we did our mending. There were only thirteen students and we were soon a family. Bobby spent half her time denying that our parents were divorced and the other half convincing herself she wasn't lying. Her fantasy had Daddy out of town working for the United States Government and eager to rejoin us. She continued this through our college days. In Yankee land in that day, divorce was considered a disgrace—something to be hidden.

I remember well that when Mother left us that first day of school, the full meaning of our new life hit us. That first night at Crestalban, Bobby and I clung to each other like orphans in a storm.

My first Christmas there I was Santa Claus. I had no idea that I would play him all my life. At Crestalban it was my role for three years. The third time was almost the last. The tree was lighted by real candles as there was no electricity at the school. That dates me! Under the tree were our gifts from the faculty and each other. I had been told not to go near the tree— my curiosity got the better of me and in an attempt to find my presents the cotton batting on the sleeve of my costume caught fire. I started shaking it to put it out and managed only to spread the flame to my beard. Suddenly I was on fire. I started screaming in terror. I heard voices, felt myself being wrapped in a rug—and then silence all around me. Everyone was quite naturally panicked. When the rug was taken off, I decided to keep my eyes closed. Ever the actress! I would make believe I was blind. "Her eyes!" A shudder of delight went through me. I was in complete command of the moment. I had never known such power.

I eventually opened my eyes to the relief of everyone. Bobby, who had been much impressed when she read *The Little Match Girl*, turned away with tears streaming down her face, expecting to find her sister a pile of ashes when she looked back at me. The Whiting sisters told me to be a good sport and not spoil the Christmas festivity.

We left on the train the next morning for New York and our Christmas holiday. Then we arrived at Grand Central Station, where Ruthie recognized only Bobby and the coat and hat she had bought me. The blisters by now were filled with cinders from the train. The teacher announced seriously that it would be wise if I saw a doctor. Ruthie, swearing like a trouper, snatched me from her calm and rushed me to a hospital.

A Japanese intern at the New York hospital tenderly removed all the cinders with a tweezer and then removed all the burned skin. I looked brand-new before he greased and bandaged my face. He told Ruthie that there was only one way I would not be scarred for life—if my face was kept greased night and day. Ruthie knew what a scarred face would mean to my life. I can never thank her enough for four weeks of sleepless nights.

Uncle Paul, who was to become assistant rector of Grace Church and then minister of Trinity Episcopal in New York City, was then the rector of the Episcopal Church in White Plains. We stayed with his family for Christmas. Then Mother had to return to Miss Bennett's School in Millbrook, New York, where she was by now a housemother. She had promised that she would stay with some of the girls who were unable to be with their families over the holiday. Miss Bennett allowed Ruthie to keep us there with her for the week. Despite the torture of the burns, which hurt more as they healed, I loved my time in Millbrook and learned to ride a horse.

Mother kept my face greased around the clock and Bobby would tell me stories at night and hold my hands to keep me from tearing the bandages off my itching face.

After the holiday, we returned to Crestalban.

I learned on my triumphant return that fame can be short-lived. Once I was examined for scars, all interest in my drama faded. I learned that resting on one's laurels was a fool's game.

The next year, Ruthie decided that this was the last time the three of us would be separated. She took the bull by the horns and enrolled in Clarence White's School of Photography in

New York City, on 128th Street. She was going to make a profession of her favorite hobby. She enrolled us in P.S. 186 and moved us into a one-bedroom apartment on 144th Street and Broadway. For the first time since Winchester, the three musketeers were together again.

When Bobby and I saw the apartment with its dreary furniture and sleazy pink lace curtains at the windows, we were stricken. It was so ugly and shabby. We held our tongues and then hid in the bathroom. As if on cue, we burst into tears. We didn't want to hurt Mother's feelings.

"Do you really think Mother thinks *this* is beautiful?"

"How can she do this to us?"

What little snobs we were. We had lived in the country all our lives, and New York took a lot of getting used to—the New York that Ruthie could afford.

P.S. 186 looked like a big, brown fortress. Forbidding, impersonal. Each crowded classroom had fifty children—quite a change from Crestalban. When the classroom doors rolled back for assembly, the mass of children was terrifying to me. I can still smell the steam heat mingled with chalk and children.

Bobby and I both felt deceived and lost, but we adjusted and came to enjoy going to school there. The maze of middy blouses and bloomers became Esperanzas and Esthers. The knickers and Norfolk jackets were Seymour and Nuncio. Foreign to us, yes. But warm and friendly. When we were asked to go roller skating down the great hill from Broadway to Riverside Drive, we went. A right turn would extend the trip down a long incline parallel to the Hudson. For two cents, we could buy paper cones filled with shaved ice and have it colored with sweet tonics of any hue or combinations we chose. A little Italian man with an umbrella stand on wheels would seek us out to sell his rainbowed wonders. How he made a profit I will never know.

Bobby and I liked our new friends and eventually adjusted to life in New York. By December, when the hill made perfect sledding, we were having a glorious time.

Even our depressing little court apartment came alive. Ruthie went to the five-and-dime and brightened things up. She then taught us how much fun a dark, depressing court apartment could be. After dinner, Mother would pass some candy around, turn out our lights and pull up all our shades. Presto! We had front row seats to a vaudeville show—unlike Keith's Hamilton Theatre, for free.

Left stage, one floor up, a young man stood in front of his bureau mirror putting stickum on his unruly hair. He appraised himself with lowered lids and some mute dialogue that he was rehearsing for his sweetheart. Below was a big, fat woman spanking two little boys who could have been the Katzenjammer Kids. Their round faces were covered with flour and from the rolling pin lying near her, it was obvious why she was furious. Her exasperation was comical and Mother giggled. "She only beats them when they sneeze." To the right, one floor below, a man sat in his Morris chair, his collar off, his striped shirt rolled at the sleeves, reading his newspaper. By the play of expression on his face we guessed at what he was reading. What an unconscious pantomime artist he was! Just across the way, a girl our age sat—supposedly doing her homework. It consisted of sticking her pencil through her Mary Pickford curls and pulling it out again. God knows what she was dreaming of. All I know is that we rocked with laughter. Ruthie had made our dreary place into the first box at the Palace.

I enrolled in the cooking class at P.S. 186. Later I entered a citywide contest the New York Board of Education was sponsoring. I chose to make cookies for the contest.

Mine were going to be the holy wafers with which I would commune with the greats of the world. I thought of nothing but cookies. It was my first contest. There were thousands of entries; I won first prize. I was in seventh heaven. The will to win was the one ingredient not to be found in Fanny Farmer.

Bobby and I attended Sunday school at the Congregational Church nearby. Our teacher was the stand-in for Lillian Gish at the Biograph studios and her name was Una Merkel. I had a real crush on her.

During that winter I became a Girl Scout. I became the most dedicated Girl Scout that ever lived. I would have tripped an old lady in order to pick her up. I have never embraced a cause in my life. I tackle it. So with the Scouts. It was a life-and-death affair as always. Competence has never been excellence to me. I wish today's critics would consider that. Doing a job well is to be expected. Adequacy has become today's high standard.

I brought home dozens of badges of merit and spread goodness, cheer and patriotism throughout Manhattan. It became
my reason for being. In no time, I was a golden eaglet. I also
became a patrol leader. I worked my patrol like a top sergeant.
I'm afraid I developed the reputation of one. But I got what I
wanted. When our patrol was chosen to march in the compet-
itive dress parade for Mrs. Hoover at Madison Square Garden,
we won. Now I could relax. I had to be the best. Nothing less
ever satisfied me.

During this period Ruthie's close friend, Myrtis Genthner,
was often with us at the apartment on 144th Street. Myrtis was
a great reader. She knew of my love of reading and helped me
expand my taste. She helped me over the bridge between the
Bobbsey Twins and the Corsican Brothers. The next bridge to
the Karamazovs was easier. It was Myrtis who suggested, while
she was reading Balzac's *La Cousine Bette*, that I change the
spelling of my name "to set you apart, my dear." Hence Betty
became Bette. The fact that M. Balzac's Lisbeth Fischer was
a horror didn't come to my attention until I read the book some
time later.

I wrote Daddy a letter soon after the change in the spelling
of my name. In his reply he laughed at me and claimed it was
a passing fancy. That did it—it always has. Just tell me I'm
not going to do something. I do it. My name forever after was
spelled B-E-T-T-E.

When summer came, Ruthie sent us to Camp Mudjekeewis
in Fryeburg, Maine. We went there for three summers. Miss
Perkins and Miss Pride were the owners. We swam, rode, went
on canoe trips, hiked up mountains and along country roads.
A camp in Maine is a glorious experience, and Mother gave
it to us.

Miss Pride taught piano in East Orange, New Jersey, during
the winter and Bobby, who had done so well under her tutelage,
was given a chance to continue her studies. We now moved
to East Orange where we had to re-enter school. I was to have
graduated from P.S. 186 in January, so I was six months short
of high school requirements. When I discovered that the Jersey
girls who had failed to graduate from their own elementary
schools because of bad grades were taking entrance exams in
the hope of starting in high school, I got an idea. I went to the

high school and asked to see the principal without telling Ruthie. I wanted to surprise her by passing the entrance examinations. The principal interviewed me—and as a result of my grades and a high regard for the New York school system, gave me my chance.

Armed with a cheese sandwich and a glass of milk furnished by a thoughtful monitor, I took the daylong examinations cold.

That afternoon, Bobby had long since returned home from her public school and Ruthie started to worry about me. She knew I could take care of myself. But we had only been in the city for a day. At five o'clock, I rushed in triumphantly. I had passed the examinations and I was a full-fledged freshman in the East Orange High School.

I did not find living in East Orange stimulating, however. I felt a tugging inside that I could not explain to anyone, least of all myself. Something had always told me I was going to be important. I didn't seem to be getting anywhere. I was bored!

I tried to conjure up earthquakes and floods to bring some excitement into New Jersey and my drab life.

We were living in a boardinghouse. Our rooms were on the top floor and we ate in the "dinning hall" downstairs. This was our first experience in a boardinghouse.

I escaped into my books after school. Otherwise I was trapped. My energies were growing and there was no suitable outlet for them. My drive took the form of plain willfulness. I was not always the most agreeable of daughters. In fact—I was being a bad sport.

Ruthie, as usual, was making the best of everything and handling me with kid gloves. She recognized her own will in me and decided, after conferring with a doctor, that I was "a high-spirited race horse and needed a free rein." She decided to let nature take its course. She had little choice. The filly became a bucking bronco.

Ruthie has told me that she was petrified of me during my teens. Her every suggestion, her mildest reprimand, would disintegrate into glares from me. She would always giggle nervously. I sensed my power over her and my irritation grew greater when she surrendered. There was no pleasing me. Her nervous chatter, meant to buck us up, insulted my intelligence and earned a smirk of contempt when I was in a mood. Poor Ruthie! She worked so hard at both jobs. She was doing retouching work for Pierie MacDonald, the portraitist in New York, and commuting. After a tough day's work she would return to Bette of the Baleful Countenance—and try to brighten my life.

One night as a new form of entertainment, Ruthie suggested that we exchange clothes and personalities for the evening. We changed from head to toe. Bobby and another little girl swapped jumpers to get into the act. The masquerade was on and down we went to dinner.

It was all vaguely amusing until I realized that the ever voluble Ruthie was sulking and glowering into her spinach ramekin and being generally obnoxious. Her characterization of me was excellent. I had to admit that. I was imitating Ruthie by interrupting every few words with a giggle. Our performance ended when I exploded, "I'm not like that. That's *not* me!" But I knew it was. Mother reverted to a tentative laugh and I stormed out of the room hearing the laughter of the other boarders as I left. Mother had hoped by showing me myself I would change my ways. It was an idle dream. I couldn't help the way I was acting. I felt like a misfit. I longed for something. My imagination took me round the world and I was stuck in a boardinghouse in East Orange, New Jersey.

CHAPTER

3

Mother, realizing how desperate I was with my existence in East Orange, New Jersey, made plans to "unstick" me. Soon the three musketeers were off bag and baggage back to New England. We stayed with Uncle Myron and Aunt Mildred in Newtonville for a few days until Mother found us a place of our own. Battle-weary, she went to see Daddy in the hopes of financial aid. She found him as cold and disapproving as always.

For the record, it was Ruthie's only admission of defeat to Daddy. She never made the same mistake again.

I was entered immediately into the high school in Newton. I had the great good fortune on the first day to hit a home run at baseball practice. I was immediately "rushed" by one and all, to be part of their gang. I have to add, to their dismay and mine that was the one and only home run I ever hit during my two years at Newton High.

Mother rented an apartment on Washington Street in Newton and scrounged around for people to photograph by sending out announcements saying: PORTRAITS WITH A PERSONALITY—AT YOUR HOME OR MINE. I might add most days after school our living room was occupied with an assortment of photographic subjects. Mother was an excellent photographer and was always busy at her profession. Plus all this, she kept house for us, made three-quarters of our clothes, and always allowed us to have our friends in whenever we wished.

A short time after entering Newton High School, I attended my first dance in the gymnasium. I was very apprehensive, as I was a newcomer and had no beau of my own. Mother rightfully urged me to go. Also, I had for the most part been in girls' boarding schools and—to say the least—was petrified of boys. I remember well my corduroy jumper, my long yellow hair worn simply hanging down my back, flat shoes, plus little or no dancing experience. I arrived in a bewildered state, and stood around for what seemed like hours praying someone would ask me to dance. Finally, a sympathetic soul, aware of my predicament, did. We danced and danced and danced— not from his choice. Those were the days of "cutting in" and no other brave soul came to his rescue. I finally decided he had a nervous tic until I caught our reflection in a mirror. He was gesturing wildly to the stag line to be rescued. At this point I pleaded something—I do not remember, probably to powder my nose—and fled home.

I burst into the apartment and had complete hysterics. "Ruthie, I'm a wallflower. I'll be one all my life." After calming me down, and hearing my complete tale of woe, she very cheerfully said, "Bette, I think it's time you put your hair up and started to dress like a young lady. Your little girl days are over."

The next party I went to was in the evening. I came home from school that day and found hanging in my closet a long, white, full-skirted chiffon dress trimmed in turquoise, with a low neckline, for me—just below the collarbone. Grandmother was there when I first tried it on. I was ecstatic. I felt like all the princesses in the storybooks. Grandmother, however, said to her daughter, "Ruth, you might just as well let Bette go to the party in a nightgown." Not even this dampened my spirits. That evening, hair piled high—cheeks bright pink with excitement, a long chiffon party dress—as I looked in the mirror I can well remember being horrified when I admitted to my image—you're pretty. I was fourteen and an unqualified triumph that evening. The wallflower was no more. Every dance was taken. I was "cut in" on over and over and even acquired two beaux that night—Gige Dunham and John Holt.

Gige was the winner that evening—he walked me home.

How vivid it all still is. The harvest moon, bright orange, my own excitement, the newness of my first conquest. Gige asked if he could be my beau. I was dizzy with happiness. I must have said yes, judging by the dance programs and poems I have in my teen-age scrapbook, signed by the name "Gige."

The social life in Newton was active and I merrily rushed to sleigh rides, hay rides, football games, picnics and dances in a lovely glow. I adored dancing always and was, fortunately, a good dancer. No one was frantically signaling the stag line any more. Rereading the love letters I received during this period, also carefully saved in my scrapbook, I am convinced I slayed them. I had "It."

Love was a very real thing to me. I moved from crush to crush, always declaring myself eternally involved with the current one. Mother would attempt to break it up by inviting the current flame to be our house guest for a few days. Overexposure would usually accomplish what Ruthie set out to do— I would come running to her, "When is he going to go home? Will he *never* leave?" It never occurred to me why Ruthie had invited him in the first place.

It is a fact—I zealously guarded my own chastity. I also was a tease. On sleigh rides I would take a flashlight and wait until a couple were really in the throes of necking—and then flash it on them. I had been brought up according to what age I was at the moment. At fourteen, beaux meant dancing, skating, toasting marshmallows, etc. Anything beyond this I felt unsuitable to my years. I was part of a gang and, interestingly enough, found the boys of my age delighted that I was interested in something besides necking.

The mysteries of womanhood were confusing to me. Ruthie, advanced in so many ways, was a true Pilgrim in this department. She was her mother's daughter. What little knowledge I had of the "birds and the bees" was gleaned from schoolmates, in hushed whispers—giggling over the world that was to come to "us women." This is the frightening way to approach the intricacies of womanhood. This gradual process of learning started back as far as Crestalban. So inexpertly did I garner my information that, when thirteen, after having been kissed by a boy one moonlit night in Southwest Harbor, Maine, I was sure I was pregnant. My tummy even got larger and

larger. Quite like the false pregnancy of an animal. My terror—
the possible disgrace to Ruthie—is indescribable. I had heard
many times talk about girls who had strayed—now I was one
of them. Every generation has its own expression for the
"monthly it"—in my day it was "falling off the roof." Having
never been told of this phenomenon, when my day arrived, I
thought it was the end. I practically said a choking farewell to
all I held dear. At the peak of my horror I ran to Ruthie to say
good-bye forever, only to be told that what had happened to
me was a "part of growing up"—this was the burden women
must bear in order to have children. I thank God there are
books today and doctors who help parents manage all the information about growing up in a sane and unfrightening way.
At least Bobby, being the younger, was saved the same jump
into the unknown. My favorite way of teasing her before she
"fell off" was quoting a line from Songs of Solomon—"My
little sister, hath no breasts, what shall she do in the time she
is spoken for?" I still say it to her. Falling off made no change
whatever in her structure.

Bobby was even more dazed with my new life than I. I
would catch her often just staring at me. I was the belle of
every ball. I joined every club at school. I even organized a
girls' football team. We were called the "Coffee-Colored Angels" for some forgotten reason and I was right tackle. Ruthie
was happily ignorant of this, and Bobby was sworn to secrecy.
We had sweat shirts with large C.C.A.'s on them. I hid mine
in the closet high on a shelf.

The boys on the high school varsity team laughed at us.
Furious, we challenged them to referee a game. They roared
with laughter but accepted.

It was a rainy day and we found ourselves playing in mud.
Women play games for keeps. They can be ferocious. The
C.C.A.'s awed and horrified the varsity that day. We played
football, we did. I was put on the bench due to the fingernails
of an opponent in my eye. Women's tactics—purely the jungle
female. I emerged head unbowed—we felt the C.C.A.'s had
won the battle. The varsity did not laugh at us—they knew we
were for real. The next day a hysterical mother called Ruthie
to say this had to stop. It did. The jig was up and that was the
end of the Coffee-Colored Angels. We retired undefeated.

That spring Mother started thinking about where we would

spend the summer. Ruthie was always the optimist and I never knew her not to feel that tomorrow would bring us all to the crest of the waves. I am just like her—and thank her for this.

She ran across an ad in a Boston paper: A *minister in Provincetown, on Cape Cod, will give a housekeeper and family free board.* What could be more ideal? This was an answer— a house for the three of us costing nothing! Plus a summer by the sea.

Ruthie answered the ad and received a response quickly— "Yes." At the end of June the three musketeers drove off to the Cape barely visible in the maze of valises, wicker baskets and photographic paraphernalia.

One would have thought we were the most carefree family in New England and we were.

Our summer in Provincetown was fun—our Pastor Grant approved of us and we of him. One thing for sure, we went to church every Sunday, and I will never forget one particular Sunday. Bobby and I became hysterical over the misuse of the word unique—it came out *eunuch!*

That summer I met the local high school football star. Jim Allen was a *next year's Harvard freshman!* I was fifteen and never before had had a prospective college man as a beau. He was a very nice guy. The greatest compliment from a Yankee dame.

How wonderful that July was. And August. I stood on the edge of life and Bobby watched, with her earnest little face, her furrowed sunburned brow. Bobby made a child's sailboat that summer with a cretonne sail. One day we went to the beach to launch her craft.

She sailed so well. She was drifting out to sea. She was drifting too fast. Bobby couldn't swim swiftly enough to rescue her. I will never forget Bobby's face as her little cretonne sail became a speck on the horizon, still perfectly balanced, heading straight out to sea. Bobby never got over it. Bobby was always a "tucker." I was the luckier. Ruthie was more *simpatica* with me; Bobby she never really understood. There, that day, Bobby stood at the water's edge without expression watching her ship sail away. Years later she wrote a story titled "My Cretonne Sail." She lost her childhood that day.

Bobby was always trying to catch up to me. I was a natural

leader—she a follower. It is possible only she grew up that summer.

Mother earned our keep in the Reverend's home in Provincetown. She cooked for him, did his laundry, kept his house plus entertaining our house guests, my beaux in particular— Gige among them. This was the first time my mother and I became rivals. It was perfectly expressed by one beau. "If you were you but had your mother's maturity, that would make you ideal!" No question about it, Ruthie was a rival—not from choice, I'm sure. A very embarrassing situation for any attractive single mother. And unavoidable with young men.

At the end of summer we returned to Newton for my sophomore year at Newton High. We lived that year on Lewis Terrace, in a two-family house. We were on the top floor. Mother continued her photography as a supplement to our meager contribution from Daddy. I continued on my gay way with the friends I had met the year before. I supplemented the family income that year by posing for a sculptress on Beacon Hill in Boston. She always sent her chauffeured car for me, and I was so overawed by the whole procedure that as I was nonchalantly stepping into the limousine the first day, I fell flat on my face on the floor of the back seat of the car. The impeccably mannered chauffeur seemed not to notice. I was grateful for that. Whenever he called for me, I would ride through Newton hoping some, or at least one, of my friends would see me sitting in state in my chauffeured car. No one ever did, alas!

I posed for a statue of Spring! My only difficulty was with a male assistant of the sculptress. He was, I know now, impersonal about the whole thing. But to me it was torture. Somewhere in Boston I stand—Spring! Naked! Standing on one foot hours at a time was not easy, but I was contributing to the family exchequer.

The following year Ruthie decided to put Bobby and me in a boarding school once more. She chose Northfield Seminary. It was unique in that all races, creeds, colors, were admissible. A sound reason for a choice of school. I remember with pleasure my roommate Ducky Seager. I remember with displeasure much else. Suffice it to say it was a bad choice for the Davis girls. Its temptation to Ruthie was its low tuition; for our purposes, Bobby's and mine, it was over-religious, the students were overworked with housekeeping chores—and the food was hopeless. We were miserable. We tried to write Ruthie happy letters but we did not fool her at all. One great day she arrived at school and in less than a shake of a lamb's tail we were whisked away. We felt we were being released from a jail sentence.

We plunked ourselves once more on Uncle Myron and Aunt Mildred for the Christmas holidays, at the end of which, after much thought, Ruthie decided to send her two daughters to Cushing Academy, in Ashburnham, Mass., a school she had attended. The fact that it is a coeducational school was, she decided, important to us since there were no men in our lives. I might add at this point that Ruthie, a most attractive woman during all these years, had many offers of marriage but made the fatal mistake of asking Bobby and me if we would like this man or that man for a father. Naturally as kids, we said, "Heavens, no!" She let us wreck her personal life. How could we know *who* was a suitable father? In other words, she never thought of herself, only of us—which was unfair to everybody concerned.

I felt at home at Cushing immediately. No doubt a lot of my enthusiasm had to do with the presence of males. The surrounding countryside was to my taste—brought back my happy years at Crestalban. Bobby, who was never as quickly at home in new surroundings, did not love Cushing as I did. Moreover, as a sister I was definitely competition. For a long time no one realized we were sisters. She was always in my shadow. Nowadays two such totally different members of one family would not be in the same school. I feel trying to keep up with my popularity was very detrimental to Bobby during these years. As usual, I became part of all activities. My goal, however—and I always had to have a goal—was to be leading lady of the senior play. I had two years to make it.

At Cushing we had dances on Saturday nights—the cut-in variety. I never lacked for partners. Bobby was popular also and had the devotion of one student, whose devotion she did not return. He was always cutting in and interrupting any future alliances. I liked many of my partners, two or three in particular. The seniors all had a go for me, which I found flattering in itself—but also found no desire for any of the older boys as a "steady." I didn't believe in having just one beau, anyway. The three most desirable young men—football heroes of course—were insulted by my lack of interest, plus the fact I was not fast enough for them, and they soon left me alone. They got even at their graduation for this turndown from a mere junior, however. In their Class Will they left Bette Davis two dozen handkerchiefs to blow her "No's" with. I cried for hours in humiliation.

I was beginning to understand the machinations of jealousy in my first year at Cushing. I was ever the perfectionist. I was a good student, I was popular with the boys, I was President of my sorority—in fact into everything. I was too much. I was starting to make enemies, through no real fault of my own. It has ever been thus through my entire life. My greatest heartbreak was the election for President of the Senior Class. I will never forget Dr. Cowell, our principal, standing on the platform in the assembly hall and reading the results of the voting. Bette Davis—1 vote. This was a beginning of self-examination and guilt. I found it cruel and hard to understand. I was thought to be "stuck up." I wasn't. I was just sure of myself. This is and always has been an unforgivable quality to the unsure.

One day early in the school year, Dr. Cowell sent for me to come to his office. He suggested that I help earn my own way through school by waiting on table. He had nothing but praise for Ruthie's efforts in our behalf, with which I genuinely agreed. I thanked him, left the office and decided to write Mother immediately, secure in the knowledge she would *never* want her daughter to be a waitress. After I mailed the letter I thought no more about it. To my utter amazement, a week later I received my *very* wise mother's reply. "By all means, Bette, how wonderful of you. Thank you so much." At that point in my life I was extremely aware of one's station in life. A waitress was on one level, a doctor another, and so on. I was most certainly not in the waitress class. However, there I was—faced with it. No escape. I sat in my room for hours contemplating what I thought would be my disgrace in front of my fellow students.

Next morning, up at six, I strode down the hill to the dormitory dining room assigned to me. With head propped high and a forced smile on my face, I started my career as a waitress at Cushing Academy. It was hard for me to take orders from anyone—I was far more inclined to give them. After the initial shock of my imagined change in station was over, I started to

learn how to be a good waitress—the best—and found pleasure
in serving well. I also found friends I had never known before.
Girls who had mistaken my efficiency and absorption in whatever I was doing as a sign of my conceit and superiority liked
me for the first time. Ruthie had proved her point. It is not
what you do you are judged by—it is what you are as a person
that matters. This is one of the great lessons to be learned by
anyone. Never look up or down at someone merely because
of his profession. Judge the person by what grace he or she
does the job at hand. I had had my primer in racial prejudice
at P.S. 186. At Cushing I had my primer in pride. I graduated
on both counts with honors.

As I think of Cushing, I am swept from one memory to
another in a kind of montage. The sorority debates—which I
won. I had inherited from Daddy an ability along these lines
plus my ever present doggedness to win. The many hours of
talks at meetings of the Christian Association of which I was
the President. The most famous of these meetings was attended,
at our invitation, by young men of the freshman class at Dart-
mouth. It was indeed a heated and frank discussion period,
dealing wholly with sex. We had found an ideal group to
interrogate as to their idea of whether a girl "should or
shouldn't." They entered into the spirit of our earnestness and
everybody benefited. They definitely returned to college feeling
those Cushing girls were no sissies. Actually it was a revolutionary idea and a rewarding one for all present. They knew
more about women and we knew more about men as a result.
Somewhere along the line, as events proved, I must have forgotten some of the things I learned that night.

My montage of Cushing however, when all is said and done,
revolves around my becoming Ham's girl. Ham I finally married. He was a senior and therefore at school only one year of
my two there. He was a lone wolf as far as the girls were
concerned. He was also working his way through school, by
playing piano for our Saturday night dances. I had noticed him
vaguely from time to time, but as we were not in the same
classes I seldom ran into him. He was not one of the "football
heroes." He told me later he had often noticed me at the dances
but never imagined I would find him attractive. Ham was tall,
lean, dark curly-haired, with a funny nose and beautiful brown
eyes.

I was a member of the Expression Class under the guidance
of Miss Lois Cann, a truly remarkable dramatic coach to find
in a small New England school. She is still there, and came
backstage to see me when I was touring in *The World of Carl
Sandburg*. Ham was always busy with his music. He started
learning to play the trumpet at Cushing. This was a definite
agony for all concerned. My dormitory was across from his
and on many a summer night while in my room trying to study,
I would hear floating across to me "taps"—played just for
me. By then, of course, I was wading in those velvety brown
eyes. I was truly in love. So was he.

I first got to know Ham when he was given the job of putting
on an evening's entertainment for the school. He asked one
and all to pitch in. I showed up for rehearsals and he suggested
I sing a song. He would accompany me and help me with the
way of presenting it. He chose "Gee, I'm Mighty Blue for
You," a popular tune of the day. What a prophetic title. Many
times in the years since our divorce, I have found myself singing
this song which takes me back to those early years with Ham.
Such nostalgia—so in love—so in love in a way one can never
be again. A woman's first love is it, they say. I agree.

The same night Ham sang "Paddlin' Madeline Home." His
was a truly beautiful voice. He is a gifted musician. His only
handicap for success in this field was his lack of drive to reach
the top. I will always feel he could have. Our eventual divorce
was due to the fact that I *did* have the drive to reach the top—
and this is a dedication few can cope or compete with.

Ham graduated that year. I have the program—each dance
marked with an X. I danced every dance with him at the graduation ball. The night before, I had played Lola Pratt in Booth
Tarkington's *Seventeen*. Ham had played Uncle Georgicums.
Rehearsals meant, of course, we saw a great deal of each other.
At his graduation I was given a huge "ham"—I'm sure I
blushed. I learned to play on the piano a song entitled "I Can't
Tell Why I Love You, But I Doo-oo." I would rush to the
piano in the assembly hall, if possible, when I knew Ham was
near, and play it to him. The graduation song was "Moonlight
and Roses." Ham sang this. And the current great song of the
day was "Always." These were our songs—they still are mine.
I often wonder if when Ham hears them they make him travel
back through the years to that graduation in 1926 when we

were so gloriously in love. My mother requested "Always" to be played at her funeral. How I cried—for all of us—each dead in different ways.

Mother was faced once more with the problem of where we would spend the summer. Ruthie and her sister Mildred had in the spring been on a motor trip in the area of Peterboro, New Hampshire. They were enchanted with the town. It so happened they passed a church at the moment the bride and groom were about to come out. Ruthie grabbed her ever present camera and took photographs of the bride and groom. She often said she didn't know why she did this. There was a charming inn in Peterboro where Mother and Mildred spent the night. Ruthie was incredible—always saving money on the one hand and being extravagant on the other. She believed to get money you have to spend it. Certainly the money she spent for the expensive Peterboro Inn proved her point. She found out there was no photographer in this town—that Mariarden, a school of dance and the theatre—was on the outskirts of town. She could very probably photograph events at the school. In other words the possibilities for financial gain plus the charm and activity of Peterboro would be a most satisfying summer for all three of the musketeers.

Early next morning Mother started the search for a house, and with her usual deserved good fortune she found a lovely two-hundred-year-old New England house—fireplaces, brick floors and all. Large enough for a studio and a darkroom as well. With a sigh of relief Mother and Mildred returned to Newton, Mother secure that her two girls would have a charming home for the summer. She picked us up at Cushing after the close of school and drove us to Peterboro, car filled as always with the usual rigmarole including our Boston terrier, Babs, and a grin from ear to ear as she told us of the summer to come—its possibilities, its fun. Ruthie always followed a dream and more often than not, her belief made them come true.

Upon our arrival at the magnificent house, Bobby and I ran from room to room inspecting the many fireplaces and antiques that would be perfect "backgrounds for my subjects." Mother hung out her sign THE SILHOUETTE SHOP and thus our summer began.

Mother was stimulated by Peterboro. A world of artists was

what she had long dreamed of for herself. She became the Ruth
Favor of her childhood. Peterboro offered her a feast of cultural
and creative opportunity.

Bobby would be placed with a fine music teacher and Bette
would study dancing at Mariarden. Next day off she went to
Mrs. Guy Currier, director of Mariarden, to enroll me for the
season. I had always loved dancing and was excited at the
prospect of studying it.

Roshanara, the dancing instructress, was actually a Britisher
named Jane Cradduck. She was a brilliant dancer and also a
designer who had done the George Arliss production of *The
Green Goddess*. I auditioned for her and she accepted me. The
tuition was prohibitive, however, and I was placed more fru-
gally with Marie Ware Laughton's Outdoor Players to learn
nature dances à la Isadora Duncan.

One day during one of my dancing classes, on the green
lawn circled by pines, Roshanara visited us. I can still see her,
dark and stately, moving with that incredible grace. Wearing
a long, softly girdled robe, she seemed to look neither to the
left nor right. She was a muse. We were all so awed that we
could barely dance and then she glided off.

The next day, Ruthie received a letter.

MY DEAR MRS. DAVIS.
    Would you bring your daughter to see me at four o'clock
today, Tuesday.

                                        (Signed) Roshanara

I read Mother's mind.

"Now stop dreaming, Mother. She just can't believe I was
that bad and wants to suggest that I take up crocheting."

But we were there at four sharp. Roshanara's dark eyes
passed over me like a warm breeze.

"Mrs. Davis, I want Bette for a student. I saw her dance
yesterday. She has talent."

Her crisp pronunciation was as surprising as her pronouncement. Ruthie's heart started to pound. Mine all but stopped.
Roshanara continued:

"I do not mean to embarrass you, but I know you are short
of funds; I have heard. Your daughter Barbara can play the
piano. We need a rehearsal pianist three hours a day. I will

pay Barbara five dollars a week and waive Bette's tuition."

Bobby was thrilled with the opportunity to contribute to the family exchequer and very expertly played for Roshanara's classes that summer.

I worked harder for the next eight weeks than I had ever thought possible. Heat or no heat, we danced eight hours a day every day and I loved every single minute.

Mariarden was a magnificent setting for outdoor drama. The E. E. Clive Players of Boston performed for part of the season in the outdoor theatre. The rest of the time the theatre was at Roshanara's disposal.

Ruthie, Bobby and I went to see her first performance. She was a revelation of spiritual beauty. Her "Prayer" a study of profound serenity. She conveyed the wonder of Faith as no sermon could.

I have never thought of Dance as anything but an esthetic release of energy—fun. Roshanara's repertoire of emotions conveyed through movement and wedded to music made my head reel. Her Hindu dances—so exotic to me—ranged from Punjab kite rituals to the classic Hindu *Nautch*. There under the stars, her setting the elms and pines lit mysteriously from behind moss-covered rocks, she shone like the moon.

I was completely carried away by her art. It seemed impossible that I would ever share a stage with her.

Two weeks later, I made my first appearance with her company. I was one of the dancing fairies in *Midsummer Night's Dream*. I should have known it would be a lucky moment. It rained incessantly for three days and nights before we opened. There was doubt we could give the performance; but we did.

What a production it was! Roshanara arranged the ballet, Richard Whorf designed the sets and costumes. He also played Snug. Alan Mowbray was Lysander; May Ediss the Puck; Frank Arundel and Lucy Currier were Oberon and Titania; Cecil Clovelley, Flute; and our director Frank Conroy played Bottom. What a beautiful actor he has always been. He has the head of a falcon and the heart!

My next appearance with Roshanara's company was as the Moth—a dance made famous by the Fuller Dancers and performed before all the crowned heads of Europe.

As a moth, I wore a white silk gown whose immense wings were attached to balsam sticks, which I held in my hands, and gave great extension to my arms. The effect was one mass of shimmering silk. I danced on a lighted, multicolored glass floor that turned me from blinding white to amber and blue to the eventual orange flame in which I fluttered to my final self-destruction. I remember the excitement of performing that night in front of an audience—the applause thrilled me. Roshanara was pleased with me and kissed me after the performance. I was quite naturally on Cloud 9. Ruthie and Bobby—I suppose they were prejudiced, but I recall their looking at me afterwards as if they'd never seen me before.

That evening after the performance Frank Conroy sought Ruthie out.

"Mrs. Davis," he said. "I seldom tell a mother what I am going to tell you. You must see to it your daughter goes on the stage. She belongs there. She has something which comes across the footlights."

The pictures that Mother had taken of a bride and groom her first night in Peterboro she had developed soon after our arrival there. When the newlyweds returned from their honeymoon she had found them easily, in such a tiny town, and they ordered a wedding book of her pictures. This was Mother's start there and led to photographing other weddings, which led to taking photographs at Mariarden off and on during the summer. Even Roshanara sat for Ruthie and was most generous in her order for prints. The greatest excitement of all this fabulous summer was the fact that the Shawn Dancers were living on the same street with us and were nudists who never pulled down the shades. Bobby and I were fascinated as we stood across from their house, well hidden under a leafy elm, and learned about life in the raw!

Ham visited us for a few days that summer. We were still in love. I was lonely thinking of Cushing without him but he promised to come up for the dances, and would see me in Newton at Christmastime. Other beaux visited me—and after a few days I would say, "Mother, *when* is he leaving?" She would laugh. She had heard this before.

My senior year at Cushing is not as vivid in my mind as my junior year. I missed Ham—*that* is vivid. I was voted the prettiest girl in the Senior Class at the end of the year. I did play the lead in the Senior play. I can't remember for the life of me what the play was. I continued contributing to the family funds by waiting on tables. Ham was at Massachusetts Agricultural College and we corresponded frequently. He came to my graduation dance. When we said good night, we both felt it was an end of something—a parting of the ways perhaps. No new boy had as yet taken his place. During the Christmas holiday he visited us in Newton as he had promised. I remained Ham's girl.

In order to have enough money to pay my tuition *in toto* before the end of school, so that I could be given my diploma, Ruthie took all the graduation pictures of the Senior Class for the yearbook. This, plus the individual orders she hoped to get from the students, would more than pay the bill. This meant she photographed her subjects, developed the negatives and made the prints herself. As long as I live, and my greatest incentive to become a success in the world, was the sight of my mother sitting in the assembly hall at my graduation. As I received my diploma, I looked down at her from the platform. She had developer poisoning very apparent on her face—she weighed about ninety pounds—as a result of finishing all the orders for the graduating class in time, a last year's dress and hat, and a tired but proud smile on her face. A braver, more exhausted mother was not there that day. I wanted to cry.

I remember thinking as I looked down at her that I must repay her for all these years of blood, sweat and no tears. I am grateful I was able to—but give her back her youth I could not. She had guts and dreams for her children. The guts made the dreams come true. There never was the word "can't" in her vocabulary.

The summer after my graduation, the musketeers rented a tiny fishing shack in Perkins Cove in Ogunquit, Maine. The shack consisted of one large room with a fireplace, loads of atmosphere, a kitchen, and one bedroom. Ruthie, as was always the case, gave Bobby and me the bedroom and slept on the living room couch.

This was a carefree summer. I took the Red Cross senior life-saving test, the one girl in a blush of boys taking the course. I passed and wore my emblem proudly on my bathing suit. It was this summer that I met Marie Simpson, who was waiting on table at the Sparhawk Hotel, a student at Hood College in Maryland, auburn-haired, Southern—and the definite belle of the beach in Ogunquit. We are still the best of friends and I'm sure that her husband Brownie was not surprised when I told him his wife had all the boys of Ogunquit gaga that summer. All but one—Fritz Hall. He was mine—a boy from Yale. I fell in love for the first time since knowing Ham. Besides, Fritz was there and Ham was far away. In a burst of honesty, I sent Ham's fraternity pin back to him with a full declaration of my new-found love.

That summer we met the Stanley Woodwards who had a studio across the lane from us. Stanley is one of America's top marine painters. We have always remained friends, and in the years since then I have bought many of his canvases. My favorite is a moonlight of the sea painted in Ogunquit, near where we lived.

It is remarkable that Stanley got any work done that summer because of the racket Bobby and I made on the rocks outside his studio window.

There was a theatre in Ogunquit run by an actor named Bennett Kilpack. Since Frank Conroy's advice to Ruthie, I had thought of the theatre more and more. I still felt as I always had that I would do something with my life. Suburbia, husband, children, bridge clubs, would never be for me. One day I went to call on Mr. Kilpack to see if he wouldn't let me play some parts at his playhouse during the summer. He was most pleasant but most emphatic that I was too young, and as I was also totally inexperienced, the whole idea was impractical. Years later we became friends and worked together in the Seth Parker picture *Way Back Home*. He was horrified and amused to find I had come to him in Ogunquit those many years ago and he had so calmly dismissed me.

This particular summer stands out in my mind for two other reasons. I went to a gypsy fortuneteller in the nearby town of York, Maine. After much silence and shaking of her head, she said to this Yankee, eighteen-year-old girl, "You will someday be known in every country in the world"—a very perplexing statement for said young girl to figure out. As a matter of fact, Mother and I sat up into the wee hours of the morning, in front of the fire in our fisherman's shack, trying to figure out what I could ever do that would make the fortuneteller's prediction come true. Motion pictures, one of the few ways possible to be known in every country in the world, never entered our minds.

This was also the summer I went on my first date unchaperoned. Mother was very old-fashioned about unchaperoned dates, even for her day. One evening, after much persuasion from me, I was allowed to accept a date with a boy alone. He brought two friends with him. As a matter of fact, delighted as I was, I was frightened to death with my freedom and apprehensive about what would be expected of me that evening; even more so when the numerous bottles of liquor were gone to work on the minute we drove up the cove away from our shack. We went to a dance at the hotel in Kennebunkport, about 15 miles away. My escort and his friends soon were spiffed. I was frantically trying to decide how to get away from them so that I could avoid the drunken ride home. One of my beaux that summer was Dick Thomas. Mother had gone to the Playhouse in Ogunquit that evening and happened to sit behind Dick. In the middle of the third act she leaned over and asked him if he would drive quickly to the Kennebunkport hotel and bring me home. Something terrible was going to happen. She would explain later. In the midst of my dilemma as to how to get home sans my looped beaux, Dick cut in on me and said he was taking me home. Mother needed me right away. A certain amount of antagonism was caused by this announcement even though I was grateful for the out, but home with Dick I went.

In the car driving back to Ogunquit he told me Ruthie had sent him to get me because she had a premonition something terrible was going to happen. I might add at this point that Ruthie had great psychic powers. She also read tea leaves with an accuracy that was awe-inspiring. Next morning my erstwhile escort of the night before came to see me. He was green around the gills and cold sober. He embraced Ruthie, saying, "Thank God, you sent for Bette last night. One of my friends drove the car home—and completely smashed it up. Bette would most likely have been killed." Ruthie was always a lifesaver in more ways than one.

When summer was over we returned to Newton. I was a free agent—a graduate with no money for college. Bobby decided she would rather finish her high school years at Newton High and live at home with us. We rented the top story of a two-family house on Cabot Street in Newton. The Stanley

Woodwards—our newly found friends from Ogunquit—lived on the lower floor.

This started a continuation of my blue period in East Orange, New Jersey. I cooked, kept house, missed Fritz—who was now at Yale—and at this point pictured myself in the white cottage with Fritz not Ham. I was in a backwash, going nowhere, and saw no hope of any change. My chums of my gay Newton High days were involved with their own lives and had forgotten my very existence. Often they would walk right by my house and never even call up "Hi." It hurt and made me that much lonelier.

Ham drove down from Whitinsville during his Christmas holiday. Seeing him again made me forget Fritz. The boy nearby is a great factor with youth in love. A beau—on hand— is worth two in the bush. I remember sitting looking at our Christmas tree in the darkened living room and dreaming our dreams of the future—hopeless dreams at this point. Here I was for the second time in my life stuck in suburbia, with no mission in life—no goal—no hope of one. It took money to go to New York and study for the theatre. Money Mother just didn't have. I worked for an authoress that winter, typing her manuscripts. Roshanara's mother had advised me to study shorthand and typing in high school as an alternate way to earn a living if my attempts to become an actress were not successful. It stood me in good stead that winter. I was able to add to Mother's income as well as keep busy, which helped me not to lose my mind with ennui.

Ruthie took Bobby and me to the Jewett Playhouse in Boston that winter to see Ibsen's *The Wild Duck* starring Blanche Yurka, with Peg Entwistle as Hedvig. I had never seen Ibsen before and I was fascinated by his power of characterization and the magnificence of his brooding emotion.

It was my first serious theatre and a whole, new world opened up to me. I was thrilled with Miss Entwistle's performance.

The curtain rose and Gina sat sewing, unaware that forces were at work to shatter her whole life. Near her on a sofa sat a frail young girl. Her hands shaded her eyes as she read. Miss Yurka's mezzo voice was greeted by applause.

"Hedvig!"

No answer. The child was engrossed.

"Hedvig!"

The child looked up as her hand slipped to her lap. My heart almost stopped. She looked just like me.

"Hedvig, you mustn't read any longer—"

"Oh, Mother. Mayn't I . . . just a little?"

She was me.

"No . . . No . . . Father doesn't like it."

I was watching myself. Miss Entwistle had lost herself in Hedvig. Now I did too. There wasn't an emotion I didn't anticipate and share with her. As the play went on, I slipped further and further into this Norwegian family. With Gregers' pious revelation of my bastardy, I suffered unbearable pain. In some incredible fusion, Entwistle, Hedvig and I were now one.

When "the little wild duck" shot herself in the breast, I died with her. I had no pulse whatsoever as Hedvig was carried from the stage in a little casket. It seemed as though everything in my life fell into place and I was in focus for the first time. There had been a glimmer here and there; but this was the vision. Mr. Conroy had known before I did. I knew now that more than anything—despite anything—I was going to become an actress.

"Mother! Someday I will play Hedvig."

Not so many years later I did.

CHAPTER

4

Ruthie had a mission now. She left no stone unturned to pave the way for me. She went to see Daddy to tell him of my ambition to be an actress.

"Let her become a secretary! She'll earn money quicker. Bette could never be a successful actress."

This was my second reason for succeeding—to prove Daddy wrong. He truly challenged me.

Aunt Mildred and Uncle Myron felt Ruthie was making a mistake, but they agreed to keep Bobby with them while we went to New York to storm Broadway.

Grandmother understood. Her pronouncement had the ring of the old-time religion: "Believe in something. Work for it. It will be yours!"

Ruthie and I drove to New York in September, 1928, after having made an appointment for an interview with Eva Le Gallienne to see if she would accept me as a student at her 14th Street theatre. I had a million doubts but Ruthie was never more optimistic.

Miss Le Gallienne's Civic Repertory Company was then one of the bright hopes of the theatre. Her interest in an actor meant the start of a career. Best of all, acceptance by her meant free tuition since all of her students paid their way by appearing in productions of the Company.

Our bags were left at Uncle Paul's house in New Rochelle where we would be staying for the night. Our hopes were high as we entered the theatre on 14th Street. I wondered what the interview would be like. My desire to start studying for the theatre was so overwhelming, I was certain I would be accepted.

Ruthie waited for me as I was ushered into the audition room. Everyone was terribly tweedy with flat heels and broad A's.

Miss Le Gallienne and her secretary soon arrived for my interview. She talked to me at length of my aims, background—asked me if I knew why students of the drama should study the movements of animals, where and how I would live in New York. I answered the last question by saying "with my mother." All this had made me feel very insecure, especially the question about the animals. I had no idea what that had to do with acting! I'm sure she felt in me a pride and a lack of yield that might become a difficult problem in a future student. The truth probably was that, as this was my first experience in a dark, unlighted backstage of a theatre, I felt strange and uncomfortable, besides the fear of not being accepted. I'm sure I was very much on the defensive.

I have never functioned well when anyone is doubting my ability to do something. Like a small child, approval is still a major requirement for my best efforts. I felt that day Miss Le Gallienne was interviewing me as a knowledgeable actress, not as an inexperienced girl wanting to learn how to become a good actress. She made me feel stupid and I was not used to this. The frosting on the cake was her request for me to read the part of a Dutch lady of sixty-five as a test of my acting prowess. A little heatedly I burst out with, "That is why I want to come to your school, to learn how to play a part like this." Silence was her reply. I gritted my teeth and started in—and drove myself to finish. I was politely thanked, told I would hear from the school in a few days, and dismissed.

Driving back to New Rochelle after my interview, I gave Ruthie a blow-by-blow description of my interview. I was positive I would never be accepted by Miss Le Gallienne. Mother found every reason to feel the opposite. We spent the night at Uncle Paul's and motored back to Newton the following day to await the letter from Miss Le Gallienne which would most certainly decide my future. The waiting was agony. I so desperately wanted to get going on my career. This was the only dramatic school in New York that Ruthie could have afforded. What would I do if I was turned down? And I was. A week later *The* letter came. I dreaded to read it. The upshot was that Miss Le Gallienne felt I was not serious enough in my approach to the theatre to warrant my attendance at her school. I was heartbroken, furious, defeated. If ever I could have become a mental case it was at this time.

I was doomed to a life in the suburbs of Boston, and would never become that something I always felt from a child I was destined to be. At Uncle Paul's the evening after my interview, Ruthie by some chance, I imagine facing the fact I might not be accepted by Miss Le Gallienne, was looking through the want ads in the local paper. She came across one which had requirements she could meet—doing retouching work for a photographer in Norwalk, Connecticut. At the end of another month or so in Newton, Ruthie knew something drastic had to be done. I was each day becoming paler and more silent. I went about my household chores automatically, feeling no hope for the future.

Bobby was still attending Newton High School. Even she didn't know me. Her gay, zestful sister was a thing of the past. Mother decided in a flash we would go to Norwalk. She would try and get the job with Mr. Jackson and have Bobby finish her senior year at Newton High by staying with Myron and Mildred. It would be near New York, a change of scene for me which might shake me out of my doldrums, and New Haven and Fritz were nearby. Our worldly possessions were put in storage, and two of the musketeers were on the march again. We hated leaving Bobby. Poor Ruthie was always torn when feeling the necessity of separating any of the three of us. Upon our arrival in Norwalk, we found a place to live within our means. Mother applied for the job with Mr. Jackson and got it, so we nested in. Mother went to her job every day. I existed. Fritz was delighted to hear we were so nearby. I saw him most every weekend—certainly the highlight in my life at that moment. Ham was once more forgotten. Ah woman—how fickle is she, an important factor in the young male-female race.

My average day started around nine or ten. I would sleep late—this made the day shorter—get dressed, straighten up our rooms, then walk downtown, a matter of six or eight blocks,

to a one-armed lunchroom for my breakfast. This boardinghouse did not serve meals. I suppose technically it was a roominghouse.

Mother's place of business was right across the street. There
she would be in the window, because this made the light better,
crouching over negative after negative, hour after hour, doing
her retouching work. It is another image of Ruthie's gallantry
I never forgot. She would come back to our diggings every
evening after work, eyes strained, back aching, but always
cheerful—always hopeful. Something was around the corner
for me. What, I didn't know. And I'm sure even she at this
point was whistling in the dark. It was soon apparent to her
that neither the change of scene nor the weekend visits with
Fritz were changing my attitude in any way. I was without
purpose—inactive—a ship without a sail bobbing about on a
stormy sea.

That fall in Norwalk it never stopped raining. Drip, drip—
I walked for miles those weeks, alone, always eating at my
one-armed restaurant and seeing Ruthie at her work across the
street. I was gradually going mad!! Rain, however, I was su-
perstitious about. It had always brought me luck. I felt somehow
that something was about to happen. My spirits were better
about the future. And I was right. One morning I was awakened
by Ruthie, standing over my bed saying, "Get up, Bette. Dress
in your best. We're going to New York today." I looked out
the window. The previous six days had been an out-of-town
tryout for the storm that was now raging. It was pouring and
the wind was howling. Ruthie added, "Rain is your good luck
sign. Hurry, our train leaves in an hour."

What was Mother up to now? Asking no questions, but
obediently doing as I was told, we were on the train for New
York in an hour. Mother had called Mr. Jackson and pleaded
illness. I knew one thing only—Mother had blood in her eye.
She obviously meant business. Ruthie loved surprises, and she
gave me no inkling of the day to come.

We got into a taxi at Grand Central Station and drove to
58th Street, between Park and Lexington avenues. The sign
outside the building where we stopped said ROBERT MILTON-
JOHN MURRAY ANDERSON SCHOOL OF THE THEATRE. I flipped.
Without a word between us we went inside and directly to Mr.
Hugh Anderson's office, John Murray's brother and the man-

ager of the school. Ruthie had called and made an appointment
with him the day before. She went into the inner office. I waited
outside. Mr. Anderson himself told me later a woman named
Mrs. Davis walked in, sat down, said, "My daughter Bette
wants to be an actress. I haven't the money for her tuition but
will assure you, you will eventually have it. Will you accept
her as a student?" Mr. Anderson claims he was so stupefied
by Ruthie's guts that before he knew it he had said yes. He
never knew what possessed him. But accepted I was. A miracle
happened on 58th Street that day. Ruthie found a way to open
the door so I could pursue my dream.

We returned by train to Norwalk that night. Mother explained
to Mr. Jackson that she would have to give up her job. We
packed our things at the roominghouse, put them in the car,
and the next day drove back to New York. I was registered in
all my classes, was assigned a room in the brownstone boardinghouse next door replete with a roommate, Virginia Conroy
by name. We were not the right casting for each other, that
was obvious at first glance, but we became fast friends, and
learned much from each other. She was a Clara Bow type, a
true flapper, who entertained few serious thoughts and bounced
constantly in rhythm to the jazz she always heard whether the
radio was on or not.

Mother once more looked for a job and was fortunate enough
to find one quickly. She was engaged as a housemother at St.
Mary's School in Burlington, New Jersey.

Our room was in utter chaos when I first saw it. It remained
that way—Ginny's half of it. She didn't believe in picking up
anything. Her ukulele was never far off; and she would sit
playing by the hour cross-legged on her bed—a John Held yogi
singing "Won't you do do do what you done done done before?" All this while I would be doing my best to do my voice
lessons, memorize lines for next day's class, or whatever. She
was basically delicious—and a dear.

She would often say, "Bette, you could be the bee's knees
if you wouldn't take life so seriously."

Mother never understood how it didn't all end in tragedy—
Virginia and I; but it didn't.

I'm afraid I got much more out of the school than Ginny
did. The faculty included Martha Graham, Michael Mordkin,
Robert Bell, George Currie—and of course, John Murray An-

derson. The first day I was there and every day, Mr. Currie, our dramatic teacher, would deliver a scathing attack on the theatre. He informed the seventy kids in our class that we were heading for the toughest, least glamorous life imaginable. His picture of the artist's life was a pointillism, whose dots of color were sweat, jealousy, competition, disillusionment, insecurity and more sweat. It was a lecture of futility that he repeated over and over again.

It was really the most discouraging pep talk ever delivered to a group of novices. The class was soon decimated. The little society girls folded up their tents and silently stole away. There were twelve of us left at the end of the semester. It was then that Mr. Currie told us that a real actor—a real artist—needs no pep talk. If anyone really wants to be an actor, nothing can discourage him.

"A real artist brings his own conviction and hope. He may be encouraged along this line. He *cannot* be discouraged. If you've stuck this term out, you've at least got the stuff."

Tough! But so is the theatre. Everything he said was true. Any artist who doesn't know that the greatest reward is his own satisfaction in work should choose an easier way of life. Acting is work. But work when you love it and fulfill yourself is life at its best.

Along with dramatics and warnings against the very goal we were pursuing, there were classes in everything including the bar sinister movies. We made one two-reeler that season and we acted in a play a week. We were constantly at work, rehearsing and memorizing while we forged ahead in our studies.

Our instructress for dancing was Martha Graham. Her job was to teach us how to use our bodies properly.

"To act is to dance!"

I worshiped her. She was all tension—lightning! Her burning dedication gave her spare body the power of ten men. If Roshanara was a mystic curve, Miss Graham was a straight line—a divining rod. Both were great, and both were aware of the universal. But Miss Graham was the true modern.

I had already learned that the body via the dance could send a message. Now I was taught a syntax with which to articulate the subtleties fully. She would with a single thrust of her weight convey anguish. Then in an anchored lift that made her ten feet tall, she became all joy. One after the other. Hatred, ecstasy, age, compassion! There was no end, once the body was disciplined.

What at first seemed grotesque to the eye, developed into a beautiful release for both dancer and beholder. To me, Martha Graham is one of America's few authentic geniuses. I will always be grateful that I was lucky enough to study with her.

A mutual friend recently repeated this great woman's happy observation that amongst dramatic actors, I have always expressed an emotion with full body—as a dancer does. If this be so, I would like to remind her that it was she who made it possible. Every time I climbed a flight of stairs in films—and I spent half my life on them—it was Graham step by step.

The proper use of body and voice can be taught. George Arliss was one of the many celebrities who lectured at school. I recall his admonition not to "adopt that exaggerated speech we hear so much of today on the stage. Be simple and clear!" And Mr. Anderson himself, who conducted one class a week, felt he could do nothing more constructive than yell, "LOUDER!" We could use him today in theatres where the actors, deep in self-analysis, share the dialogue only with that part of the cast near enough to catch it.

Frankly, I feel that the dramatic school is important only for the basic education it imparts. The alphabet must be learned. How to talk. How to move. How to sit and stand. Grace, poise, give an actor confidence. One has to learn how to comport one's self on a stage in a different manner than if it were his own living room. The alphabet! Fine. But knowing all the letters from A to Zed does not make one a writer. The mastering of the dotted I and the crossed T does not make one a poet. There are things that cannot be taught. Or rather, there are things that cannot be learned.

There are various schools that lay claim to revelation. For the talentless, it is true that a chart gives them direction. It can even guide them to adequacy. I watch young men and women today in all three media struggling through a psychological maze and they do not excite me theatrically.

One can draw just so much from one's personal experience. The actor has his instrument—yes. If he has no intellect, no passion, no expansion of soul, he can hardly understand a part in which these elements take precedence. He cannot even understand a part in which they are absent. One must be aware of the negative areas. How, for example, can a stupid, phlegmatic bigot be played well unless the actor, his opposite, uses selectivity and observes the accents of the character, thereby bringing him to life.

The present trend of the actor to personalize all tragedy and recall the moment in which his puppy was run over or her doll was broken in order to convey misery is sad to me. Although man has a basic repertoire of emotion, the subtleties in each individual are blessedly countless.

Blanche Dubois and Ophelia both liquefy before your eyes; but they melt entirely differently. Oedipus and Lear both break at the end. One cracks in half; the other crumbles to dust. Can the recalled death of the actor's sweet old Uncle William really approximate the singularity of each character's wretchedness?

I am not a teacher. I only know that an actor feels. He galvanizes his energies and his faculties and then goes *out* of himself not *in*. He pretends to be this other human being. If he has insight, he intuits and projects himself into the character, never losing the lifeline, the umbilical cord, without which he is a raving maniac and even worse—an amateur. He must always know he is pretending. Some part of him retains this knowledge; but he must suffer as the character just as he must move like him and speak like him.

An actor without insight is a mannikin; and there isn't a school in the world that can give it to him. The real actor—like any real artist—has a direct line to the collective heart. This isn't pretension. This is the whole thing in a nutshell. After reading a script, the actor has been told by the author who and what the character is. Assuming it is a good script, the meaning is clear and the actor starts to work on the masquerade. His costume is made up of a thousand and one details that fall into place when his own identity is sacrificed to the other's. This is how the actor creatively helps the playwright breathe life into the play. Every thought and physical accessory must reflect the personality and emotional drive of the character and *not* the actor. It is a portrait the author has created, not an eclectic figure.

I have heard actors cry, "This is impossible for me." "This is foreign to me." "This doesn't come naturally." "May I change the line to make it more comfortable?" "I'd *never* say that at that moment.'' Who cares what *he* would say? It's not his biography.

Many of the girls and boys today come over quite genuinely and charmingly as themselves, which is an accomplishment of some sort. But take them out of their environment and they are lost. The classics are impossible for them. Any change of locale or time throws them.

They have simply learned to express themselves; and I'm terribly happy for them. When they learn to express the character, I shall applaud them. All the walking like a cat and flying like a bird isn't going to mean a thing if the actor meows in a Brooklyn accent or quacks like Donald Duck when he is supposed to be Francis Drake.

Then there's the question of style. Without it, there is no art. As personal as these troubled actors are, there is—aside from much of a muchness—the same of a sameness. They are all so busy revealing their own insides that, like all X-ray plates, one looks pretty much like the other. Their godhead, the remarkably gifted Marlon Brando, may bring (as all true stars do) his own personal magnetism to every part, but his scope and projection are unarguable. He has always transcended the techniques he was taught. His consequent glamour and style have nothing to do with self-involvement but rather radiation.

The purists have much to say about personal magnetism, style and star quality. I will defend all three to my death. This is not a contradiction, either. The actor must learn to play a variety of melodies on his instrument. It is hardly tragic if the audience comes to recognize the tone of his Stradivarius. One can be just so lofty and arty about the "theatuh." The public makes its stars and loves them. They should recognize them and welcome them. It doesn't take one whit away from an honest portrayal.

In character work, you must of course alter yourself; but in straight drama one would have to have repeated plastic surgery to keep from being "the same in every role." This is obviously insane and only a cavil aimed at some other critic's choice. Any actor of stature and power, despite the borrowed gestures of a legitimate characterization, should command the recognition the public enjoys. I've never known one who did not.

This is not to say that there aren't performers opposed to actors. But that is a horse of a different color and can always be found running on the same track.

I return to that spark that is the individual. An actor must be true to the spark he finds in himself. And with it, he must illuminate another man and then all men. To the beginner, I would say: learn the rules, conquer the techniques and then throw yourself into a part and let go. I fear that I shocked a student recently when, at a lecture, he asked how I prepared for a role. I answered, "I learn my lines and hope for the best."

If you are an actor, all the preparation goes on underneath somewhere. The reflexes work. I can't sit down and analyze exactly how I jump out of the way of a flying object. I may know that my last remark caused its flight; but that is after the fact. I don't know how, but I jump. I play a part. It comes. The greatest thing a school or method can do for an actor is to dispense with the barriers that block its coming. That's all. It's enough.

There was another girl who greedily devoured every class at Anderson's school with me. I think it was her name that first made me single her out as something special. Rosebud Blondell. She worked like a demon and had talent. Her father was a vaudevillian and she wanted to become a legitimate actress.

One night as I was making up for the midseason test play, *Their Anniversary,* that we were both in, Rosebud rushed into the dressing room laughing hysterically.

"Wait until you get a load of your 'husband' tonight, honey. That's going to be a love scene worth watching all right."

I had no idea what she was going on about. The boy playing my husband was an Italian. During the performance I got the full meaning of Rosebud's hysteria. Michael had consumed a good Italian dinner before the performance. He almost knocked me unconscious. I will never know how I got through the play between Michael's breath and Rosebud's wide-eyed, upstage grimaces. I thought I would explode.

Rosebud changed her name to Joan later, and Joan Blondell arrived at Warners a year before I did.

There was another girl, namèd Blanchard Bartlett, in my class, whose father was President of Hobart College in Geneva, New York. Oddly enough it was Blanchard, not Virginia, who arranged my first date with a man-about-town.

My romantic life had come to an abrupt halt. Fritz had proposed marriage, and I had proudly worn his engagement ring for three days while he pleaded with me to give up all thoughts of the theatre. John Murray Anderson had just announced in the press—with accompanying photographs—that I was the perfect modern Venus, whatever that meant. The notoriety did not make Harlow Morrell Davis feel more like Zeus, nor did it please the patrician Fritz.

After college, Fritz was going into his father's business. He needed a wife and a hostess. This acting business was all very well as a premarital lark but not to be taken seriously by the future Mrs. Hall.

Now in the first place, I cannot abide an ultimatum. And what did he think I was, one of those spoiled little darlings who folded their tents and stole away after Mr. Currie's speeches about the hell of an actor's life? I was serious about theatre. I couldn't understand his unwillingness to have me continue.

Fritz even sent me a news clipping about Katherine Willson, who announced that she was giving up her promising theatrical career to become Mrs. Richard Barthelmess. "'A woman's place is in the home,' opined Miss Willson as she reclined on her davenport like a beautiful oriental flower." Every word was underscored by Fritz to bring home the point.

I would never have had to worry about money again; but I returned the ring, answered Ham's latest letter from Amherst and dusted our room—ukulele and all. Ham had enclosed my Venus clipping with appropriately irreverent remarks that made me roar.

Blanchard asked me if I would go out on a double date with her. The men were "true sophisticates—men with *savoir faire*." She made it clear that I was a desperate replacement for another girl who was ill.

"You *can* handle yourself with a man of forty, can't you? And you do drink?"

I couldn't see any reason why I would have to drink. I never had as yet, and what was this about a man of forty? I felt I was intelligent. There was nothing I hadn't read. I could hold my own in most conversations.

I thanked her and accepted. She told me we were going to the Ritz. I was thrilled! It was definitely a first for me.

My wardrobe was limited to the point of being nonexistent and Blanchard lent me an evening wrap. She was unfortunately much taller than I and it dragged to the ground. I was perfectly costumed for a Halloween party.

All the while trying to convince the skeptical Blanchard that I would pass muster, we joined our hosts in their hotel suite, where corsages of gardenias awaited us. The first real ones I had ever seen. Drinks were distributed—I said neither yea nor nay. Blanchard watched me closely to be sure I was drinking mine. She never caught me pouring it into a plant on the table. I didn't need whiskey to intoxicate me. I was having a marvelous time.

Suddenly I found myself saying, "This is the most thrilling evening I've ever had. I've never been to the Ritz before and this is my first date with—"

Blanchard could have murdered me. I had spilled the Boston beans. My date rushed to the telephone. I thought we were going to be thrown out.

"Young lady, an evening like this demands the best."

With that, he had the florist send orchids to me and the whole night took on a different tone. These sophisticated men might have looked like Lew Cody or Lowell Sherman, but they turned out to be the sweetest men in the world. They were going to give a green kid the time of her life. We went to every "hot spot" in Mr. Walker's town and finished up at the Club Alabam. They were like adoring fathers. I lay claim to being the only girl in Manhattan that night who consumed twelve bottles of pop. Blanchard was wrong. No one could say I wasn't full of the old moxie. I had been honest.

This one night covered my whole social life while I attended John Murray's school. There was too much work and too much at stake. Ruthie wasn't going to be a housemother at St. Mary's for nothing.

Mr. Anderson gave, every year, two five-hundred-dollar scholarships. One for a girl, one for a boy. This represented six months' free tuition. I made up my mind that I had to win the girl's scholarship to help Ruthie.

By the end of the term I had won the role of Sylvia Fair in *The Famous Mrs. Fair* which Margalo Gillmore had played eight years before on Broadway. James Light, of the Provincetown Playhouse in the Village, was the director. As the term examination play, it was to be presented to an audience of theatrical visitors as well as parents and teachers.

I gave the preparation of this role the works. My performance in this would win or lose the scholarship. Two days before the performance I developed a cold with threatening laryngitis. The corner drugstore became my second home. There wasn't a patent medicine or an old wives' tale I didn't try.

On the evening of the play, my voice was in good shape. It bore up for two acts.

Sylvia Fair, because of World War I and the moral disintegration that followed it, changes from a sweet young thing to a bitter and corrupt woman. By the third act my voice was very hoarse. As the play neared its end, I could hardly struggle through the last speeches. Sylvia's decay was now complete—down to her larynx. The entire audience assumed that I affected the whiskey baritone deliberately. They were stupefied by my vocal range. So was I.

Ruthie was there that night, and knowing the truth of the matter, offered up a few silent prayers that I would make it—the first of a myriad of silent prayers she offered up during the many years of my career.

The announcements as to who had won the scholarships were made that evening after the performance. Ruthie's face of gratitude when my name was read as the winner was worth a lot to me. She spent that night in our boardinghouse on an improvised bed of three chairs tied together with string. She always refused my insistence that she have my bed. She was wrong. It made me very uncomfortable to see her always taking the worst. But change her, I could not.

The director of *The Famous Mrs. Fair*, James Light, about a week later sent for me to come to his office at the Provincetown Playhouse. He told me he was doing a new play later that spring and wanted me to play the girl in it. My happiness knew no bounds. My first professional engagement! He could not give me the exact date, but if I was willing to leave school I could have the part.

Having won the scholarship, I had a big decision to make. I went to Hugh Anderson and he did not hesitate to advise me to do the play with Mr. Light. I stayed a few more weeks and then was on my way to play my first professional part in the theatre. I have been asked many times during my career by

mothers of daughters who want to become actresses whether
or not I believed in going to a dramatic school. I most certainly
do.

I left John Murray's school knowing at least the rudiments
of my chosen profession. The voice and diction lessons alone
were worth the year—to say nothing of the grace of movement
Martha Graham had provided me. I had acquired at least a kind
of technical security on stage—impossible without any training.

My speaking voice had been the least likely voice to enhance
an actress. A high, tiny sound came out—I wouldn't have been
heard in the first row. To say nothing of my Yankee accent.
Any sectional speech is a handicap for playing all kinds of
parts. The King's English—in purest form, as exemplified by
the great English actors—is truly the only thing accepted. The
first day in speech class, I was given a sentence to read—
"Parker parked the car in Harvard Square." The entire class
roared with laughter. My Boston A's were too much. Four
months later, having learned the proper A's, I was sent to other
speech classes in the school—to show how much can be done
to change one's way of speaking if one has the desire and the
diligence. I spoke every word slowly and exaggeratedly for
months and months until it all became natural to me. Whenever
Ruthie and I would drive back to Newtonville to see Bobby,
all my friends would tell me I sounded ridiculous—they gave
me up as a lost cause. Their ridicule wasn't easy to take, but
the end result justified the means. John Murray Anderson had
a nickname for every student. From the first day we met, he
called me "the little Southern girl."

I left school and when Jimmy Light called and said he was
ready to start rehearsals, I was thrilled. Complications arose—
of what nature I never knew—and the play was postponed until
fall. Having burned my bridges behind me, I could hardly go
back to the school. I decided to try and get another job.

Frank Conroy was in a current Broadway production, so I
wrote him asking if he could introduce me to anyone who might
be doing a play. He very generously sent me a letter of intro-
duction to George Cukor, who was casting for a production of
Broadway, to be done in a few weeks at the Lyceum Theatre
in Rochester, a stock company which he owned and was the
director of. The smallest part in the play was not cast, and as

a favor to Conroy—and I think a bit fearfully after interviewing me, judging by the way he looked at me—he gave me the part. A week's work. I was ecstatic. I called Ruthie at St. Mary's. She came to New York to help me pack and to see me off on the train.

She couldn't go to Rochester with me. She had to finish out the school year at St. Mary's. As the train was pulling out of the station she said, "Learn the part of Pearl. The actress playing the part is going to have an accident."

"Oh, Mother!" I said laughing. "You and your hunches." But I started studying the part on the train. I had learned by then that Ruthie's hunches were not to be sneezed at.

George Cukor, eventually one of Hollywood's top directors, owned and ran, with George Kondolf, the Lyceum Theatre. It was one of the very successful stock companies of the day. If nothing else, Mr. Cukor increased my vocabulary greatly. Dorothy Burgess, the leading lady of the company, realizing that this was my first professional job in the theatre, very kindly took me under her wing. She even translated Mr. Cukor's language for me. She was Fay Bainter's niece and a talented actress. She went to Hollywood not long after.

The play was a backstage melodrama that had been a big success in New York. I was one of several chorus girls. I almost swooned when I saw my costume. "Teddies" and a brassiere. I chewed gum to help me have the necessary toughness I knew I needed to be convincing as a chorus girl.

I also had to learn to do the Charleston; and though I had proven I was a good dancer, I was the anachronism of the Roaring Twenties. I had never run into the hip flask or the dances symbolic of the age. I was a romantic who preferred to dance to the music of Guy Lombardo.

How I wished Virginia Conroy were in Rochester with me. Why didn't I learn the Charleston while I was her roommate? I did the best I could, but never really mastered the art of this intricate dance. Rose Lerner was the actress who played Pearl and, according to Ruthie's prophecy, was headed for tragedy. I was letter-perfect in her part, and watched her like a hawk—hoping, I'm afraid, that Ruthie was right.

We opened successfully on a Monday night. At the Wednesday matinee it happened. Rose Lerner twisted her ankle badly in a fall down a stairway, which was part of the business of the play. She finished the rest of the show. That evening, she played with a cane.

I felt no sympathy, and felt a heel that this was so. My only panic was whether or not Mr. Cukor would give me a chance at the part the next night. I remember pacing back and forth backstage during the performance that evening. This was my chance!

No one approached me after the show, and desolately I went to my little hotel room that night. But I *knew* it—*every word* of it.

Next morning I got up at eight, dressed quickly, had breakfast, and went to the theatre and waited. I was soon rewarded. Mr. Cukor arrived, yelled at his stage manager, "Get that dame who has the smallest part over here right away." He didn't even know my name. I spoke up. "I'm here, Mr. Cukor." He asked me if I could learn the part by evening. I told him I already knew it. He ignored this remark and said, "Come on up here. Do you know how to fall down a flight of stairs?" Thanks to Martha Graham's class, we had learned all these physical tricks. I said yes. He said, "Show me." I did—and then we rehearsed. I knew every line and went on that night.

There was only one fly in the ointment—Pearl had to kill her lover. My fear of guns and gunpowder had always made even the Fourth of July a fright to me. I could hardly have changed the plot of the play to accommodate my phobia so I steeled myself.

Poor Robert Strange! He was the lover in question. He was to be shot twice by me near a door and then stagger off into the wings. It happened early in the act, and getting offstage saved him from lying dead in front of the audience for the rest of the act. In my terror at both the gun and my first performance of Pearl, I kept firing one bullet after another so fast that— being mortal—he was so dead he was forced to hit the dust onstage. He was in agony holding his breath for the rest of the act. At the end of the show, he sent for me to come to his dressing room.

"Miss Davis, tomorrow night will you do me a favor—only fire two bullets, so I can get offstage?" I apologized profusely. I had expected he would hit me. I wouldn't have blamed him. I was always grateful he was so nice to me—a green kid.

Saturday night brought an end to my contract, but Mr. Cukor

was so pleased with my performance of Pearl that he engaged me as the ingenue lead for the company the next season. God bless Ruthie's gypsy ways!

Many of the boys at Hobart College came to see the play, *Broadway*. My hard-boiled, gum-chewing chorus girl made them eager to meet me. They thought I was hot stuff! This was the college where Blanchard's father, the Blanchard of my Ritz date, was the President.

I was invited to come to tea at the college and was introduced to a mob of students who had known I was coming. My arrival was waited for with bated breath.

I entered sans makeup, sans spangles, sans chewing gum, sans everything that looked like an actress. I was just offstage me. It was truly a storm in a teacup. It was amazing how quickly my prospective admirers drifted off to something stronger. Poor Blanchard gave up after that. I was forever letting her down.

After I returned from my one-week engagement in Rochester, I was most anxious to find a job in a stock company for the summer. There was a need to earn money until I started my job at the Lyceum in the fall.

For the first time, practically an unknown, I started to make the rounds of agencies. I would invariably hear, "You look so young." There are worse things to hear, and I've heard them, but at the time I would gladly have sold my soul for a few crow's feet. I went from agency to agency and waited in line with the rest, only to hear ringing in my ears at the end of the day, "Come back tomorrow." I was sure tomorrow would never come again.

The out-of-work actor wears out more than shoe leather. The very sensibilities that make him an artist are shattered by the disregard he is shown as a human being.

Even now, so many years later, our government, proudly richer than any other, has done nothing to create a national theatre and a *modus operandi* that would not only enrich the theatre in our country, but produce an outlet for the talent and energy of its young artists. A theatre in which creative managers aren't always grubbing for money from the people who control the taste of their betters. England, France, Japan—even Russia! All of them understand the need of a national theatre. I remember with great nostalgia President Roosevelt's Federal

Theatre which should have proved once and for all that there were no bureaucratic pressures and no ideological strings. There was the seed. The Depression watered it. The Recovery blighted it. Like nobility, it seems it is only possible that man and nations rise to an occasion when it is an unhappy one. Miraculous as it is, must we wait for the rose to break through the broken pavement and stop planning gardens!

If there is anything tougher than being an actor, it is trying to be one. Hook and crook plus luck gets to the top. A young actor today may be lucky enough to get into a play every couple of seasons. What chance has he to improve his art?

I was sneered at in many a cubbyhole—crowded like cattle in the marketplace; but after making an utter nuisance of myself at one particular agency, the casting director looked at me and asked me if I was interested in summer stock. Indeed I was.

He gave me the name and address of the director of the Cape Playhouse for the coming season and made an appointment for me to go to his hotel next day at 3. I, like Elsie Dinsmore, saw nothing out of line about this. When I arrived for the interview, the director was in his undershirt and lathered for shaving. He apologized for his dishabille, asked me many questions about my career up to this point—and finally, with no further requirements, gave me a job with the Cape Playhouse in Dennis, Massachusetts, for the summer. Ignorance *is* bliss! My delight knew no bounds.

Having a few weeks before I was to report for my engagement at the Cape Playhouse, I earned my keep by putting on the graduation play at Crestalban. In addition to this, did household chores for Miss Whiting's mother, who planned and cooked meals for the students. Spring in New England is one of Nature's greatest accomplishments. Oh to be in England, now that April's here— Same thing! The rushing of the brooks from the melting snow, the sap running from the maple trees, the cowslips, arbutus, the smell of it all—the rebirth. One feels truly privileged to be a part of it. A person can be also reborn— spring is a birth; fall, the dying—an end of spring. I didn't even mind peeling barrels of potatoes and apples—or washing the mounds of dishes.

The waiting on the table came naturally to me. All of this took me back to the years when I was a little girl there. I felt, so *many* years ago. I was only nineteen. I might add the play was a great success. I had fun directing. I might add it is the only time I directed a play officially—if you know what I mean. If you don't, there are a few directors who, if they read this book, will know what I mean!

When the school year ended for Ruthie at St. Mary's, she picked me up at Crestalban in the car and we went to Bobby's graduation from Newton High. We saw her play Phoebe in *Quality Street*. I was so nervous for her before the curtain went up. She was adorable. Mother and I were very proud. We stayed a few days with the ever-generous Myron and Mildred, packed Bobby up and were off to the Playhouse for a season of summer stock. As usual, the Chevie was piled high—a puppy, tripods, cameras, etc.

The Cape Playhouse was, I believe, the first successful one of its kind and attracted such names as Peggy Wood, Violet Kemble Cooper, Basil Rathbone and Romney Brent as stars. I was a part of the group that played each week with a visiting star. Ruthie had no doubt about the laurels I would gain. I was always the more skeptical as to my success in any venture. At least, however, I was to earn money—and the three musketeers would have a summer together.

With Ruthie's usual luck, we found a cottage by the sea that we could almost afford. After unpacking the car and sprucing up a bit, I presented myself at the Playhouse.

I asked the man in the box office if I could see Mr. Moore, the owner.

"I'm Mr. Moore."

"I'm Bette Davis, reporting for work. When do we start rehearsals?"

"Never heard of you," said Mr. Moore.

"I'm your new ingenue. Your director hired me in New York. Mr. What'shisname."

"But he had no authority to hire you. There must be some misunderstanding. The company is full for the season."

I was dumbfounded. I was also speechless. Mr. Moore stared at me helplessly for a moment. My voice shook.

"He told me—I've come up here—rented a house for the summer—"

It was obvious to him I was sincere, and I knew he felt sorry for me.

"Well, if you—if you want to stay here, you can be an

usher in the theatre. We will pay you."

I couldn't have been more relieved. I had a job for the summer after all.

Usher or actress, I secretly memorized every part the ingenue had. I rehearsed in the outhouse at the cottage. Mother often asked what I was doing in the john all the time! I dreamed of sprained ankles nightly; but Mother didn't have a hunch left.

I felt like Molnar's Good Fairy as I ushered people down the aisle with my little flashlight. I have often since carried a torch.

The summer wore on and there wasn't a mishap in the cast. In July, I was asked to join the Junior Players and did Elise Benedotti in *The Charm School*, which was presented at Sears Memorial Hall in East Dennis. It was a benefit performance for the Methodist Church; Bobby played one of the other students. We were such a success, we were invited to play in three or four nearby towns. Our stage was usually a church-supper table on wooden horses. One time in the middle of a scene, our stage collapsed—no injuries—lots of laughter from cast and audience.

I watched and studied every play that was done. I knew every gesture, every cross. I heard they were going to do A. A. Milne's *Mr. Pim Passes By* with Laura Hope Crewes. I was really envious. The part of Dinah, an English girl, was perfect for me; the ingenue of the company was truly not the right type.

Laura Hope Crewes was not only starring in the play but was directing it as well. Miss Crewes had obviously felt the ingenue was not suitable as she demanded from Mr. Moore that a young actress "who will be believable as an English girl" be produced—from New York if necessary. Mr. Moore, who had been most sympathetic to me all summer, as well as pleased with the good sportsmanship I had shown by taking my ushering job seriously and becoming a good one, introduced me to Miss Crewes as a possibility. Mr. Moore of course told her I was a hopeful young actress with training, an actress turned usher.

"Well, my dear, if you can play and sing the English ballad, 'I Passed by Your Window,' by ten o'clock Monday morning, the part of Dinah is yours."

The ballad was not in the script and no one in the theatre

knew it. My interview had been late Saturday afternoon. The nearest town was Hyannis, ten miles away, and would there be a music store in a tiny summer town? It was too late to order it from Boston. Ruthie, Bobby and I drove to Hyannis at top speed. There was a music store; but they had never heard of "I Passed by Your Window."

I was suicidal at this point, but Ruthie—Ruthie! She had made up her mind that she'd find it.

"A church! An organist! A music teacher!"

We rushed from church to church—there were only two— in search of the organist. At the parish house of the Episcopal Church, the organist was not only there but knew the song, and after three hours' searching, found a copy of it for me. We had no piano at our cottage, so the rector of the church allowed me to use his. All Saturday evening, and all day Sunday, I practiced this song. I can still play it and can remember every word of it.

On Monday morning, I arrived at rehearsal and told Miss Crewes I knew the song. Miss Crewes wafted one of her lovely hands toward the Steinway on the stage and I sat down to play—my heart pounding. When I finished, Miss Crewes congratulated me and true to her word, the part of Dinah was mine.

The company was charming to me during the rehearsal week and thrilled that I had been given the chance to make the leap from aisle to stage. Leonard Mudie played Mr. Pim; Alden Chase was Brian Strange, my beau; and Jane Burbie was Lady Marden.

Miss Crewes, famous for the use of her lovely hands, made it very clear from the start that no good ingenue waved her hands about. To tell me this was something. The Le Fievre blood didn't pulsate through my body for nothing. From birth it had been impossible for me to talk without using my hands. But I tried. I didn't want to lose the job.

I was tempted to point out that I was not playing a cripple, but I held my tongue. At dress rehearsal, I concentrated on letting my hands hang like dead fish, but in an emotional moment I lost my head and moved my hand and arm forward slightly to emphasize a point. I was stunned when I felt a very definite slap on my wrist. I looked around, furious—Miss Crewes had done it. I not only counted to 10—I counted to 50. Mr. Moore thought I had forgotten my lines, which quite naturally made him nervous about his unknown usher-actress and apprehensive about the opening next night. The opening was a great success. I received an ovation. We had a subscription audience and they were thrilled to see their usher turned into an actress. I was good as Dinah and I knew it. My ecstasy knew no bounds. I had been rewarded for being a good sport. But best of all, Mr. Moore asked me to return the following season as the company ingenue.

I fell in love that summer with a boy who has become very famous. I don't think he'll mind my using his name. Henry Fonda. He played the juvenile lead in *The Barker* with Walter Huston as the father—and I was only the usher. He came for dinner at our cottage once. We served him his first steamed clams—in our book the greatest of gourmet treats. I don't know whether his instantaneous dislike of the clams rubbed off onto me, but he didn't return my passion. He *never* did. Our paths have crossed many times. I have to admit I did not remain faithful to Hank forever, but that summer he was the most beautiful boy I had ever seen—besides being *such* a good actor. He still is of course. His daughter Jane is such a replica in appearance of her father at that age that just looking at her makes me feel far older than I truly am.

Bobby had chosen to go to Denison University in Granville, Ohio. She was showing signs of wanting to go far away. I think she had a desire to establish an identity of her own. She was fast becoming Bette Davis' sister. Also, the turmoil and drives of her mother and sister were, I'm sure, exhausting to one of her temperament. Love us she did—"wanted out" she did also. I would be working all winter in Rochester, so we could afford to have her go. Once more our little Chevie, bulging from the seams—even more so with all the name-taped equipment required by the college—started forth for Granville. There we tearfully parted from each other, and Mother and I drove to Rochester, New York, to my job as ingenue with the Cukor-Kondolf Stock Company.

CHAPTER

5

Our future was a bright one as we motored to Rochester—under contract for the whole season! Ruthie searched, first of all, for an apartment. Paying a month in advance, she rented one that was inexpensive and completely wallpapered in broad red-and-white stripes. When I saw them, I almost lost my mind. The nervousness I was feeling about starting as the company ingenue made me unable to stand them.

"If you put out the lights, darling, you won't see them!"

"I'll see them in my *sleep,* throughout eternity!"

It was pouring cats and dogs that night. It harbored well for me as usual, as Ruthie thought of a way to break a three months' lease. We were on the ground floor. Ruthie put on her overshoes, threw a raincoat over her nightie, found a flashlight and climbed out the window. She then made large boot prints in the mud that stopped in front of our bedroom window. My hands were cupped over my eyes to soften the stripes; I watched her—fascinated—when she came back into the apartment as she wiped every trace of mud from her galoshes. She then let out a bloodcurdling scream and ran to the landlady's apartment. I heard her telling of the huge man who looked like an ape, staring at us through the window. "We could have been attacked. Thank heavens I wasn't asleep—I can't have my young daughter frightened like this—"

Every once in awhile I would hear the landlady's unbelieving voice. "Nonsense! It's impossible! You must have been dreaming!"

But Ruthie went on and on.

"I'll have to have my money back. I'm sorry. I can't stay under these conditions."

Next we heard the landlady, furious and audibly incredulous, outside our window. Then from her abrupt silence, we gathered she had discovered the giant footprints. We were out by morning and not a penny lost.

While I was at rehearsal next day Ruthie found us another apartment, which turned out to be in the heart of the red-light district. The company manager, when he asked for my address, was the one who told me; but since the place was wildly inexpensive and near the theatre, we saw no reason to move.

I met a boy named Charles Ainsley. He would always park at the end of the street; but other than that, we couldn't have been more satisfied. Charlie risked his reputation nightly. He also kept my dressing room filled with yellow roses and took me to dinner or out after the theatre whenever I was free. Unlike Fritz, Charlie adored my being in theatre. He used to come to every performance.

Formerly the proprietors of Lyceum Players, George Cukor and George Kondolf, after six years, now leased the Temple Theatre and inaugurated their Winter Season. With guest stars every week, the permanent company included Wallace Ford, Frank McHugh, designer Russel Wright, Walter Fohlmer, Helen Gilmore, Irma Irving, Benny Baker and Sam Blythe, a young man who played all the butlers and detective bits and raced around Rochester in a snappy blue Chrysler and a natty wardrobe.

Wally and Frank and Benny and Sam were loads of fun. We found out that Sam was a celebrity when, on opening night, a telegram and a big red apple arrived from his mother, Ethel Barrymore.

BARRYMORE BOY FOUND ON TEMPLE STAGE was a headline in the local paper next day. And it helped bring the audience in at prices that started at 25¢ and soared to $1.50 for the choice seats.

I was exposed, as part of publicizing the company, to my first commercial tie-ups. Helen, Irma and I found our way into the rotogravure by modeling Hanan shoes and hosiery. *You probably wouldn't recognize Miss Bette Davis,* STAR *of the Temple Players, from her nether limbs. . . . As you see, she prefers Hanan's brown suede tie-Oxford with a lizard trim. . . . Above, the petite ingenue of* THE SQUALL *in her favorite Chanel Paris reproduction in cocktail transparent velvet and crepe—to be found at the Woman's Apparel Shop.*

Irma Irving and I also posed for illustrations of short stories in the local journal and they were a scream. All gussied up in clothes and capes, we would swelter in an overdecorated apartment; and the caption beneath our tableau—utterly unrelated to our expression—would read:

"Have you heard from Mabel?"

"No. Only Mabel's mother," Mona *answered* Ruth, *who had dropped in for a visit. The girls regarded each other in mutual distrust. (The young ladies are played by the stars of the Cukor-Kondolf Company now playing at the Temple Theatre.)*

Actually, it was great fun and the various dealers gave us the clothes we modeled. I adored it most because they were always referring to me as a star.

Our first play was *Excess Baggage* by Jack McGowan. The backstage tale involved a tightrope walker and his pretty wife who stood about in spangles and decorated his successful act, played by Wallace Ford and Miriam Hopkins. I also was a vaudevillian in the play—the wife of Frank McHugh. Miriam was the prettiest golden-haired blonde I had ever seen. I will never forget her before a performance—emerging from a shower and simply tossing her curly hair dry. She was the envy of us all.

I won't say that our season was distinguished for drama; but I was learning my trade. We did *Cradle Snatchers* with the never changing Elizabeth Patterson and Marie Nordstrom; *Laff That Off; The Squall; The Man Who Came Back* with Harland Tucker and Charlotte Wynters; and *Yellow,* with Louis Calhern.

There's no doubt about it. Working in a stock company will always be the greatest foundation for an acting career. An actor tackles a new part each week, and there's no time for nonsense. The necessary discipline can be found no other place, plus the confidence and the technique that is gained. Crises are met and conquered. A tempo is created and sustained. The constant tension either makes you or breaks you. Every actor knows that stock can make you slick rather than profound; but you can't play a concerto until you know your scales. There's nothing wrong with facility—no matter what the artsy-crafty claim. Stock gives an actor facility. It makes him a professional. He can go on from there. Nothing can teach you to act like acting.

The young actors today very often have a television series where for months they play only one part. They have a Broadway play and if, hopefully, it's a success, they play the same part over a long period. Then, if they're any good, Hollywood plucks them unripe from the vine. There are more "stars" today who cannot act. And it's not their fault. They've never been given a chance to learn.

The progress of acting careers like everything else has become so accelerated that amateurs are rewarded by international fame. There's gold in all this madness and the temptation is great. How many Brandos are there who will refuse, as he did, well-paying parts in plays that bored him or wouldn't encourage his growth? He also was a worker. That's something else that has gone out of fashion. Nobody wants to work. Everybody wants something for nothing. The easy way is usually the destructive way.

There is no luxury like the fatigue that follows a labor of love. Nothing in the whole, wide world as soul-satisfying as a job well done. Accomplishment. Few go all out. Few will gamble. Everybody wants security. If that were the end-all, America would still belong to the Navajos.

A good percentage of our lives is spent doing things we loathe. Marvelous! It puts starch in your spine. Who looks forward to brushing his teeth, painting the shed or changing the linens? We're making our beds all right. We are face to face and up against an astringent, dedicated society which has been toughened by sacrifice and unhappy regimentation.

I was blessed with energy and good health. I'm also a worker. I was apt to be a know-it-all as well. When Mr. Cukor criticized my work, I would always have a reason as to why I did it my way. I alibied. Dorothy Burgess, the year before in Rochester, gave me some good advice.

"You're just a kid, Bette, and there's a great deal you don't know. You don't have to be perfect. Nobody expects you to be. Listen and learn. Don't be afraid to admit you're wrong."

In the production of *Yellow*, Louis Calhern, the star, was my lover. He was practically twice my height and age and he complained, "She looks more like my kid than my mistress." The cast could have been reshuffled; but it wasn't. Mr. Cukor fired me. I will never really know why. He never told me.

My reviews throughout the whole engagement had been excellent. It was true that my dedication to my job did not make me socially an asset as the company ingenue. Ingenues in stock companies were traditionally expected to be public domain. It could have been that. I don't know. I only know I was out of a job. I was heartbroken.

Ruthie refused to let me brood about the turn of events. She advised me to wire Jimmy Light and tell him I was free any time he was.

The timing was perfect and Mr. Cukor, I felt, was only a helpless pawn, like Judas Iscariot, destined to play out his role in the Passion Play that was my life. Jimmy Light was more than ready for me. *The Earth Between* was to go into production immediately upon my arrival. I could audition for the part. Audition? He had told me the part was mine. Ruthie reassured me, feeling that he was simply annoyed that I had gone ahead with the Rochester job and not waited it out in New York until he was ready. There wasn't the slightest doubt that I would be signed. Of course, she was right again.

Jimmy Light had suggested that we live near the theatre, which was on MacDougal Street. Ruthie soon found a typical Village basement on Eighth Street; we had to go outside the garden door each day and peer up at the sky to know what the weather was like. Marie was working in the theatre at this time—off and on—and joined forces with us in our dugout in the Village.

It turned out that Jimmy Light *had* been waiting for me, and that he was not a little annoyed at what he hinted was my opportunism in going off to Rochester. I signed a run-of-the-play contract for thirty-five dollars a week and I couldn't wait until we got started.

The Provincetown Playhouse, a step below Washington Square Park on MacDougal Street, was already famous. Eugene O'Neill had been introduced there. Helen Hayes, Ann Harding and Katharine Cornell had had their start on this stage. Ruthie, of course, was already cutting my clippings. I was starting to be frightened. One could forgive a shiny, new ingenue in a stock company almost anything, but this was the real thing. I had to be good. This was New York—not Broadway, but New York! The Provincetown Playhouse was called the Theatre of Opportunity for good reason. Started in Massachusetts, it moved to MacDougal Street in 1917. A few of its playwrights besides Mr. O'Neill were Susan Glaspell, Paul Green, Edmund Wilson, e.e. cummings, Maxwell Bodenheim, Theodore Dreiser and Edna St. Vincent Millay. Its directors, E. J. Ballantine, Robert Edmond Jones, George Cram Cook, Jasper Deeter and Leo Bulgakov.

By producing O'Neill's *Emperor Jones* and Green's *In Abraham's Bosom*, the Provincetown Playhouse opened a road to the Negro actor. It created a place on the serious stage for such artists as Frank Gilpin, Paul Robeson, Frank Wilson and Jules Bledsoe.

It was passionately dedicated to the creation of theatre with quality and scope. Its success was not accidental. The management aimed high and refused to submit to the commercial manager's idea of public taste.

James Light and M. Eleanor Fitzgerald were operating the Playhouse in the 1928–1929 season. Jimmy had formerly managed the theatre jointly with O'Neill, Jones and Kenneth Macgowan. Now he and Miss Fitzgerald produced as the first of the productions, *Abraham's Bosom*, then *S. S. Glencairn* by Mr. O'Neill and, after much postponement, my play—Virgil Geddes' *The Earth Between*.

Conrad Aiken called the Provincetown "Our Old Vic." It certainly was my Theatre of Opportunity. I prayed that I would be worthy of it.

The Earth Between was a two-act play of Nebraska farm life; and—completely unbeknownst to me—the play dealt with an incestuous relationship between Nat Jennings, a farmer, and Floy, his sixteen-year-old daughter. It did seem to me when I read the play that the widowed father's compensatory demands on the child were excessive; but it never occurred to me for one moment just how fully he wanted her to replace her mother. I had never bumped into Oedipus at dear old Cushing—and certainly never in Winchester. My father didn't even like me!

Jimmy Light, treasuring my naïveté, never enlightened me

as to what the play was about. What I didn't know wouldn't hurt me—it helped me. I was as innocent as the girl in the play.

It is interesting that I never discussed my work with Ruthie. She was the first to admit that with my life, she was more than generous with unsolicited advice. But when it came to my work, Mother never interfered. That is, with any creative process. She was never a stage mother per se. Ruthie never doubted my judgment. It would have been no dice if she had. Mother might have propelled the machine, but then she let it take off unhindered.

I've always been a loner in my work. The playwright blueprints the destination and the director, if he's good, charts my course. A good director! Half my career was spent fighting for one. In *Earth* I was in excellent hands. Jimmy Light was a brilliant director. Courtly and protective, Jimmy was then about thirty-five and greatly resembled Osgood Perkins, Anthony's lean and attractively vulpine father.

Our curtain raiser was to be an O'Neill one-acter, *Before Breakfast*. I had never seen an O'Neill play. Ruthie and I went to see his *Strange Interlude*, which was playing on Broadway with a dinner intermission. I adored it.

The characters' contrapuntal thoughts made audible by the playwright in a modern variation of the outdated asides was inventive. It was the first time I saw Lynn Fontanne. I found she was fabulous.

As Mother and I made our way down the theatre stairs after *Strange Interlude,* Ruthie was chattering away, but I was silent. About to prepare for my own debut in New York, I was suddenly aware of the responsibility I faced.

I had so much to prove. To Ruthie, Jimmy Light, George Cukor, Uncle Myron and Aunt Mildred, Eva Le Gallienne, Charlie, Fritz, Ham—but most of all myself. Would I make it—ever?

Whenever I was in one of these moods, Ruthie would always say, "I wonder when Bette will come back from Canada?" When I came to, she always merrily announced "Have you heard the good news? Bette's back from Canada." Well! I was certainly in Manitoba that night. A scared kid!

As we came out of the theatre and were walking toward the

subway, I became so aware of all the names in lights along
Broadway. Would mine ever be one of them? Mother, reading
my thoughts, put her arm around me and said, "It will be,
Bette—it will be."

CHAPTER

6

Jimmy wisely chose a date for our opening that would not conflict with any uptown premiere. This assured the presence of the top-string New York critics. St. John Ervine, Brooks Atkinson, Burns Mantle and many others covered our show that night.

Ruthie, of course, was there in the audience, and so was Marie with her beau, Shep Strudwick. It was my first real challenge. Whether good or bad, I was about to become part of theatrical history. Whether they liked me or not, Jimmy Light had given me my chance.

I had to wear a rose as Floy; and Charlie had sent one with a note: *I love you*. It seemed I had everything. I was engaged to be married to Charlie. I had the promise of a career. Thank God he loved theatre and understood my dedication to it. I thought fleetingly of Le Gallienne. Then the words, "Let her become a secretary" blotted out everything else. I *had* to make it. The rain on the roof of the little theatre comforted me.

The audience that evening was not in for a night of fun. By the time I was ready to go on, they had already watched Mary Blair, as the wife of a poverty-stricken Christopher Street artist, nag her drunken, lazy offstage husband in a tragic *tour de force* that ended with the weakling's cutting his throat while shaving. All of this *Before Breakfast*.

Virgil Geddes, an admirer of Mr. O'Neill's, had written *Earth Between*, a play in much the same stark style, with settings that could have been designed by Hopper or Burchfield. The intermission was over and we were on.

I recall nothing of that first performance now except the last scene in which I stood, weak-willed and yielding, in the wheat field with my loving "Pa." Suddenly there was a clap of thunder and a frightening rumble that vibrated throughout the building. I thought the rain had caused the roof to cave in. It was the audience. It was applause.

The curtain fell and it was all over. The rest of the cast ran out from the wings to join hands for the call. The curtain became a great eyelid, blinking. Up and down. Up and down. And always that deafening thunder. Bill Challee, my ill-fated Jake in the play and his rival, Carroll Ashburn, the triumphant Nat, squeezed my hands joyously as we gravely bowed. It was over.

I materialized somehow at my dressing table in an ecstasy that has never quite been equaled. A blur of flowers and telegrams greeted my return to the land of the living and my reflexes started to work again. The flowers needed water. More roses from Charlie—my favorite yellow ones and more love. Love! I was brimming over with it. Jonquils from Ruth and Stanley Woodward: *We always knew* . . . Violets from Ned Kent along with hope. Ned was a friend from my Newton High days. An orchid from my farmhand, Bill Challee: *For Floy who really makes me feel Jake.* A lovely, little basket of spring flowers sat in front of the mirror, dewy and already in watered soil. It needed no attention and I decided to tack my telegrams on the mirror frame like a professional before I looked at its card.

There were wires from Granville, Ohio. HOW NICE TO HAVE YOU IN THE FAMILY LOVE BOBBY. DON'T LET YOUR NOTICES GO TO YOUR HEAD LOVE BOBBY. The notices! It seemed to go well, I thought; I think I was all right.

My tiny dressing room was bursting with excitement. Ruthie, Jimmy Light, Marie with Shep Strudwick, Virgil Geddes. I wrote in my scrapbook that it was a "night in a million." It was not the exaggeration of a twenty-year-old.

Just before I left my dressing room, I sniffed the spring basket that brought memories of May days in Winchester. I opened the envelope attached to the wicker handle. There was simply an engraved name. HARLOW MORRELL DAVIS.

I dreamed I was being attacked; and when I awakened, Ruthie and Marie were standing over my bed and throwing the morning papers at me. A large pot of coffee was on and we started reading the reviews aloud.

Mr. O'Neill's curtain raiser was panned to high heaven. Both St. John Ervine of the *World* and Mr. Atkinson of the *Times* suggested that an earlier murder of Miss Blair rather than the suicide she so lengthily drove her mate to might have been more appropriate. "Punk." "Tricky." "Absurd." *That for Mr. O'Neill? What is he saving for us?* Mr. Ervine went on. He disapproved of the Village, its weather and Mr. Geddes, "who has probably never come into contact with a Nebraskan farmer." He even remembered that the Provincetown Playhouse had once been a stable and was all for "restoring it to its former state." . . . He loathed the whole evening with a passion but interrupted his brilliant invective to remark that our other play was "remarkably acted especially by *Miss Bette Davis*." Ruthie screamed.

I started skipping the texts and looking for my name—unabashedly. After all, that's what mattered. One after the other— the *News*, the *Graphic*, the *Sun, Telegram, Mirror Journal*, Brooklyn *Eagle*—all of them were excessive in their praise. It had come to pass and Mother was crying.

We had saved the *Times* for last and now Ruthie hysterically quoted Mr. Atkinson. "Miss Bette Davis who is making her first appearance is an entrancing creature who plays in a soft, unassertive style." I fell back on the pillow in relief.

And so, in the Village "where a man can call his soul his own and see who cares," I knew that never again would I ever doubt my direction or the sacrifices that had been and would be made to keep me going. Ruthie's dreams were coming true; there was a chance I might make it.

I knew this was only the beginning. I also thought often of my future life as Charlie's wife.

I saw myself carried through the streets by adoring devotees in Inverness capes who dropped me gently into the kitchen of that old, tired cottage I'd conjured up back in Cushing. I would bustle around making a pot of chowder and steamed clams for my husband and then be wafted back to the flower-strewn stage at 8:40. Like Ham and Fritz, he was tall and lean and strong.

I did adore him. But then, there were other boys I adored. It came to me in a flash that I was a fickle female. I was bursting with an energy, vitality and passion that I had little understanding of.

Even Ruthie didn't see the shapes and forms my drive was taking. *Thank God for my work*. Without the emotional outlet my acting gave me, I wonder if I could have remained so antiseptic. *Oh, to the devil with boys*. The critics had approved of me. This I understood. I was where I wanted to be—on the first rung of the ladder.

The Earth Between was scheduled to run for four weeks and, because of the play's reviews, the public lined up outside the theatre, demanding an extension of our engagement. We were a hit.

I received my first fan letters. One was from an unholy student at Holy Cross; one from a math teacher in far-off Rockville Centre; and the third from an actor named Dante who evidently thought of me as his Beatrice. He was appearing with Ethel Barrymore "as the bullfighter, Juan de Dios," in *The Kingdom of God*. Ole!

One evening after the performance a card was sent in to me. The name on it was Cecil Clovelly. He had come to ask me if I would be interested in playing Hedvig in *The Wild Duck* on tour with Blanche Yurka. Interested! I had never forgotten nor not believed that one day I could play this part—ever since I saw Peg Entwistle at that matinee in Boston. The joy on my face gave no need for an answer. He asked me if I could meet Miss Yurka the next day. He had recommended me to her after seeing me as Floy. He told me to be at the Bijou Theatre at 11 the next morning. Miss Yurka was going on tour with Ibsen Repertory in a few weeks, and as Linda Watkins was not going on the road with them, they needed a replacement for her. I would, if approved by Miss Yurka, play Hedvig in *The Wild Duck* and Boletta in *The Lady from the Sea*.

On that next morning I raced, breathless, uptown to the Bijou Theatre to meet with the great star who wanted to see me. A woman of tremendous magnetism, Miss Yurka seemed like a giant bird of prey. Her long neck pressed forward and her glowing eyes devoured everything around her. After I read a few lines, she withdrew her neck and lowered her eyes in satisfaction. Her resonant voice could be remarkably gentle.

"That's fine, my dear. We'll have one week of rehearsal after you close in *The Earth Between*."

I took the Fifth Avenue bus back to 8th Street and sat on the open top deck and watched with excitement the swathe we were cutting through the city. Hedvig! I was truly in heaven.

There isn't a creature alive today who wouldn't tell me that it was anxiety that made me break out into a cold sweat and a pink rash that night. Today we see beneath the obvious. In 1929, we naïvely believed it was the measles. It wasn't until after the evening's performance that the doctor corroborated our diagnosis. It was the measles. How I got through that night, is a mystery; I was truly feeling so sick.

By the time the last scene came, the spots were showing through my greasepaint.

Backstage I collapsed into my chair, glad I had made it. The room was spinning. I bolted upright as Daddy walked into my dressing room. He, to add to everything else, had seen the show that night. He was as formal as ever and even more elegant. My head reeled as he discussed the play.

"Most interesting character analysis . . . Ashburn was excellent . . . that Burgess fellow was very fine . . . and the boy who played Jake conveyed the Cretin-like aspects. . . . Geddes is under the influence of Robinson Jeffers . . . he has power . . ."

He never mentioned Floy! Never mentioned my performance. I, of course, was hurt that he ignored it.

I stared at him in disbelief. Daddy had barely changed. A little gray at the temples, attractively lined, but the same really. He had reached the top at the United Shoe Machinery Company and was now the leading patent consultant for the Government.

We sat looking at each other, strangers. Just as we'd always been. I didn't realize then how captive he was in *his* role. I didn't realize how inarticulate he could be, for all his brilliance. His voice became even more formal, more impersonal. He was always the gentleman.

"Would—would you care—to go out with me and have a little supper?"

Oh, dear.

"I'm sorry, Daddy. I feel wretched—really."

The thought of food absolutely nauseated me. He didn't believe me for one moment.

"I see!"

"I have a chill and I'm soaking wet. . . ."

Daddy wasn't convinced. He had been carried to New York on a wave of paternal devotion and Goneril didn't care. My heart started to ache. Now I know that his probably did also. Sick or well, there was no going back. The whole visit was out of character. He refused to believe that I was ill and after another attempt to convince him, I was just too weak to care. All I wanted to do was fall into bed and find out what was wrong with me.

I fell into bed all right and stayed there. I had the worst case of measles the doctor had seen. It was undignifying, uncomfortable; and I knew it was the end of my playing Hedvig, to say nothing of losing out playing the last week of *The Earth Between*. It would be impossible to attend the Ibsen rehearsals and I was sure that Yurka would be forced to engage someone else. I decided that I might just as well die!

But Ruthie had other plans for me. She ran across 8th Street to the drugstore to get some medication and call Cecil Clovelly. At nine o'clock in the morning. Half asleep, his resistance down, he just listened. Mother dropped the bombshell and then swore that with or without rehearsal, I would be ready to do the parts in two weeks! Dr. Davis guaranteed it. Cecil listened. He wasn't sure of the whole thing. I had to replace Linda Watkins the last week in New York before the tour in *Lady from the Sea*.

Mother knew that Miss Watkins wasn't actually leaving the country for two weeks. If she could play up to the last few days—well, Ruthie would see that I was completely cured and letter-perfect in *ten* days. The bargaining was on. She sat at the telephone while the gentleman called Miss Yurka who called Miss Watkins. Ruthie tied the whole thing up in minutes. Linda was kind enough to cooperate and Miss Yurka was kind enough to wait for me. Now all I had to do was get well!

The next fortnight was a nightmare of work. The measles had weakened my eyes and studying the script was impossible. I have always loathed being read to; and Ruthie sat at my bed and read it over and over until I thought I'd go mad. I couldn't eat. I was weak, irritable, and Mother became my victim. I threw the scripts across the room, howling in despair. If Bobby had been there it would have been easier, but we could hardly have asked her to leave college. Poor Bobby. When she heard the news of my ill-timed attack, she was reading the Ibsen plays. Bobby knew what Hedvig meant to me. She sent a little wooden duck with a tag around its neck that read: *If you must have childish diseases, here's a toy to play with.*

It was the only smile that passed my lips in ten days. While I should have been recuperating, I was working harder than ever. The rash started to fade but my strength seemed gone forever. The doctor quite properly refused to release me from quarantine as the deadline approached; but I was possessed of a bug far more virulent than measles.

The tenth day was a Wednesday and a matinee day. I was due at 9:30 in the morning dead or alive for a rehearsal; and after one run-through, I was to take over the torch from Linda in the relay race I had been entered into. The theatre should have been the Coliseum. It was the Bijou and *The Lady from the Sea* was to finish out the last days of its New York engagement. At least I wouldn't have to tackle Hedvig in *The Wild Duck* until I had a few more days to convalesce.

Ruthie set the alarm clock for 7 A.M. and I was unconscious by 9. I dreamed that I was cured at Lourdes.

Considering our monomania, it is completely out of character that Ruthie forgot to set the thingamabob on the clock. We awakened like great ladies at exactly the moment I was to have walked onstage. My guardian angel had betrayed me. It was inexplicable. I sank into melancholy and my deathbed. All was over.

My own mother, my own flesh and blood—my Ruthie—had knifed me. This was the end. Clovelly would never understand and Yurka would banish me from theatres all over the world. I lay moribund, with Ruthie standing over me—grotesque in braids, flannel and treachery!

"Keep screaming! Don't give up! We can get there. I'll think of something! *Scream at me!*"

She pulled the bedclothes off me and dragged me from the bed. The next thing I knew we were standing on Sixth Avenue and Eighth Street looking for a taxi. One can never find a free one in an emergency. We stood like demented traffic cops in the middle of the street, Ruthie waving a bottle of milk in one hand and a bottle of Virginia Dare wine (to give me strength) in the other. The clock atop the tower of the Jefferson Courthouse shrieked ten o'clock and I went berserk. I bit Mother on the shoulder. My teeth dug into her flesh right through her woolen dress.

"There's a Checker, Bette! Taxi! Taxi!"

We arrived at the Bijou Theatre at 10:30—one hour late; and Cecil Clovelly's face was stretched into a Benda mask of hatred. Ruthie started to explain.

"I set the clock. It's my fault. I forgot to set the alarm."

Cecil stabbed her with his eyes. "Think up a new one, Mrs. Davis!"

"Get out, Mother! And stay out!"

The director turned in surprise—and Ruthie with her two bottles, my formula for the day, obeyed. She sat at the stage door although as she always told it, it was "the alley," and I walked onstage.

The rehearsal went without a hitch and all was forgiven. Mother had done her job. I knew every line perfectly; and though I had still to see one piece of scenery or one prop, Cecil drummed the stage business into me. My first appearance was to be at 2:30. Really cutting it close! With rehearsal over, convinced now that I could do it, Cecil thanked Ruthie, which was more than I did at that point. I didn't have a moment to think or feel anything but Boletta. And I was exhausted. We had rehearsed in the *Duck* set which was now to be "struck" so that *Lady*'s interior could be set up. I was handed Miss Watkins' costume and told to be ready for a luncheon during which Cecil would fill me in on further details.

I took one look at the costume and almost had a complete relapse. It was filthy and torn. Impossible to wear. I didn't know how Miss Watkins could have it touch her body. And, of course, no one had thought of any necessary alteration. Just, "Here's your costume." Unbelievable. I announced my displeasure which was even more incredible and crawled off to a lunch that I prayed I could keep down.

When I got back the dress was laid out for me, exquisitely cleaned and pressed, the muslin of its huge peasant sleeves crisp and white. The little high shoes of blue leather were shined and placed beneath it. A starched white cap with little wings was on the dressing table. The whole room was immaculate. It was the cure for all my troubles—and it wasn't the management at all. It was a wounded hobgoblin named Ruthie.

I plaited my hair in long braids which I wound into a crown, dressed and went onstage to look over the set and go through my initial business, which was tricky. During my opening lines I had to raise a flag on a flagpole. The way things had been going, it was only logical that the damned thing wouldn't work. Then I had to get the feel of the ramps I had to run up and down. I had visions of breaking my leg and being shot once and for all.

There were so many things to be checked. Props I had only heard about. Suddenly, the stage manager cleared the set. The strings were playing in the pit; and I realized that I was on. Up went the curtain.

The flagpole was in working order but I was not. I started raising the flag looking calm and sweet in my peasant outfit, but I seemed to have no realization that I was to start the play.

Ruthie, who was in the front row with Shepherd Strudwick, dug her nails into his hand and prayed.

After what must have seemed an eternity to her, I looked around in a surprised manner—it was at that moment I realized I started the play—and I did. The gates opened and Boletta started talking. I managed the ramps with no trouble and four acts went smoothly.

To have been in bed for two weeks and then find myself on a stage on Broadway was too much for me to take in—I was not in sync.

I had no such trouble with Hedvig. By then I had had time to get on my feet physically. Miss Yurka staged *The Wild Duck* herself; and after two days in town in *Lady*, we opened at the Boulevard Theatre in Jackson Heights, Long Island. This was the beginning of a tour that was to take us to Philadelphia, to Washington and Boston, and lastly the old Subway Circuit, Newark, 96th Street Theatre. I made it in Jackson Heights opening night. I knew from the applause. I also knew, inside myself, I was good as Hedvig.

Florida Friebus, who played my twin sister, Hilda, in *Lady from the Sea*, was my roommate on tour. She was pleasant and fun. My impossible dream had come true.

Cecil Clovelly, who played Gregers in *The Wild Duck*, was more than rewarded for his faith in me. Good taste, not false modesty, keeps me from quoting my notices; I will only say that I could have written them myself in a paroxysm of self-love. In every city, the kindness of the critics was excessive; and Blanche Yurka's extraordinary Gina, brilliant as it was, took its proper place in Ibsen's balance scheme, reminding the critics that Hedvig, rather than being a supporting role had, after all, been used by the great Nazimova ten years before as a starring vehicle.

And I was gaining real experience as an actress. Every day, my rapport with the audience grew. And with it, my confidence. In Washington, President and Mrs. Coolidge were in the audience. They came back to congratulate us. It didn't matter that Blanche Yurka, after sharing applause with the rest of us, always took her solo calls. After all, she was the star.

The night we opened in Boston—my hometown, and where I had first seen Hedvig played—was the night of nights. Daddy was even there that night. As were Myron, Mildred, the Woodwards, so very many old school friends, and friends of Mother's. Ruthie was as usual, if possible, in the front row.

There was a letter from Charlie on my dressing table when I arrived to make up. I gaily opened the envelope. My gaiety was short-lived. I read the note again. Charlie had broken our engagement. Just like that.

His father disapproved of actresses . . . we were too young . . . knew I would understand . . . and forgive . . . helpless against them . . . so sorry!

No matter how he spelled it out, I was dumped. Anger has often saved the day for me. I was angry. I was not going to allow anything or anybody to ruin my opening night in Boston playing Hedvig.

There was a knock on the door and the doorman handed me a box. I opened it and found two gardenias with a note from Miss Yurka: *To the hometown girl.* I had half an hour before the curtain went up. I couldn't let Ruthie down tonight. All her love, blood and sweat had to be proven worth it that night to her family and friends. I tore up the letter and thought of others I'd received all through the tour. Not mash notes from amorous young college boys but letters that shocked me with their genuine affection and gratitude for what I had done. I had done nothing but gratify my own desires, fulfill my own dreams. Could I conceivably do for someone else what Peg Entwistle had done for me? *His father disapproves of my acting. Why didn't he fight for me? He never loved me.*

Five minutes, Miss Davis! *But why didn't he talk it over with me? I never want to see him again!*

Opening nights! The nightmare of all actors. Lotte Lehmann once told me, "It will grow worse not better as you grow older." She was right. It is always a kind of death before the curtain goes up. That night in Boston was no exception—added to by Charlie's letter and so many people I knew in the audience. Plus Daddy!

Once the curtain was up, my only problems were Hedvig's and all went smoothly. The curtain fell and the whole cast took its bow. The applause was tremendous. Miss Yurka stepped through the curtain for her solo curtain call. Starting to the wings, I was stopped by Cecil Clovelly. Everyone was to remain onstage in case another cast curtain was justified. There seemed to be no end to this particular performance. I watched Miss Yurka slip back and forth between the curtain, her eyes cast down in humility as her public greeted her. Then up went the curtain again, and the whole cast once more joined the star. *The audience is certainly extremely responsive this evening.* There was a certain persistence in its ardor—an ungratified passion. The audience seemed insatiable.

Suddenly Miss Yurka took my hand and led me to the footlights and the curtain fell behind us. This was a tremendous honor and most gracious of her. But then she let go of my hand, smiled that secretive smile of hers and walked off the stage—leaving me alone.

The theatre now shook with applause and bravos. People actually stood on their seats and cheered—for *me*. It was really just for me. Wave after wave of love flooded the stage and washed over me. I felt my face crumble and I started to cry.

The weight that was Charlie was lifted like a miracle. "Bravo! Bravo!" I was alone—onstage and everywhere; and that's the way it was obviously meant to be. "Bravo!" My first stardust. It is impossible to describe the sweetness of such a moment. You are at once the indulged beloved and the humble lover. Alone! All those marvelous people. My heart almost burst.

This was the true beginning of the one, great, durable romance of my life.

CHAPTER
7

The Ibsen tour ended at the Shubert Riviera on 96th and Broadway in Manhattan; Miss Yurka went to Paris. Ruthie and I piled into our Chevrolet coupe and drove to Ohio to pick up Bobby at college and bring her home to be with us at the Cape for the second season.

My arrival at the Playhouse was a far cry from my earlier one. Mr. Moore had a dressing room ready for me this time. It was this year at Dennis that I occasionally stepped out of the ingenue class. I had to play a sophisticate in *The Constant Wife* starring Crystal Herne; and I was so petrified of it on opening night that I passed out onstage. Miss Herne turned playwright and rewrote the curtain brilliantly to justify my faint. The audience never knew the difference. Ruthie did and Bobby was concerned. The rest of the week I acquitted myself.

The next week I was given the lead in *The Patsy*. My first comedy. Another first and a challenge. I had nightmares every night during rehearsal that no one would laugh. I would wake up in a cold sweat. On opening night my first line got its laugh—and I relaxed. Comedy wasn't so different after all. I proved to be a laugh riot.

The next play after *The Patsy* was Bernard Shaw's *You Never Can Tell*. The imported star was an actor named Dodd Meehan. I was fascinated by him. He, realizing this, took full advantage of my adoration and had me cue him. This naturally took time away from me to learn my own lines. I, evidently, was so in outer space, this did not worry me at all until I blew my lines umpteen times at the dress rehearsal. This did bring me out of my "love-mist" a little. After the rehearsal Mr. Moore wanted to know what had happened to me. He said, "If you don't learn your lines we will have to cancel the opening tomorrow night."

I ran all the way back to our house after that. Ruthie, having been at the rehearsal, marched into my room with the script where I was lying, on what I wished were my deathbed. Bobby was trying to comfort me; but I was beyond commiseration.

"Barbara! Put on a pot of coffee and get dinner ready. We'll join you in a little while. Up, young lady!"

Ruthie has always said that I am my most cooperative when I'm ill. Sickness and tragedy sweeten me somehow. I was never sicker or more tragic. I sat up obediently as Mother threw my "sides" to me.

"You're going to learn this part by tomorrow morning."

For fifteen hours straight I worked on the lines, Ruthie cueing me. Barbara tore us from work for the best dinner anyone ever cooked and hovered around us quietly like a guardian angel— just slipping us coffee on the hour. How I didn't get caffein poisoning I'll never know; and how I slept when finished is even more of a miracle.

At ten sharp on Monday morning I arrived at the theatre. That night we opened. I never missed a line. There was a bouquet waiting for me afterwards and in it was a contract for the next summer. I learned later that Ruthie had planned seriously the perfect murder for Dodd Meehan. After the performance, she would run into him with the car on the beach road. Who would ever find out? Cecil Clovelly, my mentor from *The Wild Duck,* was our director. Evidently my romance with Dodd Meehan disgusted the whole company. They saw through him. I hadn't—and my love was not dampened by this experience!

It was fall again and Bobby left for college. Our charming little house and a fur coat for Bobby's Wisconsin winter had exhausted our funds; and we started on our first year in the theatre with no job. We had three weeks before Daddy's next check. Leave it to Ruthie.

Two friends of ours, eager to see New York, solved our problem without knowing it. Ruthie believed necessity is the mother of invention. We were asked if they could drive us to New York and we could show them the sights. Ruthie felt at this point we had been given a million dollars.

We had stayed at the Carleton Terrace, a theatrical hotel on 100th Street, during the run of *The Wild Duck* at the 96th Street Theatre. Ruthie raved about the food and the excellent accommodations there. She went on to say that although they only welcomed people of the theatre, she would gladly pretend that we were their hosts. They could repay us at the end of their stay.

What a ten days they were—with checks being signed by Ruthie. Our "guests" financed the whole whirl, hotel bill and all. On the day the Bostonians were to leave, Ruthie asked the manager for the $150 bill and our friends gave us seventy-five. Of course, we didn't pay the bill until Ruthie got her check. We bade our benefactors farewell and now had seventy-five dollars in our pockets until the first of the month.

Ruthie, Marie (now called Robin) and I took a room on East 53rd Street. Both of us were job hunting each day. It had only two beds and we kept saying it was temporary. Mother devised an arrangement for herself, using two chairs and a suitcase, that she swore were as comfortable as a Pullman berth. The first night she tried it, there was a crash. Robin and I eventually managed to disentangle her from the bedclothes. She insisted on trying it again despite our protests.

"You two need your sleep so you'll be well enough to walk your miles tomorrow. I'll take a nap during the day."

Ruthie! We also had a slight problem eating during this period. Our funds were low. Our poor beaux when they took us out for dinner! We fasted all day—and ate like horses at their expense. When beauless, the three of us ate at a one-armed lunchroom on 6th Avenue. Shades of Norwalk, Conn.

One evening, the proprietor came over to us and said to me, "You look like an actress, miss."

I was flattered. I confessed that I was, but out of a job!

"On the way up, huh?"

From that moment on, we had a feast every night we were

there and he never allowed us to pay one cent. I have often wished I knew his name. I tried to find the restaurant years later to thank him. I only hope somewhere along the line he knew he had saved not only the pocketbook but the life of what turned out to be the actress, Bette Davis. In life I find that at the worst moments of discouragement, someone will suddenly renew your faith in not only yourself, but human nature in general. Our unknown restaurant host was certainly in this category.

During this period I entered my one and only contest—with the exception of the P.S. 186 cookies many years ago. This one did not turn out so successfully. A contract in Hollywood was offered to the girl who could look the most like Vilma Banky. We studied photographs of her—Ruthie dressed my hair like hers—I was blond. I made myself up and to the Astor Hotel we went at the appointed hour. The winner was chosen instantaneously—a setup. The rest of us weren't even looked at. This was my first lesson in Hollywood-type publicity. I was to learn a good deal more about it not too many years later.

Had not an agent named Jane Broder come into my life at this point, heaven knows what else I wouldn't have tried to get a job. My luck again. She had two offers for me: the road tour of *Saturday's Children* or an interview for a new show by Martin Flavin—the author of a very successful play *The Criminal Code*—called *Broken Dishes* starring Donald Meek. The part was the ingenue lead. I was interviewed by Mr. Flavin, the producer Oscar Serlin—of *Life With Father* fame, years later—and the director Marion Gering. They all agreed I was the right type and on Miss Broder's word, as to my talent, they accepted me for the part. There is a clause in any agency contract stating that if you are not satisfactory in a role, the producer may replace you at the end of five days—with no redress from the actor. Those five days are always a torture of uncertainty. On the fifth day I was asked to do a run-through for the "powers that be." I knew this meant they were uncertain whether or not to keep me in the part. I was never a good rehearser. If anyone doubts my ability I fold. I knew I was doing the run-through badly. Miss Broder did a lot of talking that day and they kept me in the play. I think they were not sorry.

Broken Dishes was an unpretentious little domestic comedy.

Mr. Meek was the henpecked Mr. Bumpstead; I, his daughter Elaine; both of us eventually rebel against the domineering Mrs. Bumpstead played by Eda Heinemann.

We tried out the play on October 18, 1929, at Fox's Hempstead on Long Island for one night and the Fox Playhouse in Great Neck the next. It was Black October as any old stockbroker will tell you; but the theatre was still booming.

On October 21st we moved into Werba's Brooklyn, replacing George Kelly's *Maggie The Magnificent*, whose large cast included my friend Rosebud Blondell—and a remarkably dynamic kid named James Cagney. They survived the flop and went into another one named *Penny Arcade*. One went from job to job, play to play in those palmy days. Spencer Tracy had a flop in *Nigger Rich* and a couple of months later made a smash hit in *The Last Mile*. People forget that the boy who was in *Hawk Island*, then with the dark-eyed Zita Johann in *Machinal*, was Clark Gable. A slim, vivacious girl gave two excellent performances in the gay *See Naples and Die* with Roger Pryor and then along with Glenn Anders was even better in the dramatic *Dynamo*. Her name was Claudette Colbert. Leslie Howard stayed at the Empire Theatre after *Candlelight* closed to give a brilliant performance in *Berkeley Square* with Margalo Gillmore.

The list is endless: Walter Huston and Kay Francis in *Elmer The Great*; Edward G. Robinson in his own play, *The Kibitzer*. And an attractive young Englishman named Olivier made a sensation in his first local appearance in *Murder on the Second Floor*. Eva Le Gallienne was now a nun in *The Cradle Song*. There really is no end to the incredible list of actors soon to be grabbed by Hollywood. "Talkies" were evidently here to stay and the producers were desperate for actors who could speak.

Franklin Delano Roosevelt was New York's governor and Ramsay MacDonald was weekending at the White House on that November 5, 1929, when *Broken Dishes* opened at the Ritz Theatre on Broadway.

Although Mr. Flavin's switch to "pedestrian comedy" was a disappointment to the pundits, our reviews were still very favorable and the public loved the Bumpstead family. We were an immediate hit. The whole cast was well received but the press was particularly generous to the brilliant Mr. Meek and to me. I was now a bona fide Broadway actress—in a hit.

I loved playing Elaine and Mr. Meek was an angel to work with. As my stage father, he was the personification of all dominated husbands—the perfect Milquetoast—and his third-act rebellion against Mama (engineered, of course, by little old me) was heralded throughout the city. We became as popular as the dialogue between Hal Skelly and Nancy Carrol which went, "You wouldn't fool me would you, mister?" Answer: "I would if I could, lady, I would if I could."

Ruthie and I had rented an apartment on 50th Street between Fifth and Sixth avenues. Grandmother came to New York for the opening. This was officially my debut as an actress on Broadway. I will never forget how thrilled Grandmother was that night. She sat in a box, every inch a queen in her black lace with the high collar, her white hair shining in the dark. The flowers backstage in my dressing room were legion. Grandmother and Ruthie took them back to the apartment in a taxi while I went on to a party. I got home after two o'clock and there sat Grandmother still wide awake—waiting to see me before she went to bed. She died not long afterwards and I was always grateful that she lived to know I had a good start on the road to success in my chosen profession.

Poor Donald Meek. One night, a famous night, he arrived at the theatre and confessed that he had lost every penny he'd ever made that day in Wall Street. He was stone broke. It was the night of the crash. I almost felt lucky I had no money to crash with!

My salary was seventy-five dollars a week. It was doubled after three months of our run. Like salmon going upstream, Ruthie and I went on a shopping spree. My idol in those years was Mrs. William Rhinelander Stewart. I used to dream that through some miracle, I would awaken transformed into her image. That being impossible, I was willing to settle for Mrs. Harrison Williams or Constance Bennett. They were to me the three most chic women in the world.

I loathed having a beau who had little money spend any on me. New York prices were outrageous to this Yankee and I was the Big Town's cheapest date. My escorts would walk me home from the theatre or take me to Child's on 57th Street for eggs and fried potatoes. Potatoes! I've always adored them more than caviar. For years, I was called "Spuds."

If we didn't go to Child's, it might be a soda at Park and Tilford. On rare occasions we would go tea-dancing at the Biltmore, but that was terribly special. My beaux were usually college boys on small allowances. They couldn't have been more appreciative of my simple tastes. On many evenings we would take a ride on the top of the Fifth Avenue bus. Then there was Bowling Green and the Aquarium which were a delightful prelude to the nickel ferry ride to Staten Island.

I had something in common with Shirley Booth at this period. We shared a beau—Charlie Ritchie. I inherited him after Shirley broke her engagement to him.

Ruthie always trusted me even in the "Big City." She knew I was a self-styled goddess. But she guarded me anyway—in every way. And the red carpet was never laid at my feet in all the years of my success as an actress.

One night, after I felt I had given a particularly good performance, I came home beaming and told Ruthie how good I had been that night. I didn't know that she had been in the audience. She let me finish my story and then announced that I had given the worst performance I had ever given of the part. She then went on to say, "You enjoyed yourself too much."

We didn't talk for days. But underneath, I knew she was right; and that was why I was so enraged. The moment an actor allows a part to take over and just has fun—sails—he never gives as good a performance. It's a trap easy to fall into but shows lack of discipline.

The audience has paid to see you perform, not have fun. You must always try to be at your best. Besides, you never know who's going to be out front. One night, Arthur Hornblow, Jr. was in our audience. Samuel Goldwyn had sent him to see me as a possibility for the leading lady in *Raffles*—a film in which Ronald Colman was to star.

Hollywood held no allure for me. I was happy with my success in the theatre. Also, I hated being photographed. I had been Mother's model so often I had a phobia about it. Mr. Hornblow offered me a test for the part in *Raffles*.

I made the test for Mr. Goldwyn at the Paramount Studio in Astoria. They sent it West for him to see. He bellowed, "Whom did this to me?"

When I saw it, I agreed with him. I had a crooked front

tooth that was not attractive on the screen. My insecurity in a new medium was apparent.

Not only was I made up for *The Cabinet of Dr. Caligari*, but I was dressed by a man who evidently had read his instructions in braille. It has always been a wonder to me that Hollywood ever discovered anyone from a screen test. Evidently they proceeded on the theory that if the result of all the inefficiency was even remotely favorable, there was no end to the glories that could emerge if the studio accepted you and really went to work on you.

By mutual, unspoken consent, the test was ignored by everyone. It was brutally clear that the movies were not for me. I did decide to have braces put on my teeth, however, in case I ever received another invitation for a motion picture test. It was no fun trying not to lisp during the first few performances after they had been put on. I was afraid I would be given my notice.

That April, on Easter Sunday morning, my grandmother died. It seemed impossible that I would never see her again. Grandmother Favor—the Plymouth Rock of Gibraltar.

Broken Dishes ran successfully through the spring and I returned to the Cape "straight from her New York triumph." It was my third season at Dennis. I was to join Mr. Meek and the rest of the cast for a road tour in the fall.

The Cape was as busy as ever and Bobby of course was home from college for the summer. Again a play a week. I had quite forgotten what leisure was. I wasn't to know again for twenty years.

One Sunday evening Ruthie, Bobby and I went to a movie in Hyannis Port. I suddenly let out a whoop that almost started a rush to the nearest fire exit. I had seen the back of a neck four rows in front of us with curly hair silhouetted against the screen. I knew it belonged to only one person. Harmon O. Nelson, Jr. Ham!

Though we had seen or heard little of each other for four years, it was as if we had never been separated.

We all went back to our cottage after the movie and talked into the wee small hours. Ham was leader of the Amherst band playing for the summer at the Old Mill Tavern on the Cape. We could see each other all summer and we did. Our hours were about the same. We would meet after our work—walk on the beach—go for a drive—sit around the house—talk of our futures. Ham had one more year of college. I was in the theatre. He did not know what he wanted to do after he graduated.

We were both growing up and marriage was no longer a distant possibility. But marriage for Ham and me seemed out of the question at this point. He came to see each play I did and was most impressed with me as an actress. That pleased me.

In September we said good-bye. Back he went to college, I to Baltimore, Maryland, to open the road tour of *Broken Dishes*. It was not unlike the city to be in the throes of a sweltering Indian summer. There was no air conditioning in those days and opening night, the temperature was so insupportable that we had ten people in the audience. Mr. Meek stepped in front of the curtain before the play started and invited all ten to sit in the front row. He then asked the gentlemen to remove their jackets and make themselves comfortable. I don't believe we ever gave a better performance and no first-night audience ever responded more enthusiastically than this meager group of ten.

A week later, when we were playing in Washington, I received a call from our producer, Oscar Serlin. They needed a replacement immediately for the ingenue in a new play, *Solid South*, starring Richard Bennett. Mr. Bennett had three very famous daughters, Constance, Joan and Barbara.

I really didn't want to leave Mr. Meek and *Broken Dishes*, but an opportunity to follow up my success with another Broadway play was something I couldn't ignore. The play was to open in New York in ten days, which meant a lot of work to get up in the part in such a short time. Once again I would have a deadline and day-and-night rehearsals and—from what I had heard—a rather difficult co-worker. Mr. Bennett's temperament was well known. It was with mixed feelings that I arrived at the theatre to meet him.

But nothing had prepared me for his greeting which, I would say, lacked the graciousness of the "Solid South" to the extreme. He eyed me suspiciously as I walked down the aisle, the inevitable and naked light bulb dangling over his head like a tipsy halo. He barely moved his lips as the words came out of the side of his mouth.

"So! You're one of those actresses who think all they need are eyes to act. My daughters are the same."

I had been on a train overnight from Washington. I was tired—had come right to the theatre from the train—had a job anyway—actually couldn't have cared less. I looked right at him and said, "Mr. Bennett, I'm very happy to return to Washington immediately!"

He threw back his head and laughed.

"You'll do."

From there on in, he and I were the best of friends.

Lawton Campbell's play about the decaying aristocracy of the South was a fine play to do. And I loved my part.

Mr. Bennett was Major Follensby, my grandfather. My name was Alabama Follensby. Elizabeth Patterson, an old friend from Rochester's *Cradle Snatchers,* was my maiden aunt, Geneva; and Jessie Royce Landis, my beautiful and widowed mother. Moffat Johnson and Owen Davis, Jr. played the Yankee father and son who courted and won us.

John Murray Anderson, who had nicknamed me "the little Southern girl," must have had second sight. New Englander that I am, I have played many southern girls during my career. Alabama was the first one.

Like Richard Mansfield and Arnold Daly, Richard Bennett was a fine character actor, famous for his belligerent and articulate harangues against the most daintily critical critics—all of whom adored him qualifiedly. They accepted his ravings with all the toleration of dedicated zoo attendants. An actor of uncommon gifts, his lack of discipline was legend, his excesses outrageous. The real show always started after opening-night notices.

The press was again very kind to me and the rest of the cast, but the critics perpetuated their tempestuous romance with the star. The highly respected Percy Hammond of the *Telegram* called *Solid South* a "shiftless improvisation" and found Mr. Bennett's blustering old Major Follensby "as shoddy an impersonation as a fine player could give." Brooks Atkinson unearthed "enough montebankery to make it palatable for unprincipled playgoers." Burns Mantle in the *News* thought (as everyone did) that the julep-drinking Major was good fun "but not a faithful likeness of *any* human being." Stark Young in the *New Republic* insisted that "the fine actor allowed himself on occasion to be vulgar, actorish and extraneous.'' Mr. Young also noted that Owen and I tried desperately to make ''two nobodies interesting and became stage lovers who could give birth to nothing but an asbestos curtain''; but I managed to go on with my life. Not so with Mr. Bennett. The second night his makeup was war paint.

He was so furious at the widespread blasphemy that he stormed onstage. When he couldn't find a prop, he stepped out of character and thundered into the wings, ''Stagehand! My cigar!'' It was quite a night and the first of many. There was a surprise and a tantrum every performance and they built in crescendo to one particular Monday night.

We were playing a scene together and Mr. Bennett delivered one of the Major's endless, windy speeches. It always got a big laugh from the audience. This evening it was greeted with silence. This can happen in any play and often does. There are audiences who sit like stone, daring you to breathe life into them. They fight you all the way. An audience like this can be a challenge. It can also be utterly disheartening. An actor tries a million ways to win them. I never knew any other actor to do what Mr. Bennett did.

When his speech failed to provoke the slightest chuckle, he stopped dead, walked down to the footlights and said to the audience, ''I guess I'll have to tell this audience a dirty story to get them to laugh.''

Then he turned on his heel and exited, leaving Elizabeth Patterson and me alone on the stage. We were frozen with shock; but after what seemed like hours, we pulled ourselves together and went on with the play.

He had already sounded off about the critics. The second night he informed the audience that all the critics should be taken out beyond the 12-mile limit. This was at the curtain call, not during the play. Now he was letting the public have it. It couldn't have gone on for much longer and it didn't.

We closed in two weeks because of ''Mr. Bennett's indisposition.'' Our contracts were canceled by ''Act of God.'' Not Jehovah however. This one's name was Bacchus.

During this limited appearance, David Werner, a talent scout for Universal Pictures, came to a performance. Again I was offered a screen test.

Universal had purchased Preston Sturges' hit play *Strictly*

Dishonorable, and from publicity photographs, Carl Laemmle, the head of Universal, thought I might be right for the young girl. I had absolutely no delusions this time. I consented to take another test, feeling that talking pictures were becoming more and more important and I would be foolish to turn down any opportunity to broaden my horizon.

I have never made the same mistake twice except, of course, where it has counted most heavily. This time, my teeth having been straightened, putting on my own makeup and wearing one of my own dresses not only made me feel more comfortable, but made me look more like myself.

My test was given official approval by Mr. Laemmle and I was offered a contract at three hundred a week with three-month options the first year if the test of my legs proved to be satisfactory. I had worn a long dress and they were afraid I was hiding some deformity. My legs— What had they to do with being an actress? My Puritan blood curdled as I followed instructions for the silent strip of film of my legs. Higher, higher—as quarter inch by quarter inch I raised my skirt. It was truly humiliating to me, the whole performance. There was an interval of about a week before word was sent back from the Coast to Mr. Werner that my legs had passed muster and to go ahead with the signing of the contract as planned.

I was serious about not wanting to leave the theatre which I loved. However, with the show closed, I was out of a job. Ruthie reminded me what the fortuneteller in York, Maine, had told me—that I would be known in every country in the world. This is what she must have meant. Motion pictures. The money was the most I'd ever earned—and it was another challenge—and it was either Hollywood or job hunting again.

It is extremely ironic that in the one country in which, shamefully, there is no Federal Theatre—no National Company—it was a handful of suit and clothing merchants who gave the actor the only semblance of continuous financial security he had ever had. The destructive aspects of some of these men are properly infamous; but in debt we are to their gambling instincts. The ceaseless work, the constant exposure before the public who came to know us intimately, the illusion of permanence that eschewed rent and job worries, attracted the troubadors of the world. It wasn't just gold the real actor was

interested in. It was a permanent roof over his head for the
first time.

The possibility of having a home for Ruthie, Bobby and
myself was paramount in my eventual acceptance of the offer.
I liked the idea of a home of my own, something I had never
had. If the worst happened, a few motion pictures could only
increase my reputation on Broadway. Talking pictures were,
after all, like the stage—and so I made up my mind to join
the exodus from New York.

Any misgivings I had were more than shared by my discov-
erer, David Werner. He knew I was a gamble. Talent he knew
I had—but the usual glamour connected with a Hollywood
actress I did not have. He knew I was different. Had I known
how different I would turn out to be, I would never have crossed
the Rockies. The Rockies were simple to cross as compared
to the mountains I had ahead of me to climb. The day I went
to his office to sign my contract, I took my wire-haired terrier
along with me. Boojum was his name. As I was putting my
name on the longest contract I had ever seen, Boojum left on
the carpet his personal comment. What a critic he turned out
to be!

It was and had always been understood that my first film
would be the girl in *Strictly Dishonorable*. This was the only
thing in the whole collective memory of mankind that was not
incorporated in the twenty-pound document.

"That's understood, Miss Davis . . . there are technicalities
. . . the property is still being negotiated . . ."

My decision had been made. My moving finger writ and
having writ tapped nervously that evening as all my friends
warned me that what I had spelled out was a sentence that
would make San Quentin a vacation spot.

"*You*, Bette! Do you really think you'll be given a chance
to do anything worthwhile?"

"Now you've done it. Darling! Don't you know you can't
lick them there and you won't want to join them?"

After all, I wasn't some jazzed-up little thing. If they wanted
another Jean Harlow, they couldn't expect that from me. There
are good actresses out there. Ruth Chatterton; Garbo; Jeanne
Eagels just did *The Letter*; Claudette Colbert. I'll be in *Strictly
Dishonorable*. They're just jealous. Universal has great plans
for me!

I heard the first of their plans when I kept an appointment to see Mr. Laemmle's publicity men that Wednesday. The gentlemen looked me over across the great desk and through the upraised soles of their shoes. Our dialogue was a revelation.

"Now about your name."

"What about my name?"

"No glamour. Bette Davis. Ugh!"

"It is spelled with an *e*—instead of a *y*. That's unusual!"

"Doesn't have appeal. Picture names have to excite the public—intrigue 'em. *Bette Davis!* It's a great name for a secretary."

So we were back to that, were we?

"And what," I asked, having no intention of changing mine ever, "would you consider a name full of excitement and intrigue?"

"We've given a lot of thought to it and we've come up with the perfect name for you. It's a natural. Bettina Dawes."

"*Bettina Dawes!* I refuse to be called 'Between the Drawers' all my life!" They did laugh and they did skip any more discussions about changing my name.

There were things to be done before Mother and I could leave for the Coast. Our car for one. "But dearest, the down payment is negligible" had long since become a monthly "How are we going to meet the payments?" Ruthie had just put another three hundred dollars into the car and now we were going away. She was lucky enough to sell the car back to the dealers, and realized fifty dollars on it instead of the hundred and fifty she had hoped for.

Then there was the lease on our apartment, and no one we knew—including ourselves—could afford it. Not only did we plan to sublease it, Ruthie intended to make a profit from the transaction. "We have to." Only our tickets to California were free. Until I received my first week's salary, we would have very little money; just enough to take care of meals and tips en route and a week's hotel bills.

Ruthie put an ad in the classified section of *The New York Times*. In three lines, she managed to make our flat sound like Xanadu. A day before we had to leave and were getting frantic, the telephone rang. A man's voice asked if he could see the apartment immediately. When he arrived, Ruthie and I were breathless. We had practically drawn him a tub and prepared his dinner. Ulysses never had such a homecoming. That wonderful *New York Times*. That wonderful man.

Mr. X was small and dark. Though he was close shaven, his blue beard surrounded his small, flat nose and tiny eyes right up to his low hairline. The features were set in this little island like a monkey's. A star sapphire shone from his thick, hairy hand, freshly manicured. His little feet and head were both black patent leather.

He took a quick tour of the place, Ruthie, Boojum and I waiting with baited breath. He grunted once in each room and then turned quickly, almost knocking Ruthie over.

"Do you have a closet I can lock?"

This was something of a surprise, but we led him to the hall where up to now, we had stored our baggage and Ruthie's photographic equipment.

"Have a padlock put on it."

We were about to speak when he continued.

"I will require a dozen sheets in pink and a dozen pillow cases and a dozen towels. In pink, of course. Also a dozen cakes of pink soap. I will want a maid [no color specified] from nine till twelve every day and she must be punctual. I said nine till twelve. Not nine-fifteen to twelve-fifteen. I expect her to keep things immaculate.

"The rent will be placed in this desk drawer and so will her salary, on the first of every month. Here are your first and last months' rent now. I want everything to be left exactly as it is including your name on the mailbox. I will be ready for occupancy by twelve noon tomorrow."

With that he was gone.

We stood speechless. We hadn't opened our mouths. Ruthie clutched the two months' rent in both hands. I clutched my throat in disbelief.

I must say that whoever he was, he lived up to his bargain to the letter. We will never know to what use our apartment was put that season and we never moved back. But neither Mrs. Hughes, our landlady, or the maid ever caught a glimpse of him. The money always materialized in the drawer and the cakes of soap became slivers. The laundry bills were astronomical but Mr. X paid them. I must say he never washed his dirty linen in public. To Mr. X! I hope he's still in the pink. He saved our lives, that's for sure.

While Ruthie ran around to Wanamaker's and bought all the requested supplies, I picked up the train tickets and last-minute instructions at Universal.

The office was wood-paneled and red-carpeted and bursting with Universal love. I was assured in extravagant terms that I would never regret my decision to go West. Hollywood was Eldorado, Paradise. Mr. Laemmle was going to guide my career to dizzy heights.

The splendors of my imminent life were enumerated in words usually reserved for three sheets. Sensational! Colossal! Gigantic! The tickets were my keys to the kingdom. The expected artistic triumph of Erich Maria Remarque's *All Quiet on the Western Front* would give me a faint idea of the stature—the *class* of the company. *Strictly Dishonorable* would be a prestige picture that would make me a star overnight.

Clearly, my future was dazzling. I sat wide-eyed, luxuriating in the wonders that were in store for me.

Next day, we boarded the train for California—two rather frightened people. I remember sitting on the observation platform as we pulled out of Chicago and feeling I would never see my beloved East and my friends ever again. Hollywood seemed to be the end of the world. It almost was the end of me.

CHAPTER

8

After five days—that's how long it took in 1930 to cross the country—Ruthie and I arrived at the Los Angeles station. We had left a snowy New York December five days before and here we were in the tropics. The green, the flowers, the sun—it was all unbelievable to me. Mr. Werner had told me in New York the studio would send a car and someone to meet us and get us settled in a hotel until we decided where we wanted to live. We waited half an hour. No one came.

We took a taxi to the Hollywood Plaza Hotel at the suggestion of the taxi driver. I hung out the window, gaping at everything. I had imagined that Douglas Fairbanks, Mary Pickford, Norma Talmadge and John Barrymore would be running in and out of their elegant bungalows, Bebe Daniels and Ben Lyon chatting with Vilma Banky and Rod La Roque as they picked oranges off their trees. Nothing. No one! Hollywood and Vine was Main Street. We registered at the hotel, ordered luncheon and then called the studio.

They were horrified. They had sent a car and a representative to meet us. They hadn't seen anyone who looked like an actress.

I replied, "I had a dog with me—you should have known I was an actress." I was told to report to the studio on Monday. They would send a car for me.

Ruthie and I went to a real estate office to ask about finding

98

a house. Mrs. Carr was the broker. After we informed her of
our top price, she took a few keys off a board and said, "I
know just what you want. But *first* you've simply got to see
the *most* adorable house. It's far too expensive but as newcomers to California you'll be fascinated with the place. It's
on Alta Loma Terrace."

Alta Loma! How Exotic!

Well! It was the sweetest house I had ever seen in my life.
Completely furnished, replete with linens, silver, china and a
grand piano, it had everything including a beautiful outside
porch which we learned was called a patio. From it we could
see the Hollywood Bowl. Flowers were wildly abundant and
it was midwinter. Ruthie and I looked at each other wretchedly
while Mrs. Carr hummed innocently to herself.

Ruthie got me alone for a moment.

"Can you borrow on your salary? It isn't *that* much. And
eventually—"

"No!"

"But you're a contract player, Bette. They'll advance you
money on your salary—"

"No! Mother, I can't."

Ruthie had an expression on her face I knew well.

"No! Mother!"

It was impossible to find any other house that would compare.
I was heartbroken that we couldn't take it. Mother told Mrs.
Carr that we would let her know on Monday, which was sheer
insanity. What could we let her know? That we only had enough
to live on until my first week's salary—and that was already
half spent!

When we left Mrs. Carr, Ruthie was positive we were going
to live there. I certainly wanted to but I could think of no
solution.

"I'm going to wire your father. It's the least he can do at
this point. What's more we need a car out here. You can't even
go to the corner drugstore without one."

It was true that the corner drugstore or movie house or laundry was always a mile away at the least, and there were no
taxis in the way you could get one in New York. As we talked
she somehow steered me to a Ford car agency. In a moment
the two hobos from the East were sitting in an adorable green
phaeton.

"You look just right, Bette, sitting at that wheel."

"We'll be sitting in jail if you keep going on this way."

We left the showroom after Mother repeated her promise to get in touch with the salesman on Monday. She was planning a busy day for Monday. It was the day I was to report to the studio and I was nervous.

Now Mother tried her wiles on me again. She thought the sight of the car would encourage my borrowing money from the studio.

"*All* you have to do is *show* them your *contract*."

"*No*, Mother!"

"But if they see your contract—"

"*No*, Mother!"

Back at the hotel we had such a to-do that Ruthie called downstairs to complain of the noise, hoping to throw the management off the scent. I was tired and went to bed. It wasn't until months later that I discovered what Mother was up to while I slept.

Carl Milliken, Governor of Maine ten years before, was an old friend of the family; and Ruthie had heard he was in Hollywood, staying at the Roosevelt Hotel. She called the hotel at five-thirty in the morning to be sure he was registered there. He was. Carl always played tennis with his Japanese teacher at seven A.M. and Ruthie dressed herself hurriedly. I awoke as she was sneaking out of the apartment. In semiconsciousness, I asked where she was going. "For a walk" was her reply.

I learned later that Mother ran from Vine Street to the Roosevelt Hotel and "ran into" Carl as he was leaving for the tennis court. His surprise at seeing her at this hour was tempered by his fright at her expression. When he asked what was wrong, Ruthie simply said, "I need five hundred dollars immediately." Now, we're all New Englanders and we like to know *why* someone wants five hundred dollars. Ruthie explained that we needed a place to live and a car to get us around. The loan would be for a short while. Carl, eager to get on with his tennis, peeled off five bills and handed them to her. What an angel he was. If I had known what she was up to, I would have had a fit. And she knew it.

Ruthie now went to Western Union where she paid someone to write out a message from Father. The telegram sounded exactly like him. WIRE RECEIVED. SENDING MONEY NEVER ASK

AGAIN. HARLOW M. DAVIS. The wire was slipped under our door. As I was reading it, Mother came back to the room and supposedly read it too. I ordered a huge breakfast, called Mrs. Carr, bought the car, signed the lease and moved from the hotel.

In two days we had become the proud owners of Alta Loma Terrace and a green phaeton with yellow wheels. I took the wheel and our first stop was at Mrs. Carr's. In seconds, we were driving to Alta Loma Terrace. We had our first tea and the unsurprised Governor Milliken was our first guest. A most discreet one. Ruthie! Ruthie! The originator of nothing ventured, nothing hath!

Now I was ready for anything. On Monday I drove to the studio. I was whisked through the gates. Word had spread that the "Davis girl" had arrived and one by one studio executives found reasons for wandering in and out of the reception room to get a glimpse of the "find." I waited and waited and, at last, Mr. Laemmle opened his door and I was ushered into his office.

I was wearing no makeup except lipstick. I had never plucked an eyebrow. I had never even seen the inside of a beauty parlor. My hair was worn simply, with a knot in back. Mr. Laemmle's face was a study. He was immediately convinced that I was not right for *Strictly Dishonorable*. That was apparent to me.

Mr. Laemmle later said, "She has as much sex appeal as Slim Summerville!" I was in the outer office and heard the remark. It was a long time after that before I regained my security. I had been convinced he was right.

After a tour of the lot, I was photographed in the still gallery, introduced to officials and one actress, Genevieve Tobin, and saw a few others I recognized. I was told the studio would call me tomorrow and arrange for some tests. It was rumored on the lot that Bette Davis was "a little brown wren." I think Mr. Werner was sent to Siberia. The rest of the week was spent making what they called photographic tests. They supposedly found out your good angles and your bad angles. All I wanted to do was *act!*

The following week I was sent for and told I was being tested for a part in a picture. I was not given a script for the test, which I thought odd. I was simply asked to lie on a couch. Vague doubts assailed me as one male after another bent over me whispering, "You gorgeous, divine darling. I adore you. I worship you. I must possess you." He would then make ardent love to me and end lying on top of me.

"O.K. Cut!" I would hear the director say. "Fine. Who's next? *Who's next*?"

WHO'S NEXT!

The most compulsively dedicated harlot never had a morning like mine. No less than fifteen men—all of them well-known names—repeated the scene. Only Gilbert Roland had the sensitivity to see how shocked I was. Before he started that awful monologue, he whispered, "Don't be upset. This is the picture business. We've all gone through it. Just relax!"

I didn't understand. Was it like going across the equator the first time? Was it an initiation? Relax? My ancestors were revolving in their graves. Aside from my mortification, the fact that I might just as well have been a dummy further enraged me. The camera was concentrated exclusively on the men as they ravaged this anonymous thing. From any angle whatsoever, it was disgusting. I wasn't even a woman. I was a mattress in a bawdyhouse.

This was the dizzying depths to which Universal with all its promises had brought me. Boojum! Boojum! How he had known. He had studied the fine print in the contract—the print so fine that only dogs could read it. The proof was in the pudding.

I crawled back to exotic Alta Loma and moodily surveyed the Hollywood Bowl. *Eldorado!* The flowers were scentless, the sun relentless. My heart cried out for the East and a snowy winter. It was the end of December and the weather was obscenely balmy. I loathed the whole place and cried like a baby. Ruthie, my own private Dr. Pangloss, was sure that everything was happening for the best. She was sure that I had nothing to worry about.

Bobby came from college to spend Christmas with us and arrived with a terrible chest cold. We had to put her to bed immediately. Now the two of us were sick, she of body, I of soul. Bobby coughed all night and I sighed all day. It was the unhappiest time in our lives.

The cheap, pastel decorations on Hollywood Boulevard were a mockery of a New England Yuletide. It was all so unreal. I had always adored Christmas. But not this one.

"We'll just make believe it isn't Christmas, Mother. Anyway, we can't afford to give any presents."

But Ruthie, in spite of my edict, bought Bobby and me a few trinkets—a pathetic, scraggly little tree costing little, which greeted us on Christmas morning. It was pitiful. I remember thinking that it was "from its mother's womb untimely ripped" and this depressed me further. Everywhere there was tragedy. One string of blue lights and a few ornaments—that was my life.

During what was laughingly called the holidays, I was called to the studio. One of Mr. Laemmle's relatives, a prop man, had been given his first directorial assignment on a film called *Heart in Hand*, starring Walter Huston. I was removed from the shelf and sent to wardrobe, where I was dressed in a cotton dress much too revealing in front. I complained about this. I felt I looked common—but nothing was done about it. Hot and embarrassed, I was rushed down to the set where the dark little director stopped brooding long enough to glare at me and say to one of his assistants, "What do you think of these girls who show their chests and think they can get jobs?" This was my first meeting with William Wyler. This also made it impossible for me to do a good job with the test. He gave the part to Helen Chandler and back on the shelf went I.

Then word reached me that Universal had bought Booth Tarkington's story *The Flirt*, and I was being considered for it. When Hobart Henley, the director, sent for me, I felt my chance had come. But it was not yet my day. Sidney Fox was given the lead opposite the star, Conrad Nagel, and I was cast as her sister. I was disappointed, but at least I was going to work. I was thrilled to be in a picture with Conrad Nagel, whom I had seen so many times on the screen. I couldn't believe that I was actually sitting next to him on the set.

The Flirt was called *Gambling Daughters* by the time we started work. It should have been called off. The cast, besides Mr. Nagel and Sidney Fox, included Humphrey Bogart (also in his debut), Zazu Pitts, Charles Winninger, Emma Dunn, Bert Roach and my twin, Slim Summerville.

It was a tale of Midwestern provincialism and Miss Fox and I were sisters—she the hellion, I the timid mouse. One good and one bad. I was so virtuous, so plain, so noble and so saccharine that it turned my stomach. All that nobility and what did it get me? The second lead. As further proof of my theory, the title was again changed, this time permanently, to *Bad Sister*.

But for all my eagerness to play a *femme fatale*, I was nervous about one scene I had with the star. I was to wash a baby—a warm, homey domestic touch—and then kiss Mr. Nagel when I had the infant properly diapered. The scene oozed goodness as Conrad was to watch my wholesome sweetness. Something suddenly occurred to me, and I asked several members of the crew if the baby would be a boy or a girl. It became terribly important for me to know. It was on my mind all morning. The first day of the movie, one of the men yelled "Move that broad," and I thought he meant me. I was indignant until it was laughingly explained that a "broad" was a light. The crew already had my number. They now told me that they had no idea about the baby and "What difference does it make?"

What difference?

That afternoon when Conrad and I were ready for the scene, I noticed Zazu Pitts, Slim Summerville, Charley Winninger and that old heckler Bogey plant themselves in ringside seats to watch the take. The baby was brought in all wrapped up in a blanket. As we were about to start shooting, the infant was unwrapped, handed to me naked, and, of course, it was a boy. I thank heavens that technicolor was still to be perfected. I played the whole scene in a deep blush. If it ever appears, this brilliant epic, on television, the facts will back up my story. My face turned dark gray and stayed that way throughout the scene. Red turns gray in black and white.

Bad Sister had a sneak preview in San Bernardino some sixty miles from Hollywood, and Ruthie and I attended it, my first movie. We sneaked up to the last row of the balcony. A few more feet and I could have destroyed the projector and stopped everybody's agony. I have never liked my face and a couple of my tests had driven me wild, but this was a movie. It was going to show all over the country. All our friends would see it. We sneaked out after it was over and drove home in silence.

According to all existing Hollywood standards, my face was not photogenic. Embarrassment always made me have a one-sided smile and since I was constantly embarrassed in front of a camera, I constantly smiled in a one-sided manner. My hair, my clothes, my God! They hadn't cared. It was as if they dared you to be good. No one bothered to help.

I had been in Eldorado for three months and it was option time. As there wasn't the smallest doubt that I would be dropped like a hot potato, I got the shock of my life when I was called to Mr. Laemmle's office and told that I was to be kept on for another three months. It was several weeks before I discovered what had reawakened his interest. It wasn't the fact that the critics had miraculously noticed me and spoken favorably of my work in *Bad Sister*. That would have been logical. No. Karl Freund, the cameraman on the picture, saved the day by telling Mr. Laemmle that "Davis has lovely eyes." What better reason to renew my contract? What better reason to have faith in an actress?

The head of the studio might have been impressed by Karl Freund's irrelevant observation but word soon got to me that Mr. Laemmle, option or no, had announced that "the kid might be all right in certain roles but what audience would ever believe that the hero would want to get *her* at the fade-out?"

This kind of information always had swift little messengers only too eager to deliver it with dispatch. One of the secretaries in the office confided to me that no one ever noticed me.

"When Jean Harlow is a mile away, the men sit up and take notice. You've got to do something about yourself. You've got to look sexy."

The girl meant well but I was confused. Was there just one kind of attractive woman? One certainly didn't have to be a traditional beauty to attract men. And one certainly didn't have to be Jean Harlow. In the East I had had many beaux. Was I like certain wines—I couldn't "travel"? Did I lose in the translation? Could I have conceivably become this unappealing? The top-office news was crushing although I found I was stepping quickly to evade the grubby hands of less exacting gentlemen. Evidently these fellows had no taste and I had less for such goings on. Only Ham's letters kept me sane through this period. When would they all know that I wanted to be an actress, not a glamour girl?

In the long view, these memories amuse me; but I was utterly humorless about them then. My career was the most important thing in my life. I had had it proven that I was justified in my pursuit of that career. Had I lost everything west of the Rockies that I had had east of said mountain range?

I was accomplishing nothing in Hollywood. My friends had been right. Hollywood was not the place for me. I had been flourishing in the theatre. *What a fool I was to come to Hollywood where they only understood platinum blondes and where legs are more important than talent.*

Ruthie worked overtime in an effort to keep my spirits up. I was discouraged. I was aching to work. My energies had no outlet. I was going mad, and suicide was no answer. I had been awfully lucky up until now. I hadn't gone through the series of tortures devised as a ritual for the theatre aspirant. I had moved with incredible smoothness from wide-eyed, stagestruck dancing fairy to a modest but fairly secure position as a Broadway ingenue. I had of my own volition come to Hollywood with a contract most of my colleagues envied. It was true that my training and my dedication impressed no one; wherever I turned I was rebuffed. My sense of dignity was outraged. My self-esteem was shared by no one outside of Alta Loma Terrace. My sense of propriety made me recoil at most of the Hollywood males and my continence was an utter bore to everyone.

Talking pictures had made it necessary to hijack talent from New York but the powers that were and still are—down to the fourth generation—often don't know what to do with talent. The insecurity of most of these moguls made them wary of a literate group of kids from the theatre. They wanted younglings they could mold. They wanted to create personalities, not be challenged by them. From the evidence, they wanted us to fail. They did nothing to help us. It was abysmal, that period of my career. But I had become fascinated with pictures as an art form.

While I spent countless days posing in bathing suits and evening dresses for fan magazines, I spent my evenings at Grauman's or the Pantages watching the movies from a new vantage point. If I couldn't learn on the set I'd learn from the finished pictures themselves. Suddenly films were broken down to scenes and fragments, long shots and close-ups. I became aware of editing and transitions. Unlike most of my fellow actors who had made the hegira West, I couldn't look down on a medium which could put a hundred million people in a trance. It was the charlatans for whom I had contempt. Now that motion pictures were talking, I had a vision that someday they might say something. There were moments when they almost did. But they said it best visually. The difference between the media, intellectually understood, now dawned on me fully. I knew the moment I used a microphone that I didn't have to project my voice as much. I knew the moment I was in the limited range of the camera's eye that my movements were more restricted; but my directors at this point simply told me where to stand. The finer points I had to glean for myself. Watching movies with my new point of view, I was astonished with picture technique. From the gallery of the Belasco in New York, the stage might have looked far away, but the actor loomed large and expansive.

The canvas of the stage might be narrower than that of the screen, but the strokes, by necessity, are broader. Just as in ballet or mime, the gesture must say it all, so obviously must the actor—a block away from the farthest seat in the house— exaggerate his actions and speech as well as his makeup in order fully to communicate.

What the camera can accomplish in a selective shot has to be expressed by the stage player himself. He is free of the self-imposed discipline of screen acting. Both the ham and the artist are logical products of these liberties, and have the courage to use them.

I suddenly realized that the Broadway actress was absolutely operatic compared to her Hollywood counterpart who could employ vocal and physical restraint. Some of them might just as well have posed for stills. They never would have got past the first morning's rehearsal in a theatre which demands in its actors a self-generating vitality and projection.

High theatrical style when worn by a Lynn Fontanne or Ina Claire is marvelous. And the audience is acclimated to it. Even with the arrival of the social theatre, the artifice remained. The style simply changed from chiffon to sackcloth. The actors wore it just as rakishly. Luther Adler was as broad as Walter Hampden and marvelous Geraldine Page today is as broad as the two of them put together.

This is not to say that I am narrow. Within that smaller frame we have in pictures, I have been more often than not accused of the heroic and the excessive. Once I learned that—unlike the theatre—the slightest purse of the lip, lowering of the lid, vibration of the wrist, could convey what I wished in the Mem-

ling canvases of the movies, I tried to open the hearts of the
women I played. I had to feel my way carefully through the
strangeness of the new medium. Then came my refusal, even
under the microscope, to rob the public by being "natural."
Natural! That isn't the point of acting. Though the stage and
screen have different approaches, we aim for the same thing.
Truth. The public must believe us. They must also be somehow
ennobled. The fact that the camera picks up the smallest nuance
and the stage doesn't, simply educated me to my new craft. It
didn't make one better than the other.

I was under contract as a moving picture actress and I had
to learn my craft with Ruthie and Bobby in the dark of a
balcony. I watched Garbo now as a colleague not as the mysterious Swedish beauty. Her instinct, her mastery over the
machine, was pure witchcraft. I cannot analyze this woman's
acting. I only know that no one else so effectively worked in
front of a camera. John Barrymore, George Arliss, Ruth Chatterton, all galvanized the screen. It struck me that rather than
being a stepchild of the theatre, the motion picture was heir
apparent, the logical scion of a magnificent tradition. Certainly
the artistic and communicative potential was stunning. To be
a part of that future kept me going—or not going. I became
patient. Something inside of me told me that this was not the
graveyard of my dreams but just a valley I must suffer. My
despair dissolved into hope.

As if in answer to my newfound sense of destiny, John Stahl,
one of Universal's directors, stared at me in the commissary
one luncheon as if I were a creature from another planet. He
had been searching for a girl to complete the cast of his latest
picture. Contests in the local papers, forays into high schools
and dramatic classes and tearooms had not uncovered the right
girl. It was a surprise he hadn't tried a Chinese restaurant. It
would have been a little more reasonable than looking through
the list of actresses under contract. But thank God for small
favors. Mr. Stahl saw me over a hot roast beef sandwich and
French fried potatoes and summoned me to his set, where he
cast me as another sister in the screen adaptation of Charles
Norris' novel *Seed,* a plea for birth control that was too controversial for Hollywood and all but ignored in the film. The
theme and I met the same fate. As one of John Boles' and Lois
Wilson's five children who got in the way of Papa's literary

career, I might just as well have been arrested at the source. My part might have been edited by Margaret Sanger. Jackson Rose, the cameraman, was no help either.

There was no makeup man for me, no attempt was made to light me properly and I felt like a churchmouse next to the soignée Genevieve Tobin, who played the catalyst who broke up our dull but happy home. It occurred to me that Mr. Boles as my father could never have been the great writer his subsequent freedom inspired. The character showed so little understanding of the dynamics between his loving wife and ambitious mistress that I didn't believe that he could have written the love life of Dickie Dare. But I did my thankless job and kept my mouth shut.

It was actually encouraging to play with Miss Wilson, a lovely actress, and Miss Tobin, whose work like her appearance had such polish. Working in a picture with John Stahl as a director gave me hope also. He was a talented man.

We had a World Premiere—my first since 1908—at the Cathay Circle; and Abe Lyman, for some mysterious reason, played "The Indian Love Call." Conrad Nagel was Master of Ceremonies. He should have been delivering the last rites. There on the screen along with Zazu Pitts, Raymond Hackett, Dickie Moore, Helen Parrish, Richard Tucker and the leads was my ghost. If I wasn't dead in pictures already, this appearance was sure to do the trick.

Universal, now irrevocably convinced that they had been duped, made the best of a bad bargain and cast me in Robert Sherwood's *Waterloo Bridge* in which Mae Clarke played Myra opposite Douglas Montgomery's Roy. I was his gentle sister, Janet, who is kind to the hapless heroine. And that was that! Universal's stepchild had played three sisters and not a Mascha amongst them. Brother! Not Sister!

Now, in a burst of generosity that was not a little suspect, Mr. Laemmle lent me to RKO to play the ingenue in H. Phillips Lord's screen debut as his own Seth Parker in *Way Back Home*. Frank Albertson was the juvenile whose bucolic romance with me allowed the Jonesport neighbors their chance to shed sweetness and light and their crackerbarrelsful of wit.

We shot a great deal of the film on location at Santa Cruz. Bobby, who had decided to leave college and join the family, came along with me. This was the first picture in which I was

well photographed—and more important—was not a sister. I
was someone's girl, and you did understand why he wanted to
kiss me at the fade-out. When I saw the picture I, anyway,
was encouraged by my physical appearance. I looked the way
I had always felt I looked. For the first time. What little ego
I had, had certainly taken a beating those first six months at
Universal.

Mr. Laemmle obviously had no intention of using me again.
The movie magazines were filled with stories of me, my house,
my wardrobe, my hobbies and my "beaux"; but this was ritual
since I was currently appearing in three of the gentleman's
films. But he was through with me. I was on the payroll until
option time so he couldn't get rid of me. Ignoring Polonius'
advice, he again lent me out—this time to Columbia. I appeared
in a monstrosity called *The Menace* opposite Walter Byron and
H. B. Warner.

Roy William Neill directed this adaption of *The Feathered
Serpent*; my part consisted of a great many falls out of closets.
The picture was made in eight days. I knew I had obviously
reached bottom. But I had a surprise in store for me. There
was something lower than bottom; and Mr. Laemmle sent me
there.

The next loan-out was produced by Benjamin F. Zeidman
and the picture was aptly named *Hell's House*, a story of juvenile delinquency which took about five minutes to make
although it seemed like an eternity. My name was Peggy; and
Pat O'Brien was the guy, a cheap bootlegging idol of the
juvenile delinquent, Junior Durkin, the pivotal character of this
"quickie." Mr. Zeidman was quick but he was thorough. The
camera work was excellent, the editing expert, and playing
opposite Mr. O'Brien a satisfaction. Also from New York's
theatre, Pat was straightforward and honest. He had been
brought out for *Front Page* and, at the moment, was in as
unenviable a position as I.

God's eye might be on the sparrow, but it was certainly
ignoring the little brown wren. Ruthie and Bobby had faith in
my future. I did not. I was taking a beating all right but at
least I was learning about working on the screen in the process.
Each performance had shown some improvement, more confidence, greater ease before the camera. And most important,
the public was beginning to know me. In one year, I had made

a half-dozen unimportant pictures but had been publicized in every fan magazine.

The Davis girls decided that all in all it wasn't so bad.

Six movies were under my belt. The next role would be it. The next one would be the part to prove I really knew how to act. And then it happened. Universal did not take up my option. I had been used in only three of their films and lent out for three. Now they washed their hands of me. I had failed in the new medium which I had come to love. There is no question that this was the low point in my career. I'm not a good loser and the stakes were high. I had had a fantasy in which I returned to New York a great star of motion pictures. This dream was not any more worth thinking about—I obviously would have to return to New York with my tail between my legs. I hadn't made it.

Being a picture actress is expensive and my salary hardly had prepared me for an early retirement. We were going to be broke again. It was like old times.

The studio contractually had to pay our fare back to New York. We made the reservations, arranged to sell the car, packed our trunks. The day before we were to board the train, our phone rang.

Ruthie answered. I heard her say, "George who? Arliss? Bette, it's for you—it's George Arliss."

As I went to the phone I wondered which friend was ribbing me and very elegantly I said to the supposed George Arliss—in a very broad British accent—"Yes, Mr. Arliss, and what can I do for you?"

A beautiful English voice slightly taken aback said, "Is this Miss Bette Davis? This is Mr. George Arliss."

"Of course," I answered, "and how are you, old boy?"—never dreaming I was *really* talking to George Arliss himself.

Finally he managed to get through to me that he was for real—that a Murray Kinnell who was in *The Menace* with me had suggested my name as a possibility for a part in his next picture. He wondered if I could be at Warner Brothers at 3 o'clock that afternoon. That was in two hours. Could I be— try and stop me! The sky was blue again. The grass was green. An Arliss picture! I wouldn't have to return to New York a failure!

Mr. Arliss was having difficulty finding a girl for the leading role in *The Man Who Played God*, and Murray had recommended me as a possibility after watching me work.

I went that afternoon to Mr. Arliss' office on the Warner lot. Driving to the studio I debated whether or not to tell him how impressed I was with his lecture on speech at John Murray Anderson's school. Would it seem a device? I was terrified to meet George Arliss, who was one of the great actors of all time. The great Arliss held an exceptional place in films. Billed always as Mr. Arliss, his productions and performances had a tone and quality one only found in the theatre. His casts were carefully chosen and comprised only actors with stage experience. The productions were mounted with a dignity and authenticity that made them all prestige pictures. His *Old English*, *Disraeli*, *Alexander Hamilton* and *Green Goddess* made a fortune for Warner Brothers. This was the studio to make the first talking picture. They gambled all on its success or failure. The film was *The Jazz Singer* with Al Jolson. It was a sensational success. Warners knew what they had. Stars whose light was still to be seen had died a million light minutes ago when Hollywood broke the sound barrier. Hence the desperate hoarding of Broadway newcomers and stars. Warners already had Mr. Arliss, John Barrymore and Ruth Chatterton, all of whom made the transition to the screen trailing tradition, literacy and dignity in their wake.

The premiere of a George Arliss film had the glamour and tone of a New York opening. The critics were full of praise, the intelligent public was thrilled. To be in one of his pictures not only put one on the map, but in a dignified way.

Awesome as he was to me, I really felt I was meeting one of my own when I entered Mr. Arliss' office; and I was surprisingly at ease. I respected him as an artist and somehow knew that lucky or not, I would at least be able to relate to him on a level unheard of in my recent dealings.

Mr. Arliss rose to greet me with all the courtliness and graciousness for which he was famous. His fabulous face, incredibly contorted, opened like a flower and his monocle dropped safely on its ribbon to his narrow chest as he said, "How do you do, Miss Davis? *So nice of you to come*! Please sit down. My friend Murray Kinnell believes that you would be an excellent choice for the leading lady in my next film."

"I don't know how he could tell, Mr. Arliss, from that dreadful picture."

But what was I saying? Whose side was I on? Mr. Arliss laughed.

"Mr. Kinnell is a most discerning fellow. Tell me, my dear. How long were you on the stage?"

"For three years, Mr. Arliss."

"Hmm!" The tips of his fingers touched in church-steeple fashion. "Just enough to rub the edges off."

He then looked up at and through me in the manner of a kind diagnostician seeking out the cause of his patient's pain. How skeletal his face was, I thought. The skin was drawn so tightly that I imagined there would have to be a knot somewhere in the back of his head. His small dark eyes held an ancient sadness; but his taut, triangular mouth seemed always to be repressing an irrepressible mirth. Universal had asked to see my legs. Mr. Arliss was examining my soul. The suspense was agonizing. Would he agree with Murray Kinnell that I was right for the part? There was a gentleness in his face that warmed me. I couldn't help thinking that now he looked like an inhibited satyr—a satyr who had materialized at Eton and then Oxford, a civilized gnome as misplaced in this Hollywood world as I seemed to be.

I suspect that Mr. Arliss had twenty-twenty vision because he hummed a sound of satisfaction, turned away and, having finished looking, replaced his monocle.

"The part is yours. Go to the casting office right away. They will take you to the wardrobe department."

I was too stunned to move. I finally found my voice, thanked him, which was the understatement of the century, and got out of the office without falling in a dead faint. I somehow found my way to the casting office and deposited myself with some degree of dignity, but by the time I got to the wardrobe department I couldn't control myself any longer. I started literally jumping up and down and screaming, "I can't believe it! I can't believe it!" I even hugged several perfect strangers.

The next morning I reported for rehearsal. Mr. Arliss, through Murray Kinnell, had thrown me the lifeline just as I was going down. Like Pearl White, I was snatched from the jaws of death. Because failure to me is a death. I was now under contract to Warners for one picture and they had the right, at the completion of the film, to take up an option on my services if they wished. I knew that after all this time, this was my chance. I was going to appear opposite an actor of tremendous stature along with such fine players as Violet Heming, Louise Closser Hale, Ivan Simpson and Oscar Apfel.

Based on the play *The Silent Voice* by Jules Eckert Goodman from the short story ''The Man Who Played God'' by Gouverneur Morris, and directed by John Adolfi, the story concerned a much lionized concert pianist who falls desperately in love with a girl much younger than himself. At a command performance, a bomb meant for the King explodes and deafens the pianist, destroying his career and his faith in God. His attempt at suicide is thwarted by his butler, who pulls him back from the window and points out the beauties of life in the park below. Learning lip reading and now the possessor of powerful field glasses, he insinuates himself into the lives of the unfortunates he sees through his glasses in the park, helping them with their problems anonymously, and through his providential impersonation returning to faith. It is only when he spies his fiancée declaring her love to a younger man (played by Donald Cook) and admitting her own sacrifice to the life of the great man, that he releases her from the engagement and makes final peace with himself and the older woman who has never ceased to love him in spite of his engagement and disability.

Mr. Arliss was too old to play Royale, the pianist, but he was enchanting and you forgave him. Mr. Arliss had a fantastic rapport with his audience. He seemed to share a secret that the rest of the cast were not in on. This became very flattering to them. A most successful device for box-office returns.

Mr. Arliss personally augmented my direction, supervised my makeup and wardrobe, and showed me every conceivable consideration. He was turning the little brown wren into a bluebird. For the first time care was taken with me by the makeup man, the hairdresser and the wardrobe department. What a difference this can make.

The cast was a disciplined theatre group, and I evidently surprised the star by never being late or the worse for wear after a Sunday. I was the new kid. It seems Mr. Arliss, quite properly, was intolerant of lack of discipline in the young. I shared this view. I wasn't in pictures for the fun of it. I had a dream I was going to make real and this meant work. But when work is what you love, this is life at its fullest. Sunday was a day I studied my script. *My* work wasn't ever over when I left the set.

Long before *The Man Who Played God* opened, Mr. Arliss put the finishing touch on his handiwork. He repeated his observation in his autobiography later. I recall it with pride and no false modesty because this was the turning point of my career and doubtless, in the long view, the most important part I ever played. At the end of the picture, Mr. Arliss' eyebrows rose as he released his monocle, and he said, "My dear. Not even *I* saw all the dimensions you gave to Grace. Thank you!"

The Man Who Played God opened with great fanfare at Warners' Western Theatre and was a great success throughout the country. The critics couldn't understand the change that had come over me. It was awfully simple. I had a good part with a fine cast, a fine production, and my makeup and clothes and camera work were the best.

Warners picked up my option and Ruthie, Bobby and I breathed a sigh of relief. All thoughts of packing were forgotten for at least another year—next option time.

I was cast immediately in a Barbara Stanwyck picture at Warners. Miss Stanwyck had just starred in Frank Capra's *Ladies of Leisure* at Columbia and Warners had signed her. This was the first time in Hollywood the powers had shown any recognition of my work. It was a source of tremendous satisfaction and encouraged me to unheard-of dreams of glory.

Before starting the Arliss film, I had been introduced to the Warners publicity men, headed by Charles Einfeld. Studio press agents are your shield, your moat, your fortress against the world. How they maintain their sanity and loyalty in the face of the characters they work with is a major mystery. There is nothing they do not know about you. And they take the bad with the good, always poised to shield you from the press. When a movie is bad—and we've all made some lulus—it is they who must simulate ecstasy in the face of utter disaster. The actors, producers and director have finished their job and go on to the next project, leaving these bright and discerning fellows holding the bag. They must sell to the public whatever picture we've made, even if they feel unenthusiastic about it. I was to know many of these men and will always be in their debt.

But this was my beginning and I started to serve my apprenticeship. The Stanwyck picture was a remake of Edna Ferber's *So Big*, which Colleen Moore had made so successfully and silently seven years before. The earthy role of Salina, the pioneer farm woman, ran the gamut from schoolgirl braids to gray hair. William Wellman graphically picturized the toil-worn land and farmers of the Midwest. Salina's little boy (Dickie Moore played him) kept answering (''So big'') when anybody asked him the absurd question: ''How big are you?'' I was the artist who leads this son, weak-willed as a grownup and played by Hardie Albright, back to his destiny and his mother's dream. A newcomer to Hollywood made his first film appearance at the end of the picture as the adult sculptor whose love of Salina exceeds her own son's. He was a handsome Irishman straight from Dublin's great Abbey Players and formerly wanted by the Black and Tans. George Brent. George Brent on the night that the English captured six other Sinn Fein dispatch carriers was carrying documents in his blue-black hair. He was a young man of immense charm. We were both cast in Ruth Chatterton's first picture for Warner Brothers. As a matter of fact, I worked on the Chatterton film in the daytime and the Stanwyck film at night for a week. I never knew who I was!

Miss Chatterton had always been one of my favorite actresses. In *Madame X* and *Sarah and Son* she was magnificent. Her films were saved from bathos by her magic. In order to win her, Warners had promised her not only eight thousand a week but her choice of stories. It was probably the first fabulous contract for an actress since the innovation of talking pictures. She was a star from the top of her head to the tips of her toes. Miss Chatterton chose for her first film at Warners *The Rich Are Always With Us*, a drawing-room comedy in the best Frederick Lonsdale tradition. We were all terribly rich and Miss Chatterton, being the star, was the richest of us all, indeed the richest girl in New York. Although John Miljan was Miss Chatterton's husband, he was playing around with Adrienne Dore; Miss Chatterton was in love with George Brent. I was ''the pest of Park Avenue'' in love with Mr. Brent both on the screen and off—in both cases unsuccessfully. I had to hit Adrienne in the mouth like a sweet little debutante and then dig my heel in her back; but I didn't get George and neither did

Miss Chatterton, for that matter, on the screen—but she did off. They were married shortly after the completion of the film. The film bubbled with wit and sophistication, and I was thrilled to be appearing with Miss Chatterton.

The first morning when I arrived on the set, I was clammy with nerves. Miss Chatterton swept on like Juno. I had never seen a real star-type entrance in my life. I was properly dazzled. Her arrival could have won an Academy nomination. Such authority! Such glamour! She was absolutely luminous and radiated clouds of Patou and Wrigley's Spearmint. It was further tribute to Miss Chatterton's singularity that her regal presence was in no way marred by the gum that she chewed incessantly offscreen. She actually made it chic, *de rigeur*. I felt like running to the nearest drugstore. She was superb.

The first scene was the interior of a restaurant. Miss Chatterton and Mr. Brent sat at a table and I was to make my way through the tables and greet them in a very chic and secure way. I was actually so terrified of her I literally could not get a word out of my mouth. George was sitting there, his coffee cup chattering away. He was more nervous than I.

She kept looking at me in a superior kind of way. I finally— not meaning to—blurted out, "I'm so damned scared of you I'm speechless!"

This broke the ice and we *both* relaxed. She was most helpful in her scenes with me after that. I never forgot this experience and in later years when young actors were terrified of me, I would always try to help them get over it.

I fared the best to date in *The Rich Are Always With Us* and not without the help of Ernie Haller, my first fine cameraman, who remained my favorite throughout my career. Louella Parsons, who had been most encouraging about my work from *Bad Sister* on upward, was delighted with my great change in appearance although she became obsessed with what she called my "heavily beaded lashes and overrouged mouth." Oddly enough, they were to become my trademark. Everyone seemed startled by my change of personality, which had very little to do with me but with the part I was playing. The little brown wren could become a peacock if the situation demanded. I had had colorless roles, bad and uninspired direction up until *The Man Who Played God*.

Mr. Arliss had made some suggestions regarding my hair.

A lighter hue of blond and a slick coiffure did wonders for me although my apparent resemblance to Constance Bennett, much as I admired her, distressed me no end. I had no desire to look like anyone else and every fan magazine reveled in a triptych of Bennett, Carole Lombard and myself with the captions *Hollywood Look Alikes* and *Couldn't They Be Sisters*? Miss Bennett must have loathed us. Thank God, all of that ended and we emerged as three entirely different personalities which we certainly were from the outset. Although the studio litany "we have another Bennett" was preferable to Universal's "we have another Summerville," my ego couldn't take either.

It could however take the acclaim I was at last receiving. The movie fan had discovered me. My mail started to grow and it became pleasantly impossible to go anywhere without recognition. Ruthie blossomed with my growing celebrity. It looked now as if we were going to make it in Hollywood. George Arliss was truly "the man who played God" to Ruthie and me. My greatest moment was paying off the $500 lent to Ruthie by Carl Milliken. We now lived in a house by the sea at Zuma Beach and the Ford had turned into an Auburn—secondhand, but an Auburn.

CHAPTER

9

The Hollywood male had discovered me mildly and some of them were fun. It was not necessarily a compliment that they surrounded me. I was on the way up. There was, however, precious little time for dates; I had made eight pictures that first year at Warners.

The male ego with few exceptions is elephantine to start with. Add to it a movie contract and it soars through space and into eternal orbit around itself. Gagarin, Glenn and Titov are the three men in a tub compared with the high-flyers I have known in the acting profession. Nothing has changed in the ensuing years. The old gang is just older and the new crop is younger than it's ever been. The disease is still rampant. All those misplaced drives. Mine was going on all cylinders, aiming for the top of the Hollywood hills. The electric sign spelling the name of the magic town was something to climb, a kind of bastard Sinai on top of which I had made up my mind to stand on tippy-toe! The top was just a jumping-off point to the heights I dared dream of. Shock of shocks, early inspiration Peg Entwistle had made a lonely pilgrimage to the H and ended her obscurity in a blaze of momentary notoriety. That beautiful talent!

My passions were all gathered together like fingers that made a fist. Drive is considered aggression today; I knew it then as purpose. I looked around at the glamorous stars of the day. They brought the public in. They were the backbone of the entire picture business. To me, they were not actresses, but personalities. I don't underestimate them to this day. But I wanted much more. The very quality that made goddesses of them was not what I wanted for myself. I wanted to be considered a fine actress.

The imagination of the theatre audience transforms the green cheese cloth and netting into a forest primeval, gray papier-mâché and ruby velveteen into Elsinore. Motion pictures have an advantage—the chance for reality and scope. This was the road I wanted to travel.

The performances of the beautiful ladies of the screen were *trompe l'oeil*—effects created out of unreality.

In my frequent visits to movie houses, I found that I never identified with the actress playing the lead but with the long shot of a flood or holocaust that stunned me with its authenticity. The camera's uncompromising vision of the elements, the starkness and vividity of nature gone mad, struck me as an incongruity behind the close-ups of marcelled emotions. These beautiful personalities seemed to me to be playing a masque against a background of hard realism. The screen was obviously in transition.

Barely a few years before, Valentino had silently acted out the fantasies of women all over the world. Valentino and his world were a dream. A whole generation of females wanted to ride off into a sandy paradise with him. At thirteen I had been such a female.

Theda Bara was another dream-world figure. Surrounded by potted palms, silken hangings and blackamoors and other dust collectors, Miss Bara was Pestilence herself, her monumental wickedness would not have been tolerated by Caligula in his beatnik depths for one moment. She was divinely, hysterically, insanely malevolent.

The public fell at Miss Bara's feet. She climbed from option to option while thousands cheered. The frame of reference was accepted; and absurd as much of it is now, there is much to be preserved from these earlier films. There was a heroic "larger than life" quality to these motion pictures. After all, Heaven and Hell are extreme symbols and they have made their point over the centuries.

In silent pictures, the very medium itself had a dream quality and its artifice in acting and décor was apropos. Certainly Eisenstein in Russia and Lang in Germany realized their stylistic potential. But now talkies were in and films were in flux. The immediate logic was to imitate the Mother Medium. Photographed stage plays bridged the gap to nowhere. If movies could talk then let them clatter away. There was a trend toward naturalism. There was also a Depression when I arrived on the scene. People were jobless and hungry. The New Deal was a wave that engulfed the theatre along with the rest of the country. It was to bring in its wake Clifford Odets and the Group Theatre. The public wanted greater identification and characters. It may have been done to excess, but the legitimate theatre replaced international society with the CIO.

There were breadlines and white-collared apple sellers in the streets. Unlike the vaguely glamorous First World War, the Depression hit everyone. It was true that Hollywood and its crop of musical extravaganzas offered a twenty-five-cent escape, but the Drama took on another dimension.

New York was to make its switch to social drama with ease and to rediscover the great Stanislavsky with a vengeance. Both media embraced fantasy as well but only Hollywood remained fantastic. Motion pictures had the breadth to document the drama of our times and in *So Big*, the discovery of our bedrock made a deep impression on me. Of course city life, too, was fundamental and my next picture for Warners was a political satire in which Warren William and I made the intensely bewildered Guy Kibbee a most willing and incapable mayor of a big town. The picture was light in mood but had a rolltop-desk authenticity in its political skulduggery that called for an earthy but urbane representation of the girl.

Although Ruthie and I dreamed that someday Warners would give me the glossy productions that M-G-M gave its players, I felt that the girl I was now playing would never have a hairdo by Sidney Guilcroff or a nineteen-piece suit with a supersonic collar by Adrian. This was the period when Joan Crawford would start every film as a factory worker who punched the time clock in a simple, black Molyneux with white piping (someone's idea of poverty) and ended marrying the boss who now allowed her to deck herself out in tremendous buttons, cuffs and shoes with bows (someone's idea of wealth). A change of coiffure with each outfit kept her so busy it was a wonder she had time to forward the plot. All of this was possibly not Miss Crawford's fault, the public adored it. Hollywood had its own type of reality and the Misses Crawford, Shearer and Dietrich were gorgeously glamorous.

Part of me envied them. They were so beautiful. I knew it was possible with my ambitions for acting rather than for glamour that I might never equal their popularity. But I was I!

Ham wrote he was coming to California that summer after he graduated from college. It had been so long since we had seen each other. Shortly after this news, Warner Brothers arranged a personal appearance tour for Warren William and me in the East. Ham and I crossed the country like curtain pulleys and amongst other places I opened at the Capitol Theatre in New York. We played in a sketch called *The Burglar and the Lady*. On the same bill were Hannah Williams, Lou Holtz and Phil Baker. We did five shows a day. Mr. William of the razor-sharp profile and sonorous voice was Warners answer to John Barrymore. They were always answering, replacing or emulating someone.

Warren and I played two adventurers who accidentally meet in a fashionable flat that each has planned to rob. They joined forces in a romantic and cynical partnership that glittered with Cowardian dialogue. The surprise finish had us drop our characterizations as the "director" yelled, "Cut!" It was all a performance before the cameras. The audience loved it and Uncle Paul took me to dinner, informing me that the whole family was beside itself with my growing reputation and that Father was taller than ever because of it.

After the tour of the East, we returned to California. Ham had filled in his waiting for my return by playing the trumpet in the Olympic Games orchestra—which took place that year at the Coliseum in Los Angeles. We picked up where we left off. After my two years in Hollywood, Ham also stood taller and more genuine than ever. He was home, New England, stability. I had been homesick for the world I had been brought up in. Bobby, Ruthie and I were still living at Zuma Beach. I was self-conscious of my increasing fame and tried to make light of it to Ham, fearing he would suddenly feel inferior.

Ruthie talked to me seriously one day during Ham's visit. Obviously my virginity concerned her greatly, almost as greatly as it did my beaux. It concerned me even more. The Depression, the coming election and my chastity seemed to be the topics of the day! I had not stopped working in eighteen months and Ruthie found me more high-strung than ever.

"You can't go on like this. You and Ham have been in love for years. Marry him!"

I suppose I couldn't expected Mother to suggest that we have an affair. Would that she had been that wise. Would that Ham and I had been. I was hopelessly puritan, helplessly passionate and, with Ruthie, decided that I had better marry before I became Hester Prynne.

Ruthie now had another cause and one evening at dinner, she led a chorus of friends and family in a campaign that nominated, elected and seated Harmon O. Nelson, Jr. as my husband. He was not against the idea. The next day, Ham and I, Ruthie and Bobby drove to Yuma, Arizona, where in one hundred and fifteen degrees of heat on the 18th of August, 1932, the Reverend Schalbaugh of the Indian Mission married us. We drove back to Zuma Beach right after the ceremony.

This was Ruth Elizabeth's golden moment. The proper bliss of a wedding night was here. The union under God and everything between a man and honest-to-goodness maid was hers; and her joy was boundless. A chaste bride. I was almost the last of the species. This was what I had waited for. This is what the romantic puritan wanted. Passion formalized, love ritualized, sex smiled upon by Society. My world was tidy and there was Order. I was able to shower an object with the unnamed joy that lay simmering beneath my humorless drive without a trace of guilt, with no fear of disapproval. The sweetness of first love. It still clings like ivy to the stone walls of this institution called Bette Davis. Stonewall Davis! Alma Mater! You can't mortar bricks with treacle but I tried.

I was Mrs. Harmon O. Nelson, Jr. I felt safe. I felt historic. The lust I had feared was natural and beautiful. I was released. I now had the work and the man I loved—the best of two worlds. It never occurred to me that they would or could collide. I needed help. Marvelous Ruthie! Who imagined she had any limitations—a lapse in the all pervading wisdom? She had suppressed her own libido as all decent New Englanders did and she decided to suppress mine as well by caching it with a nice Bay State husband in a nice, antiseptic marriage. Obviously this would save my purity and my career. At the time, I was in seventh heaven. All my dreams were coming true. Our "dream cottage"—that stage set I had conjured up back at Cushing—was a house on Horn Avenue in Hollywood. It was a white, ivy-covered little English house. The guest house in the back was occupied by Mother and Bobby.

I wanted us all to be together. Even though I was now married and had been saved from becoming a fallen woman and was correctly functioning as a female, still Ruthie found it hard to relinquish the reins. She had been in charge of me for twenty-six years and it was hard for her to realize my husband now had that right. I also found it hard to get away from my family. It was undeniable that I preferred being a captive, rebellious Palomino to a free one. Ham was in a most awkward situation.

Bobby's security seemed shattered by my marriage. She felt she had lost me and her anxieties took on the proportions of a nervous breakdown. Ruthie, rather than put her in a sanatorium, went East with her and rented a house near Myron and Mildred, who now lived in the country in Dover, Mass. Ham and I, due to my contract, had not had time for a honeymoon. Warner Brothers saw to it we had a strange one!

They had just completed an expensive musical, *Forty-Second Street*, with production numbers that could only have been staged on the steppes of Russia. Lavish, revolutionary and quite wonderful for its time, the investment had been tremendous; and while the public in its misery was looking for escape, the country was in panic and money was scarce. The new President, Franklin Roosevelt, had just been elected and was about to be inaugurated. In order to entice the audience into theatres, Warners arranged a tie-up with General Electric in a stunt that was to cost sixty thousand dollars, most of it absorbed by GE. A special gold-leafed Pullman train, on its way to the Inauguration with an itinerary that included San Francisco, Salt Lake City, Cheyenne, Denver, Kansas City, St. Louis, Chicago, Cleveland, Pittsburgh, Baltimore, Washington, Philadelphia, Boston and New York, was scheduled to coincide with the picture's premiere in each city. It cut through the heart of the country like a golden scimitar. Factories were closed, millions jobless, and we really should have been publicizing the musical *Let 'Em Eat Cake*. Not only did we blind the poor with our glitter, we even had one whole car fitted out with sand, water and suntan lamps that transformed the Pullman into a mobile Malibu Beach.

Other royal personages included Laura LaPlante, Glenda Farrell, Preston Foster, Leo Carillo, Lyle Talbot, Eleanor Holm who had just won the Olympics, Joe E. Brown, Tom Mix and his horse—whom we all envied. Unlike the rest of us, he lived like Louis B. Mayer, alone in his own car. "A bevy of eleven chorus girls eleven—count them" straight from the film included Lois January, Toby Wing and Shirley Ross—who were always popping into opera hose and tremendous white polka dot halters and white coats. The poor girls had one costume apiece. They were not the most attractive sight at the end of the tour. White on a train for sixteen days! The whole affair was fabulous—traveling in such luxury during a depression. We were afraid we might incite a revolution; but unlike the eighteenth-century Frenchmen, Americans love their royalty and we were welcomed everywhere with open arms, although a few did stick their tongues out at us.

Of course, the luxury and glamour were as always a façade. We worked like stevedores. I was always in a department store in Denver or Pittsburgh, opening a demonstration of General Electric kitchens or marching in parades down the streets of Chicago or Washington at 9 A.M. It was a lovely honeymoon what with waving on the observation car at 2:30 in the morning to wide-eyed movie fans. Our stateroom was only used for lying in state. We visited thirty-two cities in thirty-two days and felt like monkeys in a zoo.

In Washington, our first stop was, of course, the freight yard. Some of us had been invited to a party given by the Canadian branch of the Roosevelt family for all the young Roosevelts. Their name was Robins, and it was there that I was introduced to the President's handsome son, Franklin, Jr., just as my shoulder strap broke allowing my dress to collapse down over one bosom. I clutched it to me as I shook his hand. We roared with laughter. Properly mended, I later met the President's mother, Sarah Delano, whose resemblance to my grandmother fascinated me. A larger woman, but the same drive and magnetism. I looked in her eyes and saw all the power that her son had inherited and was soon to share with the people of the United States and of the world.

The country was lying about in little pieces and this great

man was to institute his imaginative New Deal within hours. By the time our circus was in Boston, the banks were closed and the moratorium was on. We were all penniless and issued scrip with which we could make any small purchase.

New York and "haughty, bawdy Forty-Second Street" was our last stop and we paraded from river to river to advertise the film in which Dick Powell and Ruby Keeler would make history and start a trend of mammoth musicals that did give Hollywood a shot in the arm. Bewildered and exhausted as I was by the madness of our caravan, I learned once and for all how much movies mean to the American people. The reaction of the public in every city convinced me of the miraculous power of the motion picture. There wasn't the slightest doubt that Hollywood's stars were America's royalty and their subjects the most devoted in the world. If in moments of despair I had been uncertain that the world that I had chosen was a sane one, I knew now that my chosen field could be Elysian. I was still just a little movie girl and I was almost grateful for the long list of garbage I had been made to play. It had been my apprenticeship. It exposed me to the public. I firmly believe that the public must know seventy-five percent of what to expect from an actor. Even then in early 1933, the public was comfortable with me. The public makes stars. No one else. I arrived back in Hollywood with a greater sense of dedication than ever.

Since I continued to work at breakneck speed, leaving the house at 6:30 A.M., and Ham was working with an orchestra and returning home at 4 A.M., we were reduced to writing notes for a while.

Darryl Zanuck, who was then production manager of Warners, wanted me to play the southern girl in Richard Barthelmess' *Cabin in the Cotton,* an extremely interesting screenplay by Paul Green. It was an excellent part, mine—that of a rich, vixenish belle. Aside from its literate script, it was Mr. Barthelmess' last big picture—an A production. The director, Michael Curtiz, did not want me for the part and made it clear. But Mr. Zanuck did and made it clearer. My director made my life hell every day. While Mr. Barthelmess was easygoing and kindly, I would start a scene and Curtiz would mutter behind the camera so I could hear, "God-damned-nothing-no-good-sexless-son-of-a-bitch!" which might have little taste and less syntax but a great deal of lucidity. What with Barthelmess' wife, Jessica, sitting beside the director appraising our love scenes and Curtiz' heckling, it is a wonder I made it. Richard Barthelmess had been a great silent star but his technique was utterly foreign to me. He did absolutely nothing in long shots, followed basic stage directions for medium shots and received his talent for the close-up. When he was not being photographed, he relaxed in his dressing room.

Mr. Curtiz ignored my needs completely. During a close-up of me, supposedly kissing the star—a situation usually facilitated by the "beloved's" presence behind the camera—I was made to play the love scene into the camera, sans Mr. Barthelmess! Mr. Curtiz, with a glint on his eye that could only have been borrowed from the Marquis de Sade, made me writhe toward the camera and kiss into a vacuum. I refused to let him get me down. The part was that good.

I sang Willie the Weeper to Mr. Barthelmess as I reversed the Universal Concept and lay upon him. One of my very favorite lines was in this picture.

"Ah'd love to kiss you, but ah just washed mah hair!"

Madge in *Cabin in the Cotton* was my best role to date. The daily pressure under which I worked however was so great that I would arrive home ready to explode. Like the businessman who comes home at six o'clock, irritated, exhausted and hungry, eager to be soothed by a well-run household and a soft-spoken wife, I would walk through the door to find Ham in his slippers, relaxing. Ham, like his father, was the pipe-and-slipper type of man. He didn't wear the vizor his father wore but he seemed always to be resting. Heaven help me, I came home ready to explode and I often did.

Ruthie was on my side whenever a quarrel ensued. She knew how important my work was and refused to have me upset by any domestic pressures. No doubt Ham had his hands full but so did I. The studio not realizing from my performance as Madge that they had found a niche I excelled in, next put me in a dull "B" picture called *Three On a Match*. My school friend Joan Blondell, Ann Dvorak and I were the unlucky trio, and Mervyn Le Roy was my next unsympathetic director. He kept talking of what a great dramatic star Joan was to become and I was glad for her; but his pointed references and indifference to me hardly encouraged me in my daily work. It seems that something in me created resistance in these men. There

isn't the slightest doubt in my mind that they resented my
background and my assurance. They were used to empty passive slates they could scribble on. I was already rejecting the
Palmer method and struggling toward another form of expression. Madge in *Cabin in the Cotton* was my first downright,
forthright bitch and one would have thought that the role would
have erased permanently the sweet, drab sister type that had
plagued me since my arrival. And here I was, a stenographer.
In an effort to humanize her, I would come up against the
powers.

I had daydreams about the Director with Vision who would
see what I knew I had. I woke up to find myself once again
cast in a Michael Curtiz picture, Warden Lawes' *Twenty Thousand Years in Sing Sing*. I couldn't have cared less. I was going
to work with Spencer Tracy and I was in seventh heaven. He
was one of my few actor idols. Also Robin's father-in-law, the
great Arthur Byron, played Warden Lawes. And damn it, I
was good as the moll and my notices made that clear. My
reward was a little epic called *Parachute Jumper* opposite
young Fairbanks, the Crown Prince of Hollywood, scion of
Pickfair and consort to M-G-M's Princess Royal, Joan of Crawford. Doug was still to become Great Britain's last earl; but he
was already saying "profeel" for one's side view, which goes
to prove that people do not change, simply develop and grow.
I was again a secretary—Daddy had been right—but I also
was the mistress of a racketeer. A typist-moll. Warners were
vaguely aware, evidently, of a possible niche for me. It took
patience on my part.

At home, I was still the little woman and was being helped
enormously by the gem of my life. When Ham and I moved
to a house on Franklin Avenue, I hired my first maid, Dell
Pfeiffer. She and I grew up together in the next twenty years.
Dell was large of body and of soul. She was a great cook,
could clean better with one hand and a hangover than any three
people. She loved me and I her. She was supporting a man
she eventually married and but for Thursdays and every other
Sunday was stone sober. She said to Ruthie once that on her
days off she changed her "altitude"! She moved from house
to house, never questioning, always adjusting to new circumstances—and there were many. The most difficult thing for her

was to get used to my having a new name—and she went through this quite a few times.

My "disturbances," as she called them, she loved and learned to manage so well. There were tensions. There were battles. Our little brown-shingled cottage was the scene of many a war. Ham had known that my career was growing, and he had found it exciting and wonderful. He was proud of me. He had no idea how time-consuming and enervating it was. I wasn't earning money for nothing. I was working constantly and very hard.

Although my name was growing by leaps and bounds, I was well aware that I was not being given an opportunity to grow as an artist. It's true that we all had more creature comforts than we had dreamed of. Ruthie was able to buy her automobiles without the old concern for monthly payments but *my* drive needed new highways and I realized that I would have to help pave them myself. What I wanted couldn't be achieved from nine to six, six days a week. I worried about my stagnant career twenty-four hours a day. And I brought my worries home with me. I adored my husband but there were times when he was as distantly related to my present crises as a fur trader on the Yukon.

Mr. Arliss again materialized like a genie to cast me in *The Working Man*, as his spoiled daughter. And again with Adolfi at the helm, Mr. Arliss directed me to advantage. It was the first important picture I had made in ages. After a few days of shooting, my mentor smiled that wise smile and said, "My little girl isn't afraid of me any more, is she?"

It was true that my experience had, of course, increased my confidence. On my first picture with him, I expected every day that the ax would fall. It was never that Mr. Arliss himself had given me reason for such fears. He was a lamb. But his talent was so impressive that the young actor quaked. It is amazing that when one arrives and is elevated to true stardom, he may be the same human being but he is an ogre to the rest of the cast who now imagine they are in the presence of Genghis Khan. Of course, there are those actors who encourage and indeed justify this impression, but they are rare. George Arliss still impressed me as an actor—he no longer frightened me as a person. I was growing up; he was delighted. He taught me always to think of what came before a scene and what was to come after. Scenes being shot out of sequence are the devil to play. "Always keep the continuity in your head. It will help." It did. One had to remember pitches of voice and mood to the fraction so that scenes when juxtaposed would blend.

The Working Man was another big success and dignified my struggle to the point where Darryl Zanuck decided that it was time to give me the glamour-star treatment. It was a great mistake. I wasn't the type to be glamorized in the usual way. In an ecstasy of poor taste and a burst of misspent energy, I was made over and cast as the star of a piece of junk called *Ex-Lady* which was supposed to be provocative and provoked anyone of sensibility to nausea. As an avant-garde artist, my lover was Gene Raymond whom I discarded *au fin* for the marvelously corrupt Monroe Owsley. One disgusted critic announced that Warner Brothers could have saved a fortune by photographing the whole picture in one bed. The final scene dollied in on four feet, soles upward—for which I was grateful—and happily entwined. They may even have had *The End* written on them. I can't remember. It is a part of my career that my conscious tastefully avoids. I only recall that from the daily shooting to the billboards, falsely picturing me half-naked, my shame was only exceeded by my fury.

It was at this point I heard that John Ford was going to make *Mary of Scotland,* starring Katharine Hepburn, practically the only girl of my generation for whom I had admiration and envy. RKO was treating this thoroughbred with kid gloves. Her debut as John Barrymore's daughter in Clemence Dane's *Bill of Divorcement* was a brilliant performance. The production was literate, beautifully mounted, divinely acted by a hand-picked cast, and that marvelous face was photographed magnificently. I would have given anything to look like Katie Hepburn. I still would. After this one picture she was a Hollywood star to be reckoned with.

I had read, because of my fascination for her, every biography or play written about Queen Elizabeth. In the play about Mary Queen of Scots, which was to be transported to the screen, Elizabeth appeared. I took it upon myself without studio permission to go straight to John Ford, who simply laughed in my face. It is faintly possible that he was not as unimpressed as he seemed and simply had been told by Warners to send me home; but whatever the reason, he just laughed and told me I talked too much.

Florence Eldridge, Mrs. Fredric March, played Queen Elizabeth and I was cast in a picture called *The Bureau of Missing Persons* (which was appropriate enough title I guess) with Pat O'Brien and Glenda Farrell. I was beginning to understand why Jimmy Cagney was on suspension for refusing to play a certain part; and I even understood Ann Dvorak for disappearing from town because an infant in one of her films was earning more money than she. Our contracts were outrageous and the security I had dreamed of on Broadway had become the safety of a prison. I was being handed crumbs by the studio financially as well as artistically.

At this point Ruthie and Bobby were still in the East. Bobby was just recovering and would be back soon. Ham had an engagement with his orchestra in Daly City outside of San Francisco. I would drive up Saturday nights and spend Sunday with him as often as possible.

About this time I discovered that I was pregnant and all studio problems were forgotten for the time being. My marvelous news was greeted by Ham with the businesslike, "You're much too busy to have a baby. It would be stupid to jeopardize your career!"

I was dumbfounded.

Then he came to the point.

"You don't think I'm going to have *you* pay the hospital bills for the baby."

You, I, your, mine! My dream of marriage had no such departments. It was *our* baby and *our* money. I was certain that Mother would be just as shocked as I; but in an ironic *entente*, Ruthie and Ham made a united front against me. Ruthie wrote me that a child was a very bad idea at this juncture. Possibly harmful to my career.

With such allies against me, I had second thoughts. Certainly I saw the validity of their arguments. I saw Ham's point. Until he could afford to give his child what he wanted to he preferred to wait. I saw Ruthie's point. It was stupid to burden myself in my professional struggle. I saw everyone's point. I understood everything intellectually. I was wretched emotionally.

I did as I was told.

CHAPTER

10

When Ham's orchestra was engaged by the Werthheimers for an out-of-town club date, the gossip columnists had a field day. We were obviously on the verge of a divorce. This was not unusual. Separation was always used as a potential divorce; it helped fill columns. I decided as a joke—and an answer to all the rumors—to go to the Warner Brothers premiere of *I Loved a Woman*, starring Edward G. Robinson and Kay Francis, with eight men. I felt this would truly confuse the columnists. Two carloads of us arrived in front of the theatre—myself and eight beaux—Theodore Newton, Walter Abel, Lynn Riggs, Alex Pierce, George Comerly, Schuyler Schenck, Fred Fast and wonderful Frank Conroy. We, needless to say, were a sensation. We stole the show. It also scotched the gossip columnists for quite a while.

After this broad stroke, I spent one of my many weekends at the motel in Daly City where Ham and his orchestra lived. We cooked up a storm—my friend Liz Fisher, who usually drove up with me, and I. We even had a Christmas there once. The trimmings for the tree were cutouts from the funny papers. I'd like to find the place yet that I couldn't make seem like home. Ruthie had given me this ability. She, God knows, did it for years and money is not the biggest ingredient. Imagination and being adaptable help the most.

I was cast next in *Fashions of 1934*. I was glamorized beyond recognition. I was made to wear a platinum wig. Makeup had been given the green light with nary a "may I?" The bossmen were trying to make me into a Greta Garbo. They even dressed the wig like her hair, to say nothing of the false lashes and huge mouth and the slinky clothes.

About this time, John Cromwell wanted me for the part of Mildred in Somerset Maugham's *Of Human Bondage*. After seeing me in *Cabin in the Cotton* and *The Rich Are Always With Us,* he felt I could do justice to the role. Besides, as a heroine she was such a disagreeable character no well-established actress would play her. The picture was to star Leslie Howard.

I told Mr. Cromwell I would give my life to be in the picture and he contacted the studio. Warners absolutely refused to lend me out. How could they? They needed me desperately for such historic milestones as *The Big Shakedown* and *The Man with the Black Hat*. I begged, implored, cajoled. I haunted Jack Warner's office. Every single day, I arrived at his door with the shoeshine boy. The part of Mildred was something I had to have. I spent six months in supplication and drove Mr. Warner to the point of desperation—desperate enough to say "Yes"—anything to get rid of me.

My employers believed I would hang myself playing such an unpleasant heroine. I had become such a nuisance over this issue I think they identified me with the character and felt we deserved each other!

For the first time since *The Wild Duck* I was really thrilled with a part. My performance in *Of Human Bondage* could make or break my motion-picture career. At the outset, it was the faith Mr. Cromwell had in me that made me feel I could play it. I always did my best work when someone truly believed in me.

Mr. Maugham so clearly described Mildred it was like having a textbook to go by. However, Philip's whimpering adoration in the face of Mildred's brutal diffidence was difficult for me to believe. But that was Mr. Howard's problem and not mine. I hired an Englishwoman to work for me at home for two months before starting the picture. She had just the right amount of cockney in her speech for Mildred. I never told her she was teaching me cockney—for fear she would exaggerate her own

accent. It is always more difficult to learn to speak a strange
accent subtly. Mildred suffered delusions of grandeur and
spoke, she thought, like a "leyedy."

The first few days on the set were not too heartwarming.
Mr. Howard and his English colleagues, as a clique, were
disturbed by the casting of an American girl in the part. I really
couldn't blame them. There was lots of whispering in little
Druid circles whenever I appeared. Mr. Howard would read a
book offstage, all the while throwing me his lines during my
close-ups. He became a little less detached when he was informed that "the kid is walking away with the picture."

When we were ready to do the scene involving Mildred's
decline, I asked Mr. Cromwell if I could put on my own
makeup. I have never understood why Hollywood actors don't
put on their own makeup no matter what the part calls for. I
made it very clear that Mildred was not going to die of a dread
disease looking as if a deb had missed her noon nap. The last
stages of consumption, poverty and neglect were not pretty and
I intended to be convincing-looking. We pulled no punches
and Mildred emerged as a reality—as immediate as a newsreel
and as starkly real as a pestilence. I will be eternally grateful
that Mr. Cromwell had the foresight to gamble on my ability
to play Mildred. The Yankee in me got in my way every now
and then. At the end of the picture he said, "Your career could
have been ten years shorter if you hadn't been born in Boston."

Every actor who becomes a star is usually remembered for
one or two roles. He may give other great performances but
the public seems collectively to hoard one or two special memories that are the foundation of his reputation. In the theatre,
John Barrymore's *Hamlet* and *The Jest*, Maude Adams' *Peter
Pan*, Laurette Taylor's *Peg O' My Heart* and *Glass Menagerie*,
Judith Anderson's *Lady Macbeth* and *Medea*. On the screen,
despite a legion of brilliant roles, Charles Laughton built his
permanent fame on *Henry VIII*, *Ruggles of Red Gap* and Captain Bligh in *Mutiny on the Bounty*. Garbo means *Camille* and
Flesh and the Devil. Hepburn, *Morning Glory* and *Alice Adams;* Judy Garland, *The Wizard of Oz*, and Brando, Stanley in
Streetcar. Mildred in *Of Human Bondage* was such a role for
me. She was the first leading-lady villainess ever played on a
screen for real. I was the female Marlon Brando of my generation.

My understanding of Mildred's vileness—not compassion but empathy—gave me pause. I barely knew the half-world existed. I was still an innocent. And yet Mildred's machinations I miraculously understood when it came to playing her.

I was often ashamed of this. The famous scene between the obscene lovers in which, in disgust, I flung his deformity in his face—"You gimpy-legged monster! Do you know what you are? A cripple! A cripple, cripple!"—froze both Philip and the audience in horror. Mildred's cheapness of mind, her poverty of spirit and her prideless quivering body were loathsome and pitiable.

I suppose no amount of rationalization can change the fact that we are all made up of good and evil. Maugham himself understood Mildred so that as an artist his natural resources include the full spectrum of emotions. Acting is a make-believe world and I've been a captive since that Boston matinee of *Wild Duck*. Hedvig! Now Mildred! Up to that point, the two roles I adored most—completely opposite.

With young actors who talk about becoming the character and having themselves in a role, I must argue. There is a part of you that must hold the reins and control the projection. There is a part of you that must be aware of pace and timing. This is considered heresy today by the dedicated naturalist school.

Without discipline and detachment, an actor is an emotional slob, spilling his insides out. This abandonment is having an unfortunate vogue. It is tasteless, formless, absurd. Without containment there is no art. All this vomiting and wheezing and bursting at the seams is no more great acting than the convulsions of raving maniacs. They might as well put up camp chairs in the violent ward at Creedmore and sell tickets.

This belching, sweating and twitching may be very well in a dramatic class for the inhibited. Very good! We all know that dancers cannot arabesque without feet. But if a dancer keeps staring at them during her performance, the illusion is gone. Her feet must be birds on stage. The ballerina does not step in front of the Metropolitan's gold curtain and do her exercises. She dances. So with the actor once he limbers up. In control of his instrument, he fluctuates within his frame. He can create patterns with grace. He can create a design. He aims to please the eye and the ear. He may aim to shock, but only within the boundaries of his art.

The artist does not spread across the stage or screen like a wild cell, hoping in the mass of emotion he may, with luck, hit a vital organ. He must know where he is going. It is again selectivity and style. It must be real but, to me, it must be more than natural. There must be a statement. This to me is art. Way back in the old Belasco days, I chose realism. But to be real, the artist must sometimes embellish.

Rossellini's Italian films made their first impact on the world because the director used realism. Both *Open City* and De Sica's *Bicycle Thief* were not naturalistic films. Anna Magnani is not a naturalistic actress. She is an artist. She is always in command. Always aware of the rhythms and rhymes and reasons. A realist, yes. One never not believes her; but one also never stops wondering at her transitions, the mastery of her emotional keyboard. She is a realist but she embellishes just as Lynn Fontanne does on her elegant level.

Everyone who saw Laurette Taylor in *Glass Menagerie* raved about her performance, as, indeed, he should have. But the highest encomium seemed to be "She *was* Amanda. She wasn't acting at all." She was acting every single second. She could turn Amanda off or on at will. Disillusioning? Not at all. That is an actress. So with Magnani. Her penchant for playing the wild, uncombed virago has seduced many into believing that she plays herself. Beautifully concealed, she has a technique that matches Vermeer for clarity and delicacy. It does not matter that Magnani's hair is greasy, her dress torn. She has an inner purity. Like every real artist, she does not lose herself although the wealth of passion which is hers is poured into her work. Rossellini and Fellini, too, are not naturalistic. If they were, they would set up their cameras on the Spanish Steps and let them roll all day, can the film and send it to the exhibitor. It is *what* they see in a Roman day and *how* they juxtapose the events that create the movie's life. They may have used the people of Rome—amateurs—as their actors; but through their guile and labor, in short their art, they create the greater reality—the truth.

I was never completely Mildred or Hedvig or any other character. I was always Bette Davis watching herself become another person. We all, on occasion, find ourselves involved in a character that strikes a painfully personal chord. It is then that we must be ruthless with ourselves. A player who forgets he is pretending and "becomes" Oedipus will just as naturally tear his eyes out in the last act. It would make a gorgeous opening night triumph but *quo vadis*?

Give me Laurence Olivier's and Judith Anderson's "larger-than-life" approach to their work. I would go anywhere, any time, to watch the matchless John Gielgud whom I consider the greatest living English-speaking actor. His purity as an artist is religious. Ralph Richardson is barely a breath behind him. These men have a professional chastity and an intellectual drive that dazzles me. Their scope, versatility and humility plus utter mastery of their job make them unique in a profession that does not ordinarily suit the male animal.

I know that our age deifies the dull and the bland; it isn't even what it is claimed to be—a reflection of our barren time. No time could ever be this dull. We're off to the moon. Hundreds of millions of people are throwing off tyranny. Two ideologies battle unto death and become each other through hatred. There's madness afoot. Dull? Barren? Africa is, at last, taking its rightful place in the world community. Right here in our country, the Negro is moving from passive resistance to a more aggressive stand for his rights.

Can the self-absorbed artist do nothing better than examine and re-examine his own boring insides? Must he piddle on canvas and stage? He belongs to a species that may disappear if he doesn't wake up to his part in the whole.

I wonder how Michelangelo would have sculpted and painted today? Would all that beauty and nobility be sacrificed to the grafitto, John Loves John?

Without wonder and insight, acting is just a trade. With it, it becomes creation. Simone Signoret in *Room at the Top* truly had the universal. She wasn't that woman. She was *all* women.

It is an interesting fact that most people believe that *Of Human Bondage* was my first picture although I had made twenty-one films before it. All these pictures and my parts in them seemed to blend into one colorless glob with a few exceptions. Two years of posing as Miss Fourth of July and Little Miss Clothes Horse for the fan magazines—two years of hard work and indignities and a rival studio, not Warners, gave me my true beginning.

Bondage made movie history and I would like to add a footnote to it. Despite or because of the rumors concerning my performance, the Warners reaction to the proof of my justifiable fight for good parts was simply, "Well RKO knew what type of girl she really was." Ruthie called me from New York after the premiere of the film. She was beside herself. Once more she had seats down front at an opening of mine, and once more, she was proud of me.

The Academy of Motion Pictures Arts and Sciences nominated me for an Oscar and my home studio seemed reluctant to take advantage of the tremendous publicity that always attends such an honor. It was an RKO picture, it is true; but *I* belonged to Warners and it was to their profit if I won. The air was thick with rumors. It seemed inevitable that I would receive the coveted award. The press, the public and the members of the Academy who did the voting were sure I would win! Surer than I!

But the gods and the Great McGinty had other plans. My bosses helped them by sending instructions to all their personnel to vote for somebody else.

Frank Capra's charming comedy *It Happened One Night* captured all the trophies and its stars, Clark Gable and Claudette Colbert, won the Oscars for best performances.

Not since Charles Evans Hughes went to sleep as the "President" and awakened a private citizen was Hollywood so astonished by an upset. My failure to receive the award created a scandal that gave me more publicity than if I had won it. Syndicated columnists spread the word "foul" and the public stood behind me like an army. Not since that decision in 1934 was so cavalier a verdict allowed to take place. Price Waterhouse was asked to step in the next year to count the votes, which they have done ever since.

I cannot say I wasn't crushed once I had been that close to the prize. I had not lost my loathing for second place.

There was no change in the Warner attitude after all this acclaim. I was made to trudge through the professional swamp at Warners brimming over with frustration and rage. One skirmish after another followed *Bondage*.

With the solitary exception of *Bordertown*, which I had made before *Bondage,* a melodrama in which I was allowed some dramatic range and in which I appeared with Paul Muni, I might just as well have been any of the stock girls under contract.

Having tasted a moment of cinematic art with Mr. Cromwell, I was more and more impatient with the inanities at my studio. In *Bordertown* I was, in one particular scene, supposed to awaken in the morning and get out of bed. I smeared some cream over my face, tousled my hair and got into the bed on the set. Production was stopped for four hours while Archie Mayo the director and I yelled at each other. It seems that I looked awful—as if I had just awakened.

"But I did just awaken!" said I, impatiently.

They still didn't know that I had no desire to be just a glamour girl. They still didn't know that I didn't care if I didn't look alluring when I shouldn't.

This kind of battle was regimen at the time. Against fabulously authentic sets, anything genuine was taboo. How they adored cardboard actors and how many they cut to pattern. And how, all my life, I had detested pattern-cutters.

I won that little skirmish but I had further trouble. The character I was playing had to go insane on the witness stand. My director was not satisfied with my performance. He was somewhere back in Silents or a Hogarth print where the mentally ill really go mad with a vengeance. In a strange reversal, Mr. Mayo wanted me to play it in the fright-wig, bug-eyed tradition. I thought it wrong for the character and the general tenor of the picture.

Anyone can black out a few teeth, let her tongue hang and look demented. Children at play will say, "Look, I'm a looney," and contort their faces into a classic mold of idiocy. My director had evidently never seen anyone retreat from reality. I had. Something must be put to sleep inside, and, once accomplished, the personality blurs. One doesn't play this kind of schizophrenic by "going mad." One drifts away from shore. Though dialogue and physical incitement may be present, it can be curiously unrelated to the eyes, which work independently. I only know that for this particular girl, I *felt* disassociated. Mr. Mayo did not agree.

"They'll never know you're supposed to be insane."

Hal Wallis, who had just replaced Darryl Zanuck as head of Warner Bros. Productions, was brought into the scene, and I only asked that the picture be previewed the way I played it. If the audience had the slightest doubts as to my sanity, I would gladly redo the scene.

The preview audience hadn't the slightest doubt and it was never mentioned again.

Ham and I by now were living in Garbo's Brentwood house. I was bursting at the seams and Ham was as contained as ever. Sometimes I would stare at him as he receded into the distance.

I would come home from the studio and be so bored by his languor and resistance to my problems that I would hop in the car and drive a hundred miles.

"Don't dare come back" would ring in my ears and so it went.

I was filled with a compassion that was streaked with irritation. I wanted to stay married but our reversed roles debilitated him in its purest sense and drove me to distraction. The whole alliance had been a mistake based as it was on economic imbalance.

At the studio, I had inherited George Brent as a leading man from his wife, Miss Chatterton. And gossip, not without some foundation, implied that the bequest might be all-inclusive. Certainly George was an enchanting man with wit and beauty, and an excitement he rarely was in the mood to transfer to the screen. But he still belonged to Miss Chatterton. My little white cottage might have been in a state of disenchantment, but *that* is crooked poker in my book.

The Warners were quite befuddled by me at this point. No matter what piece of garbage they gave me to do, and no matter how much I scornfully sniffed at it, I did my job—and well. If they wouldn't help me, I'd help myself. Critics and public were making me more important and still they resisted. It seemed so stupid when I saw properties around that I was suitable for. As a complete change of pace I was eager to do *Alice in Wonderland*. With my long tubular neck and my astonished eyes I looked exactly like the Tenniel drawings; and I adored Alice, who has never been played properly by anybody—anywhere. Carroll's Alice is a little spitfire. She is rebellious, precocious, both innocent and cynical, spirited and intemperate. Alice isn't sweet. She's salty. My bosses thought me insane. And I had to be satisfied to take the Red Queen's famous advice to Alice that "in this world, one has to run very fast to stay in the same place."

My graduating contract seemed to the studio to be compensating enough to me for my work; but money was not the question. They were all used to actors who were grateful they had been rescued from diners or from under wet stones and, as long as the cash rolled in, were happy. As long as their paychecks weren't shy and their billing was bold, all was right with their world.

James Cagney had long been a problem to the Warners and now I was. But Jimmy, whom I worshiped, and with whom I had a small part in Michael Curtiz' *Jimmy The Gent*, was already a big star whose power could not be ignored. I was treated as an untractable child. On the rare occasion when I socialized in Hollywood, if I'd meet Jack Warner at a party as he was leaving he would wag his finger at me like the father of a delinquent.

"Remember, Bette. You have to be at the studio at six o'clock. Get to sleep soon."

My head would reel. In the first place, I was never late on a set in my life which he well knew; but more than that I was made to feel like a four-year-old. In all fairness to Jack Warner, I will add he was singular as a movie mogul. No lecherous boss was he! His sins lay elsewhere. He was the father. The power. The glory. And he was in business to make money. I was aware of this; but I was and am still convinced that the public will buy good work if it is presented with the same packaging that glamorizes the trash.

When the studio handed me the script of *Dangerous*, I was punch-drunk from my last few horrors. The story was hardly inspiring. Joyce Heath, a sort of Jeanne Eagels character, whose brilliant but short career in Theatre is eclipsed by her dipsomania, is picked up, washed off, and given a second chance by the elegant young star-struck architect, Franchot Tone. Convinced that she is a jinx to everyone (and she was so right) Joyce refuses to allow her loving mentor to back a comeback play for her with his only savings. His fiancée, Margaret Lindsay, got lost in the shuffle as Joyce, still married to a weakling who will not give her up, decides to kill herself and her "sash weight" in a speeding car if he does not relent. In a Chattertonian ending that finds her husband crippled for life, Joyce beats her jinx by sacrificing her love for the chronic invalid she has created.

I read the script carefully and signed. It was maudlin and mawkish with a pretense at quality which in scripts, as in home furnishings, is often worse than junk. But it had just enough material in it to build into something if I approached it properly. Franchot Tone was lovely to play with and I worked like ten men on that film, receiving another nomination for an Academy Award. Probably to cash in on the fact that I had appeared with Mr. Howard in *Bondage,* I was now cast opposite him in *Petrified Forest.* This time he was delighted to work with me and absolutely charming. It was he who refused to do the picture for Warners if they didn't use Humphrey Bogart in the gangster role he had created on Broadway. Leslie had by now become so warm and chummy that throughout one scene where we lay on the floor, victimized by Bogie, he kept nibbling on my arm.

Petrified Forest made Bogie's career and it didn't hurt mine. It was a beautiful play. But the annual awards of the Academy helped further. Ruthie, Ham and I attended the dinner. This time I was up against Katharine Hepburn's brilliant *Alice Adams,* by far the best performance of the year.

Victor McLaglen received the award for his remarkable job as *The Informer* and then, the venerable D. W. Griffith, making the most of the moment, announced the best actress of the year. There was a shout from my table and everyone was kissing me. I made my way to the stage. *It's a consolation prize.* This nagged at me. It was true that even if the honor had been earned, it had been earned *last* year. There was no doubt that Hepburn's performance deserved the award. These mistakes compound each other like the original lie that breeds like a bunny. Now she should get it next year when someone else may deserve it.

Nonetheless, this was it. I had reached the top of the heap and stood holding the statue while my family glowed with pride. I had done it. I had my career and I still had Ham. He was playing and singing at the Roosevelt Grill and the young set was giving him finally the adulation and recognition that he deserved.

Though I tried to keep our standard of living down to a scale more commensurate with his income than with mine, it was difficult. For an actress, there are certain expenses that are prerequisite even if she doesn't succumb to the excesses of Hollywood. There are servants, clothes, transportation—minimal symbols of station without which the public is disappointed. Then too, these are, in actuality, necessities when her

time is limited. I certainly could afford anything I wanted—
anything but a baby. And I tried to understand this also. I
would have understood anything to make my marriage work.
The one thing I couldn't do was give up my career, something
that Ham wouldn't have wanted either.

We were both caught up in a mess that we thought would
resolve itself if we just ignored it. This never happens and it
didn't to us. We were both human beings, subject to the stresses
and strains of a misalliance neither would admit was such.

Ham would have and did love me when I was penniless.
When we were first married, my salary was small and we
weren't even sure I would have a career in Hollywood. I mean
a career. It wasn't until *Bondage* that we were certain. Ham
married a struggling young actress. But the battles were becoming epic and the arena was now strewn with flowers.
Money, per se, meant nothing to Ham; but there are precious
few men who can resist box seats at the Coliseum and first-
class passage all the way. He may fight it self-righteously and
refuse the offer in black and white; but the daily exigencies of
life—the little things—that make up a relationship are so subtle
and seductive that he slowly sinks into the habit. Every man
has his own threshold of pride and his own point of satiety.
Personally, I have found it quite exalted. Mankind has an enormous capacity for self-justification. I understand this, too.

It would seem to be utterly irrational not to marry the woman
you love because she has money or leave her because she is
making more than you. One's values would have to be twisted
to reject love for such a reason. The classic minstrel solved
the riddle and married the Princess. He didn't carry her off to
his hovel in the black forest. He was made a Prince by her
kind father, the King. It's a fairy tale, it's true; but so is the
whole romance of eternal love and marriage. I still believed in
it.

I didn't know how disfiguring the economic pressures were
to my charmer. I only knew that, although my father wasn't a
kind and generous King, I had enough for both of us and had
no wish to live in a palace. But this princess worked like a
slave, and like all analogies, this one disintegrated like the
husband who is overshadowed by his wife. The sharing of
wealth is not in itself corrupting. The true rot sets in when he
thinks it is. He stops being a man and his wife stops being a

woman. When a woman is independent financially and eclipses
her husband professionally, the man suddenly finds it necessary
to be a nineteenth-century lord and master. He falls back on
symbols that are insupportable to the self-supporting wife. My
mistake was to attempt the duality. I couldn't be both husband
and wife and I tried.

I should have put my foot down immediately. I exhausted
myself instead. The man who waits for his wife to return home
from the jungle to cook his dinner and put away his shirts
because it's a woman's job is not displaying virility. To live
pleasantly and spend his own salary on himself is hardly sharing
the responsibilities of a home. But I was becoming used to the
role of Daddy. Harlow Morrell Davis had made me one years
before. He bequeathed it to me permanently.

Daddy came to California once on business and had dinner
with us on Franklin Avenue. It was the first time he had met
Ham. I received a letter later, one of his typically succinct little
notes. "Your husband is a nice young boy." How contemp-
tuous he could be. How superior!

Daddy died in 1935. He was too bright to enjoy being alive.
His contempt for all of humanity including himself was so great
that he abused and neglected himself physically. Ignoring doctors' orders—"Doctors!"—he worked himself to death. Father
quite willingly wore himself out. Years of asthma, self-neglect
and bitterness drove him to a heart attack and his grave at fifty-
four. In his whole life, he had loved one creature that I know
of—his vicious chow. The dog bit everyone in sight, probably
at his bidding. I recall being terrified of its purple tongue and
its sharp, fierce teeth. Daddy would laugh uproariously. How
unhappy he must have been and how insulated from the world!
He left me quite a legacy. A wife, a daughter, and now I was
married and seemed to have one more responsibility. I only
asked that some attempt be made to contribute to the household
even if only in energy. But man is a strange animal. As his
role becomes weaker his need to dominate becomes stronger.
Washing a dish, it seems, is more emasculating than having a
woman buy it.

I suggested Ham go to New York to find a job. He had a
sustaining program on radio for a while but soon was back in
Hollywood and we continued in the reversed roles that would
eventually kill the marriage.

A dedicated doctor seeking the cure for cancer, a dedicated anyone with intellectual superiority and true identity, could ignore the urbane symbols of status that encircle the successful artist. He may even laugh at them as I have. But there was the rub! There was no equity in our drives nor in our sense of sovereignty. That was the core of all our troubles.

Ham was sensitive and dear. He was talented, also. But not all who are victimized are infected to the point of fever. When the delirium sets in, save your pity for the next of kin.

I stubbornly insisted that I could beat the game and make our marriage work. After all, we were not incompatible. Ham, Ruthie and I argued again about my having a family, and I really didn't believe I had a chance. Ruthie knew that I could never bring up children halfway. She was afraid I would give up my career rather than diffuse my energies. Neither of them wanted that. I will never know what I would have done had I been encouraged to have children at this point in my career.

Waves of euphoria used to pass over me that Ham would suddenly find himself. Certainly the future looked promising for me. All of Ruthie's dreams were coming true.

At the Academy Dinner in 1935 I sought out Ruthie's face. She sat, regal and beautiful, between Bobby and Ham. Mother was truly the star to end them all. A fabulous hostess, Lady Bountiful to her family, her house was more elegant than mine. Ruthie had completely fused us into one. *If I don't still the applause and accept the award, Mother will!* In a sense, it was Ruthie's triumph and I knew it. Ruthie—whom I had sworn would never have to lift a finger when I made it. She never had to again. Mother believed the Hollywood legend. She, who had worked for me, like a demon—had known no sacrifice great enough—now relaxed into luxury. Bobby, fully recovered and with infinite lucidity, had started to call me the Golden Goose. And Ruthie believed her. To Mother, Hollywood was a playground and movie actresses spent their days floating through an atmosphere of Chanel-scented flattery, adoration and glamour. I don't believe that Ruthie ever believed I worked once I arrived. Her labors were done. She had given me this paradise and now we could all enjoy the eternal loaf.

I learned about women from Mother. Through gratitude and precedent, I believed Ruthie wise and eventually, after battle, took her advice. I was put into the position of loyal daughter

versus loyal wife. Mother never put her foot down. Mother
never took over. But in her girlish, appealing, elegantly insin-
uating way, she always convinced Ham and me that she knew
best.

My feeling of debt was so great that I bent over backwards
to take her side in any crisis. But I observed that Ruthie was
changing roles. Understandably bored with the sacrificing
mother, Ruthie was slowly, in attitude and demands, maneu-
vering me as she once had Daddy. Lovely, fractious, indolent
and increasingly self-absorbed, she spent more than I gave her
and bewildered me in her apparent indifference to my daily
struggle. Her world became higher but narrower, her interests
material and circumscribed. Always a woman of taste, she was
now the connoisseur. Nothing in my private life was ever worthy of her approval if I did it on my own. Nothing I ever did
earned her approval. Thin or fat, short hair or long, I was
always wrong and in need of her advice and direction. That I
took it seems incredible now. Certainly my husband was furious.

Ruthie never approved of my indifference to how I looked
off-screen. She insisted that it was my duty to be "dressed up"
on every occasion.

"You are a star, Bette. A great star and people look to you
to be well groomed."

Ruthie with her champagne taste now had the purse to go
with it. And when she hadn't and wanted to buy something
extravagant for me, the gift card said, *From Pinky to Pinky*
and I would know that sooner or later I would get the bill. It
was outrageous but charming and I always found it irresistible.
From Pinky to Pinky. We were obviously one and if I didn't
have the sense to splurge, she did. It became a family joke and
worse, a family ritual. Ruthie! She became my daughter, a
spoiled, enchanting little girl.

Bobby empathized completely and tried to help me all
through the years in any way she could. She had saved my life
a million times. About this time, eager to leave Ruthie and
make her own life, Bobby married a boy named Robert Pelgram. Ham and I drove with them to Tijuana and witnessed
the ceremony with heartfelt wishes for their happiness.

* * *

As I clutched the statuette that night and the applause died away, I knew a split second of serenity. Ham and I were still married after almost four years. I was pleased about this. And I had my family.

I stared at the little gold-plated man in the palm of my hand. He was a Hollywood male and, of course, epicene; but in a kind of madness his backview was the spit of my husband's. Since the O. in Harmon O. Nelson stood for Oscar, Oscar it has been ever since. During the evening I went to the ladies' room where I was followed and attacked by a lady fan-magazine editor who let me have it.

I stood, my back against the pink-tiled wall, like a traitor before a firing squad. The rat-ta-ta-tat of her mouth was a barrage that almost felled me. One would have thought that I had defiled the Academy or eaten her young. Slowly her purple rage subsided and I was able to piece together the now sputtering syllables.

"How could you? A print! You could be dressed for a family dinner. Your photograph is going round the *world*. Don't you realize? Aren't you aware? You don't look like a Hollywood star!" That again!

I was wearing a navy-and-white checked dinner dress with white piqué lapels. It was very simple and very expensive. As the hackneyed script goes, the reporter—in our privy council—informed me that I no longer had the right to do as I wished. Never say this to a Yankee.

CHAPTER
11

Now that I had received the Academy Award, I had high hopes the studio would find me a great script. My hopes were soon shattered. I was cast in an absurd adaptation of Michael Arlen's *Golden Arrow* in which George Brent and I were alternately seen with a black eye. It was called a comedy and in the brilliant fade-out, we turned to the audience during our last embrace to reveal that we both had one at the same time. The international hilarity this was supposed to provoke was further insured by a three-shot in which the hackie himself had not one but two shiners. The whole affair was a black eye as far as I was concerned.

When the company scheduled *Satan Met a Lady*, a Dashiel Hammett remake that was not to achieve any quality until John Huston directed it years later under the title *Maltese Falcon*, I was so distressed by the whole tone of the script and the vapidity of my part that I marched up to Mr. Warner's office and demanded that I be given work that was commensurate with my proven ability. I was promised wonderful things if only I would do this film. On its completion, my next assignment was the part of a female lumberjack in *God's Country and the Woman*, a script so undistinguished and a part so stupid that I flatly refused to play it. The heroine was an insufferable bore who scowled while everyone kept yelling "*Timber!*" After thirty-one pictures, two Academy nominations and one Oscar, it was obvious I would have to do something drastic to change the situation.

I was unhappy, unfulfilled and further compliance would only have destroyed the career I had so far built. Warners seemed bent on undoing all my work. It was impossible to control their vandalism; but the least I could do was to restrain from collaborating with them. I couldn't and wouldn't play this part. This time it was final. The very contract system that once offered me such security had become stultifying. One had bed and board in jail. I had not one whit of freedom as an artist. The privilege of choice had not been mine for years. Even Miss Chatterton, who had been lured to Warner Bros. not only with gold but with the promise of self-determination, had discovered that, on reflection, they had changed their minds. A proclamation was delivered that the artist, no matter how big, could no longer have this right. A few poor decisions on the part of the stars frightened the producers to death. Their own mistakes were another matter. Every picture had to make money primarily; and they rolled them out like sausages. I had never had the power of selectivity but I wanted it. I was beginning to feel like an assembly-line actress.

The studio had gained prestige through the Academy's accolade. My popularity had grown immensely. I was now directing the public into Warners' Theatres. To be submissive at this point seemed stupid. The daily skirmishes that always ended up with a truce in the commissary now ended. This was the moment of truth. It was the time for real action—an open break, a war in which one of us would win. If I never acted again in my life, I was not going to play in *God's Country*. It was now a matter of my own self-respect.

The Warners were convinced that I was simply in a tizzy. "She's difficult but she'll come around." They asked me to be a good girl. Their patronization was as undignifying as the role I was refusing. When they realized that I was in dead earnest, Mr. Warner returned to his promises. He informed me that he had just bought a property I would love and if I played the lumberjack, I'd be very happy. He told me he had just optioned a new novel about the South. *Gone With the Wind*.

Mr. Warner smiled reassuringly and waved me away.

"Just be a good girl and everything will work out."

Production on *God's Country and the Idiot Woman* began. William Keighly, George Brent and the whole unit left for location at Longview, Washington; and I left for Laguna Beach. I was on a one-woman strike. My salary was stopped and I was put on a three months' suspension as punishment.

My contract had five more years to run. The time of my suspension would be added to this bondage. In other words, unlike all other forms of employment, the right to strike was not ours. Refusal to pay us was theirs; and these unpaid months would be added to the original contract. Such a contract could be for a lifetime under this incredible arrangement.

Jimmy Cagney, Humphrey Bogart and I, amongst us, had about twenty suspensions in our years at Warners. There weren't many fighters in Hollywood; and we were punished for our unwillingness to compromise. An actor in genuine distress had no other recourse but refusal to work. One's apprenticeship had to end sometime.

By the terms of my contract, I received an annual twelve-week lay-off in which time I felt it would help my career *and* my value as a Burbank player if I made a picture for someone else. Other companies often requested my services. I felt that if I was allowed to accept one of these offers I would, at least, have some option over my material *once* a year. This, of course, under a standard contract was impossible.

This time we were at an impasse. I refused to leave Laguna, and Beverly Roberts, a new contract player, thought she was lucky to replace me in the picture. Word went out that I was dissatisfied with my salary of five thousand a week, a fictional figure that was picked out of the air. I was made to seem greedy and high-handed; the quality of my screenplays and directors was never mentioned. My lack of artistic freedom was brushed aside in a publicized story of a holdup for more money.

The whole world seemed eager to give me advice. Many Hollywood pundits told me that I would wreck my career, antagonize the whole industry and lose a great deal of money in the bargain. I was also reminded that if the trouble dragged on, I could also lose my following.

I couldn't believe that I could be this right and lose anything. It was impossible that I could feel an injustice this strongly and be wrong.

The press had a field day with this open warfare, and every

columnist had his say. More misinformation was printed concerning my demands than I ever thought possible. The verbal exchanges between the Warners and me became rougher and rougher.

There was a general feeling of unrest in Hollywood that year. Cagney—on my home lot—was already in court over his contract. Hepburn was fighting with RKO, Margaret Sullavan with Universal, Carole Lombard with Paramount, Eddie Cantor with Sam Goldwyn. Stars were learning that their drawing power entitled them to some consultation about their careers and some greater share of the companies' profits. In an attempt to protect themselves from this rising class, Warners now cast me in the role of a spoiled brat, an untractable infant who needed a good spanking, Peck's Bad Girl. Although my valid protestations prompted one savant to call me the Luther of Burbank, my bosses preferred the image of the unmanageable child.

Well, the child decided to leave home. At the height of all this publicity, Ludovic Toeplitz, an Anglo-Italian mogul who had produced, among other fine films, Charles Laughton's *Henry VIII* and Elizabeth Bergner's *Catherine the Great,* came to Hollywood to see me. Mr. Toeplitz with his bowler and George V beard offered to pay me twenty thousand pounds apiece to star in two pictures: *I'll Take the Low Road* with Douglas Montgomery and Nigel Bruce; the other one, with Maurice Chevalier. Both scripts would be subject to my approval. The plan was to film the first in Italy, the second in France.

This seemed to solve all my problems. I was being offered not only choice roles but a climate of mutual respect in which I could flourish. And I could not be stopped from working abroad.

I made up my mind to take the bull by the horns; and despite the dire prophecies of friends and colleagues, Ruthie agreed that I was right. I signed with Mr. Toeplitz and in order to avoid an injunction by Warner Brothers, Ham and I waited until late one Saturday night and flew to Vancouver: we then went by train across Canada to Montreal, where we boarded the *Duchess of Bedford* and sailed for England. (Injunctions could not be served on Sundays.)

There was some time before the first picture was to start and

Ham and I were ready for a real honeymoon. But for the hectic
42 St. Special, we had never had one. In some demented way,
I thought this might be what was wrong. Away from Hollywood, in a completely strange country discovering new things
together, I thought we might find ourselves again. I was still
on that tack—the diehard. We landed in England on our fourth
anniversary and I was ready for a sentimental journey.

We were feeling very gay on our arrival at the Firth of Clyde
at Greenock. The Scottish press called me an "unemployed
movie star" and welcomed me with a warmth and a recognition
that surprised and did not displease me. I had not realized how
well known I was abroad. We went on to Liverpool and I was
excited as a child on this first trip to Europe. A wave of op-
timism carried me ashore. I already saw two European triumphs
and the Warner Brothers holding each other's heads and luring
me back with plum tarts. I felt gloriously free of silly gun
molls, typists and lumberjacks. And I was far across the sea.
I wanted to see Wales and look vainly for kissing cousins among
the legion of Davises. I wanted to see everything.

Warners served me with an injunction prohibiting me to work
anywhere; and I was unimpressed. I was sure that England and
her Magna Carta would see to it that my slavery was ended.
This was restraint of trade and I would fight it if necessary.

We went to the Claridges Hotel in London and met with Mr.
Toeplitz and Monty Banks, the director of the first film. Then
Ham and I saw the London sights. We also visited Brighton
and saw the *Follies* on the Palace Theatre Pier; we rented a
saloon car and toured the country for two weeks. In Blackpool,
breathing that glorious fresh air, we watched a cobbler work
at Great Eccleston, played darts in a pub at Garstang and found
a real coal fire in a cottage north of Lancaster. The variety of
dialects fascinated and confused me. Some of the people might
just as well have been speaking Hindustan. I tried desperately
to learn some of the accents. In London, the assault of cockney
on Ham's ears had been too much. He had been reminded of
my pre-Mildred days when that was all 'e'eard around the
'ouse. I never knew what kind of part I would be challenged
with and I soaked up everything. A sponge I remain to this
day.

Britain was fascinating and we drove through the Lake District, starting from Torquay round the Cornish coast up to

Ruthie, who made it all possible

Daddy

thank you

A fan recently sent me this photograph. I do not remember the house where I was born. Chester Street, Lowell, Massachusetts.

Being a model for Ruthie

Graduation from grammar school. Photo: Ruthie.

Me and my John Held
Yogi roommate,
Ginny Conroy.

Miss Innocence—
Provincetown
Playhouse, 1929.

My sister Bobby who died in 1979—how I miss her still.

Mildred in *Of Human Bondage* was a bitch. No one wanted to play her, but I jumped at the chance. And it was the real start of my whole career. Leslie Howard was the leading man. 1934. Photo: Bob Watz. *Of Human Bondage* ©1942 Warner Bros. Pictures Inc., ren. 1973 United Artists Television Inc. and Bert Six.

Butternut, 1939. Still a Yankee.

A labor of love and one of my proudest accomplishments — the Hollywood Canteen, 1942.

Queen Elizabeth, one of my favorite roles. I played her twice. *The Virgin Queen*, 1955, was my favorite of the two. Photo: *The Virgin Queen*, © 1955 Twentieth Century Fox Film Corporation. All Rights Reserved.

With Anne Baxter, director Joseph Mankiewicz, and Celeste Holm on the set of *All About Eve*. It resurrected me from the dead and it changed my life, for better and sometimes worse. 1950. Photo: *All About Eve* © 1950 Twentieth Century Fox Film Corporation. All Rights Reserved.

Sitting here with Ruthie on the set of *All About Eve*. 1950. Photo: *All About Eve* © 1950 Twentieth Century Fox Film Corporation. All Rights Reserved.

Gary and my first meeting with Carl Sandburg. Photo: Bernie Abramson.

I've always kept scrapbooks and cherished photographs with family and those I care about. This picture was taken by the talented Greg Gorman at the St. James Club in Hollywood. I adore the photograph, the place, and the girl beside me. My assistant for many years, Kath. Photo: Greg Gorman.

Harold Schiff, for many years my lawyer, my best friend, and "father" to my children.

No need to explain, it's *Baby Jane*—a role that brought me added fame. And the first time B.D. saw me made up for Jane she said, "Mother, this time you've gone too far." 1962. *Whatever Happened to Baby Jane?*

On the set of *Baby Jane*. At that time, these two "old broads" were considered unbankable. 1962. Photo: *Whatever Happened to Baby Jane?*

Was I happy because Joan Crawford wasn't in *Hush, Hush…Sweet Charlotte?*
After Olivia de Havilland replaced her, Joan continually gave press releases
from her "Oxygen tent." 1964. Photo: *Hush, Hush…Sweet Charlotte*

Working with R. J. Wagner in the series *It Takes a Thief*. My name for R.J. has always been "beautiful, just beautiful." That is, inside and out. 1972. Photo: From the collection of Christopher Nickens.

Edith Head was a queen of her profession. She was Hollywood's eminent costume designer and I worked with her whenever possible. Always with elegant results. 1972.

Michael and his mother ready to go to church for his wedding. Seventeen years later, the marriage is still thriving.

Margot Merrill photographed at the Lochland School, her second home for many years.

I played Miss Moffit on the screen with great success. The stage version twenty-nine years later with Dorian Harewood (and with music) folded out of town. 1974.

On the set of *The Disappearance of Aimee*, photographed by that fine actor James Woods. Photo: James Woods.

The American Film Institute is for Life Achievement, an awesome phrase. After so many other awards, this one was the frosting on the cake. Jane Fonda and George Stevens, Jr., presented me with this award.

Gena Rowlands, my costar in *Strangers*, for which I won an Emmy. We were photographed for publicity "out of character," looking as we really did. 1979. Photo: From the collection of Christopher Nickens.

After the sixties, some of my best parts have been on television. I enjoyed playing Alice Gwynne Vanderbilt in *Little Gloria…Happy at Last,* for which I received an Emmy nomination. 1982. Photo: Courtesy of Edgar Sherick Associates.

Jimmy Stewart with me in *Right of Way*. A delightful experience costarring with him. I adore him. 1983. Photo: Nancy Ellison. Courtesy of Schaefer Karpf Productions.

I have always said my epitaph should read: "She did it the hard way."
So director Fielder Cook gave me a present, which I now take with me
wherever I work. 1983. Photo: Nancy Ellison. Courtesy of Schaefer
Karpf Productions.

1983 ARMY BALL
SPECIAL AWARD PRESENTATION
TO
BETTE DAVIS
Co-Founder and First President
of the Hollywood Canteen

Forty years later I received the nation's highest civilian service medal for the Hollywood Canteen. I was one thrilled Yankee lady. 1983.

With Kath and Robert Osborne leaving Deauville where I was honored at their film festival. And especially thrilling for a Yankee, I received France's Legion d'Honeur. 1987.

My son, Michael, with his wife, Chou, and my two adorable grandsons, Matthew and Cameron. I was honored when they decided to name their first son, "Matthew Davis Merrill."

"Little Ronnie Reagan." December, 1987. Photo: Courtesy of the Ronald Reagan Presidential Library.

I used to dress up to go dancing, now I dress up to receive prizes but I've never taken a single award lightly. Each of them is a result of blood, sweat, and tears. 1989.
Photo: Kevin Winter/DMI

In 1989, *LIFE* magazine asked Greg Gorman to photograph stars of the Hollywood year 1939 with new stars of today. I chose the talented James Woods as my junior partner. Photo: Greg Gorman.

I will always cherish the night I was honored by the film Society of Lincoln Center in New York. I've made good in the city where my acting career began seven decades earlier. Kath, my escort Harold Schiff, and Jimmy Stewart joined me in the "honoree's" balcony while I acknowledged a standing ovation. Photo: Vic DeLucia/*NYT* Pictures

At San Sebastían, September 22, 1989. (Left to right, center) Kathryn Sermak, the honoree, Mayor Albistur. Photo: Pedro Párraga.

"I wish you love."

Somerset. The color and the kindness of the West Country people caused me to fall in love with Great Britain forever. I was slightly disappointed in the mountains, which were dwarfed by our Western ranges, but the overall beauty of Devonshire was matchless. I have always been a rubber-neck but in Wales, I needed a rubber tongue. I could never quite, "make" myself pronounce, Llanfairpwllgwyngyllgogerychwyrndrob-wllelantysillogogogoch. That was the name of the town, all right. A little investigation cleared things up slightly when I discovered that it was originally a primitive description of the village; i.e., Church Mary-A-Hollow-White-Hazel-Near-To-The-Rapid-Whirlpool-Church-Saint's-Name-Cave-Red. That's a Welsh rarebit! It was impossible to find a cousin. We wouldn't have been able to communicate anyway.

When we returned to London we found the papers full of my fight with Warner Brothers. Plans for the film were going ahead. I went to Paris for costume fittings. It was odd. First the return to my Welsh origins—now France. How I adored Paris, with the linear delicacy of its architecture, its clearness of light and its air of intellectual vigor. I had the most incredible feeling of at-homeness there. The change from Devonshire cream and English beer to the escargot and vin rosé of France came naturally. I had been eating for five during my stay in England and managed to lose ten pounds through pure exhilaration. It would have been better if I'd gained some reserve flesh. On my return from the Continent I was to need the strength to withstand its mortification.

It seems that Mr. Warner met with Signor Toeplitz and had a most unromantic rendezvous in Venice. They had come to no agreement about my two contracts. Signor Toeplitz claimed that he was not pilfering anyone and was justified to go on with his production plans. His contract with me was, as far as he was concerned, legal and aboveboard. He was untouchable. Warner was adamant about the sanctity of my legal obligations. I was equally and righteously appalled at its unholiness. The refreshed thought that I could be forced into putting on a grass skirt and doing a hula if it so pleased my masters and even sent out on personal-appearance tours in that condition so enraged me that when I heard Warner was serious enough to bring this to the English courts and litigation could cost me a fortune, I still refused to turn back. Once and for all I had to consolidate my position as an actress and not a painted puppet subject to my masters' whims.

On September 9, Messrs. Denton, Hall and Burgin, solicitors for Warners and First National Pictures, obtained for their client an *ex parte* injunction restraining me from any other employment until a week hence, at which point Mr. Justice Lewis in Chambers renewed the writ until the now inevitable action in King's Bench Division of the Court.

Mr. and Mrs. Warner were staying with William Randolph Hearst outside of London. Ann Warner tried vainly to dissuade her husband from going on with the action but the die was cast. Mr. Warner engaged Sir Patrick Hastings as the company's barrister. The most redoubtable legal mind in all England, Agatha Christie later used him as her prototype for the lawyer in *Witness For the Prosecution*. It was obvious that the heavy artillery was being brought up. It was Bette against Goliath.

I needed my own barrister and Signor Toeplitz recommended tall, dignified Sir William Jowitt. Six foot four of vertical England, he was a Spy drawing and a brilliant lawyer. In the custom of his country he recommended that I immediately give him a ten-thousand-dollar retainer. I almost died. Despite the Warners' rumors of my immense wealth, I was settling down to a fight and for the first time in years, was not receiving an income. Ham and I had blithely traveled around; Mother and Bobby were living as always. We had expected a montage of triumphs and here I was going to court.

It was at this point that Ham decided to return to New York and look for work. I was absolutely dazed; but he insisted it was the most sensible thing to do. Now I *was* in a fix—over my head and alone.

"Why fight City Hall?" was the Greek chorus that sped me on my way from Hollywood. It may be the only thing worth fighting—but I hadn't expected to do it all alone. My romantic notions about marriage were myriad, not the least of which was the dependabilities of both parties. With all my monomania about my work, for all my irascibility, I was behind Ham the whole way and he knew it. I was always on his side. I surrounded him. And still he chose this moment to return to America. It wasn't often I needed him. This was the only time.

I saw Ham off at Southampton and stood bewildered on the dock as his ship pulled away. We must—each of us—give what we can to a relationship. His salary, assuming he was to get work, would be negligible in comparison to the moral support I craved at that moment. I was never so wretched as when I crawled back to my cell at the Park Lane. "I need absolute quiet," I had told the manager when I asked for a small court room. I was down to shavings.

My suspension was costing me a fortune as it was. Now the added expenses were terrifying. Sir William was very decent about a delay in payment and the War began.

There is probably nothing as awesome as an English courtroom. The wood-paneled walls and leaded windows, the "docks" and misty dignity, and the black-frocked and be-wigged barristers are all designed to astonish the guiltless and intimidate the miscreant. Its purpose was not lost on me. I felt a little like Alice in a heretofore unpublished adventure in which very serious French poodles were about to settle my fate in a jabberwocky I didn't dare to question on pain of death. And there on the highest seat was Mr. Justice Branson, whose divine detachment and arid, dewlapped countenance made me think that E. E. Clive should have been playing him. But this was not a film. No one was going to yell "cut" unless he meant my throat. This take was for keeps.

Sitting in the well of the court with Sir William, I felt the little black dots of Sir Patrick's keen eyes beneath his bulging brow beating a path to mine. His gaze could turn one to stone or jelly. I met his eye. I fixed him with a glance that was supposed to chill him. He grabbed the neckline of his domino and started speaking. It was clear that I was not just fighting the Warners but the whole Motion Picture Industry. Sir Patrick's voice belonged in the theatre. His opening remark was, "I think, m'lord, this is the action of a very naughty young lady." I wanted to kill him!

He went on: "I think it right that I make it plain to your lordship that this really is a case of great importance to the whole industry, because although the contracts vary, no doubt in some minor points, from other contracts which are the standard form in the industry in substance, it is the common form.

"It is the common form of contract with which most large film companies in America engage most big film stars. There are exceptions of people who have a position so established that they prefer to be independent. What this young lady is seeking to do, in effect, is to tear up the contract and say, whether she is right or wrong, the court will not grant an injunction against her. That is tantamount to saying that these ladies and gentlemen can come over to this country and the courts will say that they cannot be stopped from doing this sort of thing . . . a series of defenses have been put forward of this nature . . ."

It was evident that the entire Motion Picture Industry was backing Warner Brothers, for were I to lose the case, every major star would rush for the nearest exit and follow me to freedom. Not one other film company in Hollywood would touch me with a ten-foot pole. Sir Patrick's sharp tongue then slashed into my defense against "slavery." Admitting that my contract was extremely stringent, he smiled that concrete smile and spoke of my slowly graduating salary that by 1942 would reach 600 pounds.

"If anybody wants to put me into perpetual servitude on that basis of remuneration, I shall prepare to consider it. And what is more I shall not ask Sir William Jowitt, K. C., to stand up for me and argue that it would be slavery." He pursed his lips and waited for his laughs like the magnificent performer like he was. Irony was Sir Patrick's forte.

He was so brilliant. I couldn't believe that Sir Patrick really didn't get the point. He would probably have done exactly what I was doing but he was the plaintiff's lawyer and not mine.

Mr. Warner then shyly took the stand. He looked as nervous as I. For a split second, I felt sorry for him. But by the time Sir Patrick got through with my boss, it sounded as if I had been found in an ash heap and he and his brother Harry had breathed life into me. He allowed that I was exceptionally interested in my work and was a serious actress who could conceivably be distressed by inferior scripts.

"I admit," Mr. Warner admitted, under my Sir William's interrogation, "that an actress could become heartbroken if she had to play parts that were not fitted to her." He also conceded under questioning that I could be forced to eat oatmeal for a commercial tie-up and be publicized thusly if the studio found it desirable. Mr. Justice looked displeased about this and I made up my mind that I would spend my days trying to hypnotize him into complete agreement with my case. He must have thought me mad. I stared at him throughout the trial wide-

eyed and with what I believed the persuasiveness of Mesmer.
Sir Patrick was working on a different level. He made the most
of a letter which I had sent to Mr. Warner in which I mentioned
among other things that the time to be paid well was that time
before the public told you to go to blazes.

"Unfortunately," Sir Patrick smiled that ironic smile again,
"she chose to go to England!"

He then tore into poor Signor Toeplitz (whose name he
refused to pronounce correctly). He accused him of luring and
bribing me to Europe and doing me a great disservice. When
he was finished, Sr. Toeplitz sounded like a white slaver. Time
and time again I had to hear how disastrous it was to a producer
to have an actress walk out in the middle of a picture thereby
necessitating the disposal of many reels and their remaking at
astronomical figures.

I had done nothing of the sort. I had *refused* to play, in what
time and the critics proved, was a terrible movie. And still,
fellow mogul Alexander Korda appeared as a witness for Warners and once more went into a whole fantasy that had Juliet
quitting a picture and the impossibility of having Romeo finish
the film with another Miss Capulet. Mr. Korda then announced
that actresses were usually willing to be bought, sold, lent and
completely managed by producers since it was usually to their
advantage. My lawyer exacted the admission that if she didn't,
there would be a great hardship. Mr. Korda admitted further
that I worked terribly hard for a woman but "she's well paid
for it." The attendant smirk was meant to imply that *that*
justified everything.

This nightmare continued for three days during which one
Gerald Gardiner, representing Signor Toeplitz, rose out of nowhere and like the amusing Richard Hayden objected toothily
to the slanderous implications of Sir Patrick.

"Why, the evidence isn't all in!" he cried. "And you are
blacking the name of my client. This accusation is unfounded."

Mr. Justice looked like a weary basset hound.

"Your client is not on trial here, sir."

"And that is why we object to his conviction! He . . ."

"You will please to not make a speech. The court will not
allow you to make a speech. When the evidence is all in perhaps
I will preside over a case between the two companies. At
present this is irrelevant. I have allowed you a simple statement

of denial and now we will get on with the case.''

The little man was hysterical.

"But your Lordship, my client cannot wait until the completion of his trial to have his good name cleared . . .''

Mr. Justice glowered at him with all the might of his exalted position. He was bored as well as angry and he dispensed with Mr. Gardiner immediately. Even I was bored with this byroad. I was eager to hear my own side. Sir William was about to begin. Mr. Justice called a recess and we all smoked in the corridor where I discovered that in the very next chamber a divorce case was going on that was to rock the whole empire. Simpson versus Simpson. It was a unique case, I heard, because the apex of the usual triangle was a man whose name could not, by law, be mentioned in court. It was certainly whispered in the corridor and eventually broadcast to the world. A King was the correspondent!

Obviously everyone had his troubles and I returned to hear Sir William plead my case. He made a beautiful and impassioned plea for my rights. He answered all the irritating discrepancies and charges of the company and insisted by precedent that Mr. Justice Greaves-Lord—bless him, whoever he was—had found an identical contract that made the involved actress chattel. Furthermore he insisted that the question was whether those in great and superior authority could force an artist to work against her will.

"If they are forced as punishment not to work and therefore eventually to starve—that is the question of slavery. I suggest that the essence of slavery is not that it is less slavery because the bars are gilded, but because some authority says, 'You must continue to work under contract.' ''

Then Sir William came to the most important point other than my impotency in choice of material. He pointed out that if I refused to work for anyone else and waited until 1942, at which time my contract would have expired, it would only be beginning because of the self-perpetuating nature of the contract that simply added at the tag end all the months of inactivity.

"I then suggest," Sir William eloquently continued, "that it is therefore not a legal contract but a life sentence."

According to that document called a contract, if Ham took a photograph of me in back of our house, the Warners—in an extreme move to be sure—could conceivably and quite legally consider it an "appearance." Confiscation of the negative was nothing to the breach of contract I would be guilty of. It is exactly this sort of "blue law" that worries the discriminated-against citizen. A demigod can imprison you at a crucial moment for smoking on Sunday or spitting in your enemy's eye. It was proved that I could be sent to Saskatchewan or Timbuktu without any recourse. Even motherhood could automatically terminate our agreement or extend it nine months. Sir William then made it clear that I did *not* walk out in the middle of the picture but had refused a part I did not think consistent with my case. He gently hammered one nail after another into their case. The restrictive nature of my contract was such that I was not allowed to make "any private appearance in any way connected with, for instance, theatrical shows." Sir Patrick interrupted with the gracious news that he was not seeking an injunction to keep me from going to the theatre. But Sir William was proving his point. I could, by contract, not even arrange to get up a party for my favorite charity. I had to get permission to have my name used in any civic activity whatsoever. I was absolutely *owned* by Warners and under their aegis, I could be ordered to dance in a chorus line and be forced to comply.

While Sir Patrick looked bored and Mr. Warner looked uncomfortable, Sir William reached the heart of the matter.

". . . I do not know much about art or artists . . . It is a contract of very long hours and hard work. . . . I do not suppose that any artist can turn on his inspiration as one turns on a tap. His mood and inspiration have to suit. It is a contract which can be rendered tolerable and bearable by a human being only if the persons for whom the artist is working show tact, good temper and consideration." Amen! Sir William thought it unnecessary to call me to the dock. He insisted that it was purely a legal matter; and he feared that under unfriendly interrogation I would lose my temper and injure my cause. Sir Patrick Hastings was so furious not to be able to tear me apart, that he took off his wig and threw it across the courtroom. It was quite a gesture and even I was impressed. I lost the case!

Nothing worked for me, especially my attempt at thought transmission. Mr. Justice was very much in possession of himself. He reserved his judgment until the weekend was over and I returned to the Tudor Close in Sussex to await the unhappy news. I had moved there because it was less expensive and I wanted to be unbothered by the press. I was now a wreck.

When the news came, I was walking on the beach in utter melancholy. Jack Warner had won a three-year injunction or the duration of my contract (whichever was the shorter). I was his and if he exercised his options, my inhuman bondage stretched to 1942.

I lost with a vengeance. I looked out to sea grimly and then wrote Mother. I never needed her so much in my life. Everyone had warned me not to fight. Well, I paid for it. I not only lost the case but a fortune in salary. I owed Sir William his retainer and I was obliged by law to pay Warners' costs, which were tremendous. Added to all of this, I had been living abroad in the naïve knowledge that I was about to prosper with the now maligned Signor Toeplitz. *See you in court! I was so cocksure of myself. Right always triumphed.*

The day was quite properly gray and foreboding. It was October and the chilly air was gnawing at my bones. But something else was eating away at me. I was never a good loser. *Of course. Why not!* I decided to appeal. My solicitors informed the court of my decision. The case cost me over thirty thousand dollars. The appeal would bring it up to fifty. But from across the sea one could hear the sigh of relief from M-G-M, Paramount, RKO, Universal and the rest. This was something they would stick together on. Gaumont British had a big party to celebrate my defeat. If I had won, all their castles would have tumbled; and Jesse Matthews, England's greatest star, would have answered Hollywood's call.

Mr. Justice found that there was no room for application of the doctrine of restraint of trade. The injunction only held good for Great Britain. There was a possibility that I could work in Italy but there wasn't an American movie company that would release the film. Ham cabled, THE CLOCK IN THE STEEPLE STRIKES ONE and it was dated from Whitinsville, Mass. I wasn't finished yet. There was so much still to do but I was alone. I called California to speak to Ruthie.

"Mother? Mother, come over and stay with me while I fight this out. I'm going to appeal."

"Hang on, Bette darling. I'll be there!"

It seems I did nothing for a few days but bicycle and walk on the beach all bundled up. I saw no one but the press, which kept descending on my little hotel by the sea. I wanted to be alone. I wanted to think. I was exhausted. This defeat was a real blow to me. It was a one hundred percent defeat. A sock in the teeth! There was nothing, no positive aspect, I could cling to at all. Through the fog, across the expanse of water, was America and Hollywood and more of the same drivel that had driven me into all of this litigation. I couldn't go back to all that. And then I received an unexpected guest.

On my return from one of my endless besweatered trudges I found George Arliss in the lobby waiting for me. Once again he reached out and gave me his hand when I needed it. It was the sweetest gesture. He had come all the way from London to offer his condolence and his advice. We had tea and Mr. Arliss chose his words carefully.

"Go back, my dear Bette. You haven't lost as much as you think. Go back gracefully and accept the decision. See what happens. I think good things. If in time you feel you're being treated unjustly, put up another fight. I admire your courage in this affair but now—go back and face them proudly."

That wonderful man. He was more dispassionate than I and quite right, of course. It was eventually my final decision and I cabled Mother to stay in New York and wait for me. I sailed on the *Aquitania* early in November to face the music.

Ham had made one record with Tommy Dorsey and was still trying. We both agreed this time that he should stay in New York for a while and try his luck some more.

He saw Mother and me off for Hollywood where my diet of continental delicacies was only the hors d'oeuvre for a nice big main dish of good old provincial humble pie.

CHAPTER
12

It is only fair to record that Warners not only greeted me with open arms but graciously relieved me of their share of the damages. I didn't have to pay the King's ransom to Sir Patrick, and Sir William's retainer was shared by my employers who fulfilled Mr. Arliss' prophecy and bent over backwards to be nice. It was now evident to them that I never would have sacrificed so much time, energy and money unless I was indeed earnest about my career. They knew about my domestic situation and the drain it was on my supposed fortune. I realized I had to make the best of the situation and we met in the spirit of conciliation. Their generosity made it a pleasure being a good sport. In a way, my defeat was a victory. At last we were seeing eye to eye on my career. I was aching to work and they were eager to encourage me.

There is no doubt that the publicity attendant to my litigation paved the way for Olivia de Havilland's eventual court victory over the immoral suspension clause. She put up a successful fight in California some time later and, once and for all, a definite terminal date was set to all such contracts. The Emancipation was proclaimed and what Sir William had called "perpetual slavery" became a thing of the past. Hollywood actors will be forever in Olivia's debt.

In the long view, there is no question but that I won after

all. Jack Warner now offered me the excellent *Marked Woman*
and I settled down to real work. Though the title reflected the
victimization and eventual scarring of a call girl who tried to
avenge the rape and murder of her innocent sister sucked into
the racket by a gangster reminiscent of Lucky Luciano, I preferred to believe that it was a good and positive omen. I was
now marked for great things at last. I was particularly restless
and driven, to make up for my inactivity. I wanted to strike
while the iron was good and hot. But when was I not driven?
While in England, my maid Dell stayed with Bobby and her
husband. The days had slipped by unnoticeably and it seems
that Dell leaned nostalgically on her mop and informed Bobby
that "I miss Bette and her disturbances." Dear, wonderful Dell.
She was now happily back with me—and far more permanently
suited to me than my husband, who was sticking it out in New
York. She took all of my explosions with the resignation of
the Sicilians who live in the shadow of Etna.

Marked Woman was a good picture. Humphrey Bogart,
whose star was rising, played the district attorney and Eduardo
Cianelli was the slimy, elegantly obscene white slaver. I had
seen a performance at the Palmer Playhouse of Lynn Riggs'
Green Grow the Lilacs on which the revolutionary musical,
Oklahoma, was eventually based and was impressed by the
brightness of a young girl named Jane Bryan. I convinced
Warners to put her under contract and she played my kid sister
in *Marked Woman.* I made up my mind that, when possible,
I would remember what it had been like when I first started
and secure players dared me to crash the gate of the Establishment. She was excellent in the film which on the whole
was satisfactory in every respect.

I remember only one little fracas without which life wouldn't
have been the same. In the film, Janie is seduced and dies. To
avenge her murder, I inform on the racketeer who, as a warning
to the other girls, has me beaten and scarred for life. After I
had been beaten to a pulp by Mr. Cianelli's henchmen in the
awful vendetta, my director, Lloyd Bacon, had me bandaged
by the makeup men for the first hospital scene in which Bogie
was to visit me. I was to be half dead. I don't think I ever
looked so attractive. Lily Daché herself could have created that
creamy puff of gauze at the peak of her inspiration. It was an
absolute gem of millinery. After I studied myself in the glass

and weighed the possibility of wearing the creation someday at Ciro's, I smiled sweetly and left the studio for lunch. Instead I went to my doctor.

"I have just been beaten up by a gang of thugs, Doctor, and my cheek has been carved by a knife. Would you please bandage me?"

When I drove through the studio gates on my return, the watchman turned pale and picked up the telephone. Word was passed throughout the lot that production would have to be held up.

"Davis has had a terrible accident!"

They came running from all directions and Bacon saw his schedule go down the drain. I quietly walked onto the set and got into the hospital bed. A parent weeps and wails for his missing child but the safe return is usually greeted by fury.

"You mean you're all right and this is your idea of makeup?"

"You believed me, didn't you? So will the public."

And that is the way it was photographed.

My new picture was *Kid Galahad* with Edward G. Robinson and Wayne Morris. It was a story about prizefighters and a good one. Mr. Curtiz was again my director and I will never forget Wayne's knocking out a fighter in a take. "Fake fight! Retake! Fake fight—awful!" Curtiz screamed—but it was difficult to redo because Wayne's opponent was unconscious. He had knocked him out cold.

Marked Woman and *Kid Galahad* were consolidating my position with the public. Next I was cast for the third time with Leslie Howard in a comedy that loosely suggested, in our roles as a tempestuous acting couple, the glorious Lunts. Olivia de Havilland, a favorite of mine, as an actress and a person, was my rival in the film. It was a farcical comedy, but Leslie and I had a romp and I was out of the gutter and in Orry-Kelly's latest gowns.

I have always adored comedy. It was my misfortune however that, when I was given a "new facet," I was given farce, which has never been my dish. High comedy is a different story—the old Philip Barry-Frederick Lonsdale-S. N. Behrman variety had great style—the butterfly touch. High comedy seems to be a thing of the past. I suspect the world is losing its sense of humor. It is difficult to juggle hundred-megaton notions with any sprightliness. More than ever the artist either beats his breast in agony or his thighs in hilarity. We live in a time of extremes. The luxury of good taste unhappily has departed with the cane-backed Rolls Royce. The leisure class spawned the detached wits who had the time to regard the world wryly and indulge in exquisite badinage. No one dares flirt with the flame any longer. One seems intent on flying straight into it.

I myself have been burned too many times to be lofty about it. I have been far too humorless to laugh with any justification at my fellows. I'm far too square to negotiate the soft curves of gentle irony. I know my limitations; but I can decry them. I cannot linger with Persian subtlety on the rim of a rose. I must suck it dry and move on—a stinging bee, a worker with a Queen Bee complex. I do my job by instinct and demand by divine right my proper station. That is my paradox—that I am both worker and Queen. There is a dullness to my deaf, dumb and blind response to that half-forgot battle order. I am doomed to an eternity of compulsive work. No set goal achieved satisfies. Success only breeds a new goal. The golden apple devoured has seeds. It is endless.

It is small wonder that Ham was both dazzled, bewitched and then exhausted with my crises. I always had one. My latest film, *That Certain Woman*, was not good. It was a remake of Gloria Swanson's *The Trespasser*. It tasted a bit of soap and recalled Miss Chatterton's nobility that Barbara Stanwyck eventually inherited. After all those years I worked with Hank Fonda, whom I hadn't seen since my early theatre days. Hank was coming up in the world. Along with Ian Hunter, we tried; but the picture just didn't make it. Bette Davis was moving on all cylinders and Ruth Elizabeth was losing her husband. I didn't want a divorce. I no longer loved Ham—not as I had. That was long since gone. I had left home, so to speak, long ago; but I wanted it to be there when I returned.

I was too busy finding a script to preserve the unpreservable. When *The Life of Emile Zola* was prepared for Paul Muni, I read the script and was fascinated with the small role of Nana. It was unabashedly little more than a bit—but I begged the studio to allow me to do it. It also could have been a sensational stunt at that point in my career. I also begged Mr. Muni to let me play it, but he wouldn't.

About this time Owen Davis, Sr. and Warners were having

a legal battle over the title of a property that Mr. Davis claimed
was his. An amicable settlement was made between them by
the purchase of one of his plays—*Jezebel*. It was a story about
an antebellum vixen named Julie Marsden.

I will be the last to deny that the nationwide search for
Scarlett O'Hara in the now-world-famous *Gone With the Wind*
infuriated me. It could have been written for me. Warners had
dropped its option while I was in London, and David Selznick
had bought the story. When I read it and remembered Mr.
Warner's promise, I was fit to be tied. It is true that I got my
second chance to play Scarlett. When initial plans were in the
making, Mr. Selznick asked Warners if they could borrow Bette
Davis and Errol Flynn as a package. The thought of Mr. Flynn
as Rhett Butler appalled me. I refused. I was not going to be
part of that parcel. I wasn't. And that was my last chance.
George Cukor was the director in the beginning. Shades of
Rochester. He still saw me as the girl in *Broadway* and whatever
his ancient grievance, his thumbs were still down. By such
intangibles are careers affected.

The quest for Scarlett became international, and I had my
partisans. I was as perfect for Scarlett as Clark Gable was for
Rhett. And many knew this. In the face of such obvious casting
inspiration, the official decision was to find a fresh face. One
would have thought me Ouspenskaya! The story is too familiar
to belabor. Everybody's second cousin was tested and I was
used as the touchstone. That was how right I was. It was
insanity that I not be given Scarlett. But then, Hollywood has
never been rational.

I only argue with their eventual choice because it was not
I. Nor do I detract one whit from Miss Leigh's beautiful performance when I say that I still wish I'd got my hands on it.
But as luck would have it, Julie Marsden, the Jezebel in question, was a blood sister of Scarlett's. Willful, perverse and
proud, she was every inch the Southern belle. She had the same
cast-iron fragility, the same resourcefulness, the same rebellion. Julie was the best part I had since Mildred. I had no time
to be shocked by the fact that my little white cottage was
crumbling. Like a set that is struck after a performance, it
seemed like the dream it was—a façade, a temporary scene
for pointless arguments.

I couldn't believe this scene was being played by childhood

sweethearts. A boy and girl had adored each other, married and never dreamed of such an ending to it all. It made me feel old and weary. The fact that I didn't care anymore that I was finding other men attractive was heartbreaking to me. Under the circumstances, having never had any adventures before marriage, this was the logical sequence of events. We finally some months later faced the fact that I had outgrown the whole relationship. I gave Ham permission to divorce me. His grounds were: "She reads in bed. She neglected me for her work." In the final analysis, I guess this was the truth.

When my boss, Hal Wallis, announced that he had hired William Wyler to direct *Jezebel*, I was stunned. The little man who had said a long time ago to me, "What do you think about these dames who show their chests and think they can get jobs?" Saying nothing about all this, and licking my chops that I was now in a position to refuse to work with Mr. Wyler, I asked for an appointment to talk to him. Revenge, they say, is sweet. It has never been thus for me. Mr. Wyler, not re-membering me or the incident, was, to put it mildly, taken aback when I told him my grim little tale of woe. He actually turned green. He was genuinely apologetic, saying he had come a long way since those days. I could not help but believe he was sincere. With no revenge left in me, I started work on *Jezebel*. I became such a champion of his talent—and still am—that one would have thought I was his highly paid press agent. It was he who helped me realize my full potential as an actress. I met my match in this exceptionally creative and talented director.

Unlike some yeoman directors, he couldn't work with the talentless. I can hear him now, dispensing with actors of no experience.

"I am not a dramatic coach. I want actors who can act. I can only direct actors, I can't teach them how to act." How different from a Frank Capra who conversely preferred to direct personalities. That handsomely, homely dynamo, Wyler, could make your life a hell.

It was he who screamed at me, "Do you want me to put a chain around your neck? Stop moving your head!" This man was a perfectionist and had the courage of twenty. He was as dedicated as I. It is impossible to describe the contribution that Wyler made to *Jezebel*.

After all these years, I had been given a high-budget film with all the trimmings I had fought for and a talented director that I had been begging for also. The cast included Henry Fonda, George Brent, Donald Crisp, and the inspired Fay Bainter as ''Auntie Belle'' who understood Julie so well. ''She's always meanest when she's loving most.'' Miss Bainter's contribution to the film and to my performance was immeasurable. It just wouldn't have been the same picture without her.

My first appearance was in a riding habit. As Julie entering her house, I was to lift my skirt with my riding crop. It sounds simple. Mr. Wyler asked me to take the riding skirt and the crop home and rehearse with them. The next morning, I arrived knowing he was after something special. I made my entrance a dozen times and he wasn't satisfied. He wanted something, all right. He wanted a complete establishment of character with one gesture. I sweated through forty-five takes and he finally got it the way he wanted, or at least he said so, in his very noncommittal way.

Toward the end of the film, Julie and Press's wife fight over who will go with him to the plague-infested swamps. The actress playing opposite me couldn't play the scene the way Willie wanted her to. She was the giver in the scene, I the receiver. She had to convey the power of possession. She was his wife. Willie shot the scene over and over and still was not satisfied.

When I thought all was lost, Willie suddenly moved into a close-up of her. The scene still seemed unsatisfactory to me but he printed a take.

''That's it. Wrap it up!'' he shouted to everyone's relief.

That's what? I thought. But I had underestimated him for the first time. He had made a stumbling block into a stepping-stone. During her dialogue, Willie moved into a close-up all right. A close-up of her hand on the banister of the staircase. It was her left hand and there on the usual finger, glistening with symbolism, was her wedding ring. What more powerful indication of her priority could there be? What greater antagonist? I would have jumped into the Hudson River if this man had told me to, directorially speaking.

The most famous scene, however, was the Comus Ball. With all the girls in traditional white, Julie out of spite arrives in scarlet to the embarrassment of her escort and the horror of the guests. John Huston, who did the screen adaptation, merely indicated this in a paragraph. Without a word of dialogue Willie created a scene of power and tension. This was movie making on the highest plane. Insisting that my correct escort dance with me—knowing that I am making him an accomplice in this gaucherie—and his refusal to stop, once the floor is cleared by the revolted dancers who consider us pariahs, is so mortifying that Julie wants to die. But now Press is relentless in his punishment. His own embarrassment is nothing to the shame he must inflict on her. Julie implores him to take her home. His grip on her waist becomes tighter, his step more deliberate, his eyes never meet hers. And always the lilting music, the swirling bodies and the peripheral reaction shots of the stunned pillars of society and Auntie Belle, who suffers with Julie. It is a scene of such suspense that I never have not marveled at the direction of it.

Fonda's wife was about to make him a father and the film was scheduled to get him back to New York for the arrival. It played havoc with the continuity and Mr. Arliss' words echoed in my ears. I also remembered Mr. Barthelmess' vanishing act during my close-ups. But this couldn't be helped. Every time I see the gifted Jane Fonda today, I remember what she put me through before she came on the scene.

Jezebel was work from the word go. Willie was so thorough and so inventive that we were running behind schedule—Hollywood's biggest bugaboo. Of course, this can be carried to extremes from Von Sternberg to Wells; but creative artists are not capping soda bottles ninety a minute on an assembly line. Art may be disciplined but not regimented.

Warners, in a fret, decided to take Willie off the picture since the budget was going out the window. But this man wasn't going to be fired if I, personally, had to burn the place down. I wasn't going to lose this genius for anybody or anything. I walked up that beaten path to the sanctum sanctorum and announced that I wouldn't finish the film if Mr. Wyler were not allowed to continue.

"I have been raced through the picture because of Hank's baby and I will not be rushed with my part of the film. Plus, changing directors in midstream would be a tragedy."

I was willing to work late each day if necessary to keep Willie on the picture. Warner agreed. I worked until midnight every night and was back on the set early each morning. I earned the Oscar I received for *Jezebel*. The thrill of winning my second Oscar was only lessened by the Academy's failure to give the directorial award to Willie. He made my performance. He made the script. *Jezebel* is a fine picture. It was all Wyler. I had known all the horrors of no direction and bad direction. I now knew what a great director was and what he could mean to an actress. I will always be grateful to him for his toughness and his genius.

My reporter friend must have been delighted because I was dressed to the nines for the Academy dinner this time—a brown net dress with aigrettes at the neckline. It was the beginning of the halcyon years. The proof of the pudding would be the scripts to follow—and the directors. I was never surer of myself professionally than at this moment.

CHAPTER

13

With my two statuettes, critics' awards and my latest box-office receipts, I again met with Mr. Warner. It was our little Boston Tea Party. I was no longer the spunky little colonial asking for more representation from His Highness. I was now a sovereign state demanding my own tithe—a member of the commonwealth. I had never been able to keep my mouth shut, but now mine was a voice that couldn't be ignored.

My legal battle in London was concerned primarily with quality of product. My present concern was quantitative and monetary. Now I wanted money. I had looked around me at the great names who had preceded me. They had had their moment and they were, some of them, grateful to have a bit in one of my films in order to eat and keep up their self-respect. An actor's career can be a short one. His time on top even shorter. I had no idea how long my star would remain. Any clear night you can watch one disintegrate in the heavens. I was reaching my zenith—no nova, I. Over and over, I heard myself say, *Ruthie and Bobby must be secure forever. Thank God, I'm an ox; but what happens if I become ill? What happens if I lose an arm or an eye? What happens next?* Thirty is young, but it is an age at which a greater awareness of your mortality arrives along with the first line on your face. My Yankee blood

171

cried out for land and complete financial independence. *No
more peanuts! No more haggling! Jezebel* was a success and
was bringing in loot. I wanted my share. I got it.

The old, battle-worn document was torn up and I received
a new contract. It was not what I had asked for, but it was a
definite improvement over the old one.

The full-page ad for the acclaimed *Jezebel* ran side by side
in *Motion Picture Daily* with Warner's announcement BETTE
DAVIS SUSPENDED. I'd refused to do a turkey called *Comet
Over Broadway*. I knew that every star had her night; but I
wasn't quite prepared to kill myself off in one fell swoop.
Continuing their lunacy, they next offered me something called
Garden of the Moon. It was vacation time again. But then the
studio sent me the script of *The Sisters*.

It was another costume picture. Jane Bryan was again one
of my sisters. Errol Flynn was my co-star. For this particular
role of a restless, confused newspaperman, he was well suited.
Handsome, arrogant and utterly enchanting, Errol was something to watch. His arrivals on the set always reminded me of
Alfred Lunt's vaudeville turn as an M.C. in Robert Sherwood's
Idiot's Delight. Flanked by four to six blondes, arms linked,
Errol would strut in at about eleven. One expected them to go
into a routine, which no doubt they did. He was already the
stud of the Warner stable and had or would co-star with everyone on the lot. There were two notable exceptions. And I was
one of them.

In the first place, the quality of my scripts was of prime
importance to me. The studio was not in Puccini's *La Bohème*
but Warners' Burbank. I was there to work! I had a million
and one things on my mind with every picture. If I had shared
Errol's indifference to our profession, this book would be a
very different one. Infinitely charming Errol was possessed of
his own demon. His drive was in an entirely different direction
and probably enhanced by his hushed but recurrent tuberculosis
which was soon to keep him out of military service. At the
time, he was unquestionably the most wholesomely beautiful
satyr.

I was a rare bird to Errol. I confused him utterly. One day,
he smiled that cocky smile and looked directly at me. "I'd
love to proposition you, Bette, but I'm afraid you'd laugh at
me."

I never miss the rare opportunity to agree with a man. "You're so right, Errol."

He bit his lip, waved his arm through the air and bowed in mock chivalry like Captain Blood. He was extremely graceful in retreat. But it was Olivia de Havilland whom he truly adored and who evaded him successfully to the end. I really believe he was deeply in love with her. I must say that, on the whole, his average was excellent. He was certainly at the top of his class.

Hollywood men!! For the first time I got to know them better. One might say I dollied in on them for a closer look. It was inevitable. On the set of *The Sisters* I was risking life and limb daily. During the San Francisco earthquake sequence, my director, Anatole Litvak, ordered a button pressed and the ground opened beneath me and walls came tumbling down around me. If I had been a fraction of an inch off my position, that would have been that. As it was, a splinter from a crystal chandelier flew in my eye.

Bobby, my watchdog, who was knitting serenely in a corner of the set, now jumped up, ran to me and screamed, "Tola Litvak! You are a son..."

He nonetheless went on relentlessly in what seemed to be a subconscious desire to eradicate me once and for all. He probably saved the studio thirty-five dollars a day for a double. I was much too proud to show my terror and give him the satisfaction of calling me a coward. While I managed to avoid the crevasses on the set, I became involved in a far more catastrophic relationship with the prototype of the Hollywood male.

He was extremely attractive and one of the wealthiest men in the West—or East for that matter. I met him, characteristically, while working. My energies knew no bounds and I became more and more interested in civic causes, the first of which was The Tailwaggers. It was an organization that cared for abandoned and lost dogs. Its English progenitor had been started by the Duke of Windsor—now married to the lady at King's Bench.

A lifelong dog lover, I became president of the group and during my tenure of office we trained dogs for the blind. The work became infinitely satisfying and accomplished a twofold purpose. In order to raise money, Bobby helped me arrange for a dinner party at the Beverly Hills Hotel, to which the movie colony responded generously. At this affair I met the gentleman in question. His influence and cooperation were a great help to me, but this interest proved to be directed toward me rather than the case at hand.

It is important to note here that I had met at this time another man who I now know was the only man in my life. The only man I ever met whom I could respect in every way. However, his strength, his brilliance, were such that I felt endangered. I was afraid his domination would affect my career. I genuinely fell in love with this titan who shattered every preconceived notion—every single dream. He was capable of taking complete charge and I was petrified. The relationship was tempestuous to the point of madness and I resisted the loss of my sovereignty to the end. This was a man who would have run my life from sunrise to sunset. The temptation was enormous. Ruth Elizabeth was living in a fool's paradise. It was true I felt like a woman for the first time. It was true that cameramen and still photographers at the studio told me that my face had changed. "You must be in love, Bette. The camera never lies. You're beautiful." It was true all right. All the banalities became sweetly true. "A simpering, whimpering child again." That Lorenz Hart!

My one-tracked mind ruled me! My career! What would happen to it? Ruth Elizabeth had a field day. She was the dark horse; as for me, I ran like a buck steer! The man of my life married another. Afterwards I was told, characteristically, that Tuesdays would be "our day" (just like that, he said so!) Tuesdays! They weren't for me *or* Ruth Elizabeth!

Back of my restlessness, my quest for love and romance, even beneath my growing disenchantment with the male per se, there was always my work. The rigid Yankee spine that any anthropologist would recognize as the old species, Betteus Davisus, she wolf—habitat northeast coast of United States to southern clime of Pacific Ocean—noted for polygamous quest of perfect mate and ferocious independence. Belongs to no pack, condemned by duality to eternal solitude.

I started work shortly after Ham divorced me on what, in my opinion, turned out to be my favorite and the public's favorite part I have ever played. Judith Traherne in *Dark Victory*. I had begged, cajoled, peddled for months this story to every producer at Warners. David Lewis shared my enthusiasm. We enlisted the interest of Edmund Goulding, one of the few all-time great directors of Hollywood, and among the three of us we got Mr. Warner to buy the property. The day we started shooting the film, Mr. Warner said, "Who is going to want to see a picture about a girl who dies? But it is a great part and I'm happy you are having a chance to play her." Thank heavens, millions of people came and watched Judith Traherne die. I'm sure Mr. Warner was glad he was wrong.

I was truly upset, due to the divorce, during the filming of *Dark Victory*. So upset was I that after the first week I went to Mr. Wallis and offered to give up the part. I couldn't bear not to do justice to Judith. He had seen a week of my work on the screen. He said, "Stay upset."

Judith Traherne was a wealthy society girl who is told by a doctor, with whom she eventually falls in love—played by George Brent—that she is dying of a brain tumor. Eschewing self-pity, she puts her house in order and the magnificent manner in which she dies is their victory.

At the end of the story, Judith is blind. She had been warned that this symptom is terminal. She knows that death is almost immediate. In the paradise of a perfect marriage to her doctor, she has come to know, at last, mature love and a genuine life. Both know she is going to die although the nature of her disease is such that she will seem perfectly normal until the last moments. As she and her husband are about to leave Vermont, where they live, for a medical convention in New York—a convention very important to her husband's future—Judith, while planting bulbs in the garden with her best friend, beautifully played by Geraldine Fitzgerald, comments that the sun has gone under a cloud. She then becomes aware that her hand is hot with sunlight. She now knows that she is going blind— and that means her death is near. Being sure her husband does not know this, with some convincing excuse she sends him off to his triumph without a "good-by forever" to him, and with all the courage in the world dies alone, with only her dogs and the housekeeper in the house. She sends her best friend away. She wants to prove she can do it alone. Judith's strength and courage affected me very personally. My own recent loss of my husband—plus the bravery of the character I was playing— threatened to drown Judy in sentimentality. My empathy for

Judy was overwhelming. This compassion could be no part of the characterization. Judith did not know what self-pity was. It was Ruth Elizabeth, damn her. She was calling the shots.

When my energies are momentarily depleted, my docility, Ruthie contended, was refreshing. This was a most vulnerable period of my life and I was a doll. George Brent was by now a free agent. Miss Chatterton had divorced him. It was inevitable from our first meeting through the seven films we had made together, that we would one day have a romance. Often the identity of the characters actors are playing are transposed into our real-life relationship. The doctor's sympathy and love for Judith, plus her dependence on him, influenced, I think, both of us. Plus the fact that in my book, George will always be one of the truly attractive men I have ever known.

Judith won me another nomination for the Academy Award. This time, I was pitted against Vivien Leigh's Scarlett O'Hara in *Gone With the Wind*.

I received countless prizes for *Dark Victory* and critics' awards all over the country. A poll of the press called my performance the most outstanding of the year; but I knew I would not receive the Oscar. *Gone With the Wind* had been released and was the sensation everyone knew it would be. A fine motion picture, its performances were outstanding. It was going to cop every prize and I had been around long enough to know. So be it.

I was now working on *Juarez*; and the night of the Award dinner, I was dead tired. Up at dawn, I had been at the studio for the unusual makeup at six. After dinner, knowing who the winner would be, I decided to go home without waiting for the presentation of the awards. Ruthie said, "Bette! Are you mad? Everyone will think you are a bad loser!"

Ruthie always worried about what other people would think. I seldom could be bothered. But I followed her advice—I stayed. I sat there until two o'clock in the morning, at which point everyone was "surprised" and delighted that GWTW ran away with almost everything. Robert Donat as Mr. Chips won the Oscar for the best actor. The best actress was Vivien Leigh.

I joined in the applause that she so well deserved, then I turned bleary-eyed to Ruthie and said, "We're going home now."

I had only three hours sleep that night, but my sacrifice went for nil. Nothing stops Hollywood from talking when it wants to. Staying had not changed a thing. "Did you see Davis leave in a huff when she lost?" "Davis walked out in a rage!" There is nothing anyone can do to avoid the preconceived and desired reactions of Hollywood.

In the year 1939, I secured my career and my stardom forever. I made five pictures in twelve months and every one of them was successful. In quick succession, starting with *The Sisters* and *Dark Victory*, there were *Juarez* with Paul Muni and Brian Aherne; *The Old Maid* with Miriam Hopkins; and *The Private Lives of Elizabeth and Essex* with Errol Flynn. I weighed eighty pounds when I discarded Bess's ruff and hoop for the last time. I was really exhausted. I knew I must take a holiday and recharge the battery.

Warners, pleased by the gold coming in from all of these pictures, decided to give me a vacation. I think they wanted one themselves. Hurricane Bette herded the people into their theatres and brought showers of green stuff, but she howled and wrought havoc as well. I will never deny that I was on occasion insufferably rude and ill-mannered in the cultivation and preservation of my career. I had no time for pleasantries. I said what was on my mind and it wasn't always printable. It was the year of the push not the free sail. Each picture presented a problem or bred one.

Juarez, for instance, was peculiarly constructed. The antagonists never meet. The part of the film in which Brian Aherne and I appeared as Maximilian and Carlotta was shot and assembled before Mr. Muni as Juarez ever stepped before a camera. He saw our part of the picture in the projection room and his wife, Bella, observed that it was a "complete picture without ever seeing Juarez." It was true. Mr. Muni brought with him fifty additional pages of script that he wanted added to his part. He was that powerful and the studio allowed it.

The length of any picture must be limited. When the Juarez part of the film was finished, we were in trouble lengthwise. Something had to go. Brian's and my part of the film received the cuts. Although it was a good motion picture, the film, before cutting destroyed it in the abattoir, was a great one. Mr. Muni's seniority proved our downfall.

Paul was a most attractive man, I thought. Evidently he did not think so and usually retreated behind a beard. Transference

is one thing, but I sincerely believe the audience wants to
become familiar with certain physical attributes that are ever
present in each performance. Mr. Muni seemed intent on sub-
merging himself so completely that he disappeared. His wife
used to say, ''I've lived with more men than any other
woman.'' There is no question that his technique as an actor
was superb. But for me, beneath the exquisite petit point of
details, the loss of his own sovereignity worked conversely to
rob some of his characterization of blood. It is a criticism that
I aim at the naturalist actors. Paul's intellect was always at
work. He fought the good fight in his own terms and added
greatly to the dignity and respectability of Hollywood. Claude
Rains, who played Napoleon III in *Juarez*, was also a contributor to the dignity of Hollywood.

Juarez was the first time I had ever met Claude or worked
with him. This was the third time I was in awe of an actor. I
was again thrown for a loop. By this time, it must be clear that
I was hardly a meek and obscure young actress. Still he scared
the life out of me. When he looked at me during our scene as
Napoleon would look at Carlotta, with loathing, I thought he
Claude Rains held loathing of me Bette Davis as a performer!
We have laughed about it many times since. Claude and I made
four pictures together in the process of which I am proud to
say he considers me a friend.

The Old Maid, an adaptation of Zoë Akins' play based on
Edith Wharton's novel, in which Judith Anderson and Helen
Mencken appeared at the Empire Theatre, presented an entirely
different problem. For the first time since Rochester, I worked
with Miriam Hopkins, who was cast as the sister who takes
and brings up my illegitimate baby as her own while I, the Old
Maid, am relegated to the role of ''Aunt'' Charlotte. I was
never mad about the part. The finished picture proved to be
most popular.

Miriam is a perfectly charming woman socially. Working
with her is another story. On our first day of shooting, for
instance, she arrived on the set wearing a complete replica of
one of my *Jezebel* costumes. It was obvious she wanted me to
blow my stack at this. I completely ignored the whole thing.
Ensuing events prove she wanted even more to be in my shoes
than in my dress.

Miriam used and, I must give her credit, knew every trick

in the book. I became fascinated watching them appear one by one. A good actress, perfectly suited to the role; it all was a mystery to me. Keeping my temper took its toll. I went home every night and screamed at everybody.

In the first place, she never looked at me. When she was supposed to be listening to me, her eyes would wander off into some world in which she was the sweetest of them all. Her restless little spirit was impatiently awaiting her next line, her golden curls quivering with expectancy.

Once, in a two-shot, favoring both of us, her attempts to upstage me almost collapsed the couch we were sitting on. She kept inching her way toward the back of the couch so that I would have to turn away from the camera in order to look at her. If her back had had a buzz saw that allowed her retreat beyond it, I wouldn't have been in the least surprised.

Miriam was her own worst enemy. I usually had better things to do than waste my energies on invective and cat fights. When I first met Tallulah Bankhead, she said, "So you're the woman who does all of my parts on the screen! And I do them so much better." "I agree with you, Miss Bankhead," I replied.

One day, Laura Hope Crewes appeared on the set of *The Man Who Came to Dinner*. Past all power and desire to slap ingenues, she was now coaching them in speech and accepting small parts in films. Here was another moment of possible revenge. I think she fully expected most anything from me. I had dreamed of a reversal of positions for many years.

It never stopped shocking me that great theatre names whose heights once seemed so inaccessible were reduced to playing bits on the screen. I was having my day as they had had theirs, but such an encounter would always make me feel uncomfortable. They were still as gifted, still as wonderful to me, and I have never not treated my seniors with the respect they deserved. Times have changed. This is now what happens to me! Not bits *yet*. But who knows?

I decided on my course of action. I welcomed Miss Crewes warmly and with great deference. "It's been such a long time, Miss Crewes. How wonderful to be working together again."

No doubt she would have preferred not being robbed of an ex post facto justification of her high-handedness. But I couldn't have been dreamier. This, I decided, was truly the greatest punishment of all. Turning the other cheek!

When the picture was over, Miss Crewes came to my dressing room. She handed me a box—and was gone.

I opened it and inside was the most beautiful watch—pearls and diamonds on the back—that I have ever seen. This was her belated apology. She died six months later. It is one of my truly cherished possessions.

The next film Miriam and I made together was *Old Acquaintance*. We were always old somehow; everything but old friends.

Again I played the heroine and Miriam the bitch. Quite a reversal for me—but if you play the heroine you have to play it. I truly feel back of all Miriam's unhappiness and rivalry with me was this one fact. She wanted to be loved too, as a heroine. Came the scene in the script when I slap her—that's what the script said. I might add, the rafters above the stage were full of excited spectators. It was rather like a prizefight ring below. We rehearsed this scene for hours—not only her eyes were wandering but so was her body, to every corner of the stage.

I finally said, "Miriam! If I have to sit on top of the piano to look into your face for this speech, I will." The slap followed the speech and I had to be near her.

Her look of innocence and seeming lack of comprehension was infuriating, but stand still she did—and take the slap she did. To be sure, her eyes filled with tears of self-pity—but the camera couldn't see it. It was on her back!

The next day, she arrived on the set very late. I had been waiting for hours. In all contrition she said upon her arrival, "Ahm sooo sahry—everybody, but ah've bin fleuin' so terribly."

I could have *thrown* her off the roof for that one. Yes, Miriam is a caution; but good actress she is.

Another dream of mine now came true. Mr. Wallis bought the Maxwell Anderson play *Elizabeth and Essex*. I finally was to play Elizabeth—and to me the only fly in the ointment was the casting of Errol Flynn as Essex. He wasn't an experienced enough actor to cope with the complicated blank verse the play had been written in. There was only one Essex I wanted. I fought to get him as much as Garbo had fought against him some years before when she insisted on John Gilbert for her *Queen Christina*.

Laurence Olivier was in Hollywood with Miss Leigh. He was working with Willie Wyler in *Wuthering Heights*, then in Alfred Hitchcock's *Rebecca*, and after that in Aldous Huxley's superbly literate adaptation of *Pride and Prejudice*. He was perfect for the part of Essex. He *was* Essex—arrogant, beautiful, virile and talented. In all our scenes I dreamed he was playing Essex.

I was secretly a bit tentative about playing Elizabeth at this time. I was only thirty years old. Elizabeth was sixty. I studied the Holbein portrait of her and was not a little amazed at the resemblance between us. My costumes were designed by Orry-Kelly. My first round in my latest match had to do with costumes. It has always been essential that I dress a part authentically, particularly in the case of a historical character. My cry for the genuine. The director insisted that the hoops and ruffs be scaled down for fear they would be too wide in the camera. Mr. Wallis will discover for the first time, if he reads this, that Orry made two complete sets of costumes for Elizabeth. The first, according to director's order, the second according to the historical records. I tested in the first wardrobe and played the picture in the second. Tricky is a determined female.

I had never been photographed in color before. My pictures brought the public in without the added expense. Too, I have always thought color robs an emotional story of power and most of my work was of an emotional nature. History, however, is usually enhanced by color. Particularly Elizabeth—her red hair, her fascinating clothes—everything about her life was colorful.

Elizabeth was my tankard of tea. Charles Laughton visited our set one day. Henry VIII in person.

In my full costume and balding head, I swept toward him swishing my *huge* hoop.

"Hi, Pop," I shouted irreverently.

"Ah! It's my favorite daughter!"

Marvelous Charles Laughton. I will never forget his Henry. I confessed to him that day I felt I had a nerve to be trying to play this part.

"Never stop daring to hang yourself, Bette!"

This became, from that day on, a credo of mine. An artist must be willing always to take the big gamble. Without it, he can't plunge to the depths; but he can never reach any heights either. Nowadays everybody is playing it safe. No one dares to go out on a limb. From the secretary with Blue Cross to the world figure with his eye glued to the future history books, everyone is playing Follow-the-Leader on his march to security.

The actor—classically the carefree itinerant, the minstrel—now aches for solvency above all else. The successful actor today is a corporation. He is in lumber, real estate, oil, cattle. There is no criticism in terms of investment; but the Buck has become the actor's God. His orthodoxy is such that there must not be any other God before it. I wanted security also. But not to the exclusion of artistic integrity.

Sarah Bernhardt used to demand her weekly take in solid tender. No green paper for Madame. She had moneybags waiting to fill with gold pieces whose weight and indisputable value proved a comfort to her. But she earned it acting. She earned it the hard way. She could have, in her prime, lain about nibbling *marrons glacés* and become far richer through calculated romance. But she was an actress! To survive and to prosper doing what one wants is the dreamiest of lives. To fulfill a dream, to be allowed to sweat over lonely labor, to be given the chance to create, is the meat and potatoes of life. The money is the gravy. As everyone else, I love to dunk my crust in it. But alone, it is not a diet designed to keep body and soul together.

CHAPTER

14

The entire generation of movie people with whom I worked and played yielded a tiny list of artists who had integrity, the will for holy battle and the eventual triumph of major contribution to the medium which stupidly resisted its own enrichment. I can just about name them on two hands. James Cagney, Paul Muni, Spencer Tracy, Charles Laughton, Charles Boyer, John Ford, Irving Thalberg, Heinz Blanke, my producer at Warners, John Huston, Frank Capra and Willie Wyler. The producers with the executive genius to understand the need of hiring good people at any cost were Sam Goldwyn and Harry Cohn. Katharine Hepburn and Margaret Sullavan and Olivia de Havilland were fighters for integrity also.

Most of Hollywood's glamour boys spent their lives ensuring their place in the safety of the producers' arms and the hearts of the public. The masculine ego, outsized at birth, takes on gargantuan proportions in the actor. As his box-office power grows, his self-adoration has all the obscenity of a Krafft-Ebing fetish. He is so taken with himself that there really isn't room for a third part.

His world is a small one bound on the north by his own Polaris, on the south by his own twinkling toes. His longitude can be measured by the distance between his reach and his grasp. If he likes women at all he must be careful. He is, in all fairness, a target for every troublemaker alive. The most harmless flirtation holds the promise of scandal. One or two of the more enterprising males have built their reputations on satyrism and they have their own set of problems; but they are different. Most of the men, especially in the 30's and 40's, had stricter moral clauses in their contracts and found it difficult to play around. The amount of money forced out of the town's gentlemen for indiscretions has always been staggering. Whether or not the public would necessarily boycott the typical American lad who was simply caught acting like one is neither here nor there. The studio officials sincerely believe they would. Hence, the restrictions were great. The Hollywood male had his choice of female limited.

It eventually boiled down to the women in his profession or the local debutantes. Pasadena proved an excellent showcase. There were always countless pretty girls with "nice backgrounds" and low striking power. It always amused me. As far as Hollywood was concerned, a debutante was evidently a girl who owned an evening wrap and knew who her father was. But there was always the danger that she was a hysterical fan who would drive him mad. A man was far less fortunate than a woman in this department. Male fans are in much better control of themselves. At any rate, the actor's understandable fears and working hours usually drove the actor to intramural romance. Like a headwaiter he gravitated to the biggest names. Actors and actresses! All-star casts assembled for no one's benefit. The competition was absurd and the amount of flunkies in the no man's land between them absolutely forbidding.

Most of the male stars, like kings, demanded partners of equal rank. It was safer and their status was guaranteed. Arrival at a premiere with a beautiful and perfectly groomed Queen of Films was essential to their notion of protocol. And beneath the medals and epaulettes and plumed helmets, the men who *were* men weren't either. They were so busy parading their virility onscreen and in lobbies that they folded up like gilt party chairs only brought out for special occasions.

Their values shocked me. Their intellects evaded me. For all their cynicism, expediency and patina, they were the most provincial of all Americans. There wasn't a fistful I could even have a conversation with, and with the solitary exception of the powerhouse who would have threatened my career, not one

could I look up to in respect. They were on the whole a lot of
weak sisters who were attracted to sovereignty and were frightened by it. Like the rock 'n' roll music and Coca-Cola one
now finds in Sorrento, Hollywood seems to have exported its
handsomely packaged impotence. *O tempus, O mores*—oh
men, oh women. Where have they both gone? Is it truly the
end of the West? Where are the men who are stronger than
women? I lost one Ham and was presented with a townful. It
has been said that an actor is something less than a man, an
actress more than a woman. It should come out even. It doesn't.

Their vanity is effete, their self-involvement intellectually
limiting and their life's work, to the best of them, ignoble. I
have never known the great actor who wasn't aware of this and
didn't plan eventually to direct, or produce. If he has no such
dream, he is usually bitter, ungratified and eventually alcoholic.

There are and always have been a few whose gift is so great
and whose perspective so blessed that their virility is preserved.
But the majority of actors strut about like the cocks of the walk
they wish they were. I have always found it extremely difficult
to find a man attractive when he's wearing curlers in his hair.
I have always found it impossible to respect a man when he is
patting his throat. I find it impossible to be excited by a man
who becomes hysterical because his better profile has been
sacrificed to the advantage of a scene. The glamour boys have,
and always will, bore me.

I was fortunate not to have to work with many. My films—
once I reached my peak—brought the public in without a co-
star. Now, all Hollywood, London and Rome are enlisted for
each film to drag the customers from their TV sets.

In *Juarez*, the authenticity of décor and costuming was unarguable. Brian Aherne looked absolutely beautiful in the blond
beard that was a replica of the Emperor Maximilian's. He was
truly a vision. I thought I was being flattering.

"Brian, you should always wear a beard."

His eyes narrowed and he looked down from his six feet
four with naked hatred. "And *you*, Bette, should always wear
a black wig!"

No one but an actor could be so absurd. They're almost all
of them absurd. A fine actor lay dying at the end of a movie
I was in. I kneeled at his side bereaved. I shall never forget
the actor's plaintive comment to the director—

"Don't you think Bette is crying a little too much?"

A less heartfelt reaction to his death would actually have weakened his *own* characterization. The death scene is always a giveaway. I was speechless when another actor watched himself expire with a little hand-mirror under the sheet of the bed on which he was lying.

The glamour boys do their best to avoid roles that somehow will blur the image they have created in the public mind. It is astonishing. For some, the slightest moral lapse, the faintest suggestion of vulnerability or softness, make scriptwriters of them all. These are the personalities and not the actors. If they had their way, Hamlet would have made up his mind and Mercutio would simply have told the nurse it was twelve o'clock.

The dullness of these stalwart mannikins is almost surpassed by their hypocrisy. Their purity and virility have always been a fiction. Not a real ego amongst them—but vanity! Vanity! All was vanity.

Robert Montgomery and I made one picture together and it might just as well have been a ballet. An excellent actor who needn't have bothered embroiled me in a fascinating tangle of mechanics.

In motion pictures, a scene is played in medium shot with the two actors working together. After it is photographed, the cameras are set up again and the exact scene is repeated at a different vantage point. Obviously the expressions and gestures must match perfectly so that the various angles, pieced together, give the impression of peripheral vision. This process may be repeated often and always includes extreme close-ups of each actor, whose intimate, full-screen reaction adds greatly to the dynamics of a scene.

Now, each actor plays his original scene separately—in close-up exactly as he played it in two; and from this scene, the director chooses those reaction shots he wants. By tradition, the female star does her close-up scene first. It is shot directly on her face while the co-star's voice and face are offstage. When this is completed, the gentleman repeats his performance under the same conditions. Each must obviously match the original take perfectly so that the director may choose at random those desired reactions that he will blend in the final mosaic.

Mr. Montgomery, resenting, I presume, my role of a woman

in charge, purposely added elements to his close-up performance that did not exist in the original scene. By reacting to things I never did, he invalidated my close-ups, making them worthless. It was upstaging in its most diabolical form. Needless to say, it was thoroughly unprofessional as well.

I probably had less close-ups as a star than any other actress. I believed that there were emotions too great not to use full body. I believed—as onstage—that one acts with the complete body. One's back can describe an emotion. But this situation was different. The interspersed close-up does add power to a performance. The audience needs and wants the occasional intimacy.

Mr. Montgomery was ostensibly the great gentleman and very old-school tie about all these shenanigans; and so I observed the ground rules and fought him on his own terms with overwhelming graciousness. I simply relinquished my right as a female star. I let him do his close-ups first.

The competition with a male star is unbelievable. You are under attack at all times. When I made *The Scapegoat* with Alec Guinness, he cut my part into such shreds that my appearance in the final product made no sense at all. This is an actor who plays by himself, unto himself. In this particular picture he played a dual role, so at least he was able to play with himself.

It is foolish of the actress to cling to youth. But somehow an actor, damn him, can be attractive at any age without cosmetic aid. A woman—certainly an actress—clings to those things which first made her desirable. It is only when she insists on remaining eighteen that she becomes a bore.

The male star demands children as mates and as co-stars. They see themselves as permanently appealing and don't think it at all strange that they are making love to actresses who could be their granddaughters. The old boys are still at it. We old girls still are too!

I have always felt Hollywood very instrumental in America's being so wildly youth conscious. We are the laughingstock of Europeans on this score, as a matter of fact. It does become contagious—this wishing to look years younger. All the pulling and taping and scraping has produced some incredible results. One is apt to look a little like a petrified Japanese beauty, but younger to be sure.

I tried it two years ago. Perc Westmore, the dean of the Hollywood makeup artists—one of my truly great friends and the man who made me up at Warners for years—taped my face. I wanted to see what I would look like. When he was through, I was enchanted—a little expressionless but smooth as a baby. I was mesmerized. I was lovely. I rushed home feeling sure Gary would look at me in amazement and wonder what miracle had happened. Quite the reverse. He looked up from the script he was reading and said, ''What in the hell happened to you—you look awful.'' I laughed so hard that the tapes on one side of my face collapsed. I then, of course, looked grotesque. Gary then expired with laughter. That was my last attempt to put back the clock. There is no use trying to look like a college girl again. We are all postgraduates. Somehow facing the fact and looking one's age makes one actually look younger, I keep telling myself.

CHAPTER
15

At the finish of *Elizabeth and Essex*, I was worn out, almost at the breaking point. Sweet as George Brent was, he was Hollywood. Our secretaries were so busy courting each other for us that it was inevitable that they would take over our romance. I longed for my roots. I picked up and went home again like Thomas Wolfe. I couldn't either; but I tried.

I faced east and made my hegira to Lowell, Newton, Boston, Cushing, everywhere. I appeared like a ghost in all my old haunts—Ogunquit, Peterboro, Ocean Park. Nothing had changed and everything was different. I was now more tired than ever, wretched with a homesickness that only became more severe with my return to each place.

I sat in melancholy for days, watching the waves beat on the rockbound coast. What punishment these rocks take! They call me a rock. Ha! What strength, what rock, endures forever? This too will become sand, I thought. What is sand but granulated stone? And before the soft anonymity of sand, before the refinement, pieces are chipped away, jagged edges appear. What's happening to me? My marriage was a mistake. A flying horse and a surefooted burro. I want to fly alone—to be free; but I don't want to be free. I'm lonely. Why couldn't I have allowed Ham to take me over completely? I hate this life I've been thrown into. Why can't I have a husband, a man who will not be destroyed by my success? Why can't I have what every one of these fishermen's wives has? I don't want to end up alone at fifty—unsafe, desperate, pitiable—without someone who needs me.

The ocean kept crashing against the land. Summer had passed into fall and I didn't want to budge. The chill air slapped me across the cheek and all the golds and reds of a New England autumn hypnotized me. I sat like a masthead, staring out to sea. Sleepless I watched the morning come and I thought of a canvas by Juan Gris I had seen somewhere. Gray and pink boxes—dawn. It was a haunting picture and terribly sad. He must have found it painful to face a new day. The sky broke into little boxes as I thought of it. It was painful for me to face a new day.

I traveled up the coast and ended up at Peckett's Inn on Sugar Hill in New Hampshire. I needed a longer rest than I'd thought; and the studio was eager for me to regain my strength.

At this point, they would have done anything for me. Along with Eleanor Roosevelt and Anne O'Hare McCormick, I was chosen by Durward Hughes of the *American Dictionary* as one of the world's outstanding women. Awards were flowing in from everywhere. It was difficult for me to reconcile my present mood with the honors I was receiving from countless countries in both hemispheres.

"Tiger Lady" had become "Duse of the Dunes" and "Popeye The Magnificent." But these epithets were nothing to that one given me by the exhibitors, the banks and the press. It was now decided that I was the "Fourth Warner Brother." It had come to that. I was just as shocked by our consanguinity as they; but I was bringing home the bacon and was now a respected member of the family.

The motion picture industry was built on the theory that one made cheap little pictures and great big profits. It is the base of all economy that one buys low and sells high. But there are all sorts of businesses. There's Woolworth for instance and there's Cartier. Both do very well! I saw no reason why a good product couldn't also make money, and besides I never could reconcile myself to the fact that I was in a business at all. I am bored unto death with the usual evaluation of the public's mentality. The idiots who cavil to the fictional mob simply project their own limitations. Once in stride, every one of my films tried to be literate, intelligent and tasteful; and for a very long period I brought more people into theatres than all the sexpots put together. It confused them.

Hal Wallis actually looked me straight in the eye one day and said with absolute candor, "Personally, I can't stand the kind of picture you make; but as long as you sell them, we'll make them."

That was the head of production of Warner Brothers Studio—Hal Wallis! Who, amongst other talents, decreed milady's fashions. He adored the Dobbs fedoras his wife, Louise Fazenda, wore, and I kept finding them topping all of Orry-Kelly's wardrobes. Orry knew how to dress ladies as well as glamour queens. Like Edith Head, he understood that his creations were meant to enhance the actress, not be the star of the production. He designed the outfits; but Mr. Wallis designed the hats, and always the same one. I was often in the front office—if not corporally—in spirit. I subscribed to *Vogue* magazine in his name. The first of each month *Vogue* would arrive in Hal's mail. I hoped he would study the current trend in hats! I think he forgave me eventually.

I almost missed the daily madness as I vacationed on Sugar Hill. Almost! It was such beautiful country and I had met someone who did nothing to hasten my return. Arthur Farnsworth was the assistant manager of Peckett's Inn. He was definitely suited to this job with his charm and his breeding. He was a New Englander by birth. The Farnsworths were an old coast family.

I had been so tense, so exhausted, so vexed, that when I found a moment of serenity I couldn't bring myself to shatter it. I so adored Sugar Hill that I bought one hundred and fifty acres of rocky, rolling land and planned to build a house there. It would be my haven. Sugar Hill would be the place I would always return to when exhausted from Hollywood—my favorite New England! The only part of the world that has been home to me. It was here that I came out of my blue funk—here that I felt happy for the first time in years. New Hampshire and Farney were a tonic for me. I kept extending this rare vacation, hating to leave.

Bobby gave birth to a baby girl and though I lived on the phone until I knew all was well, yet I never forgave myself for not going to California to be with her. Shortly after the birth of her daughter, Bobby had another breakdown. My guilts became a deadweight. I felt I had let her down.

Her husband, Bob Pelgram, and her baby, Fay, stayed with me at Riverbottom, my California home, until Bobby was well again. Farney drove to California that year with my cousin Gordon—Uncle Paul's son—and my friend Robin. Robin stayed on with me as friend and secretary for some time after that. Farney remained a few weeks and then returned to his job at Peckett's, and I started working on *All This and Heaven Too*. There were times when my titles were prophetic.

I had Charles Boyer as my co-star, and Anatole Litvak again as my director. But there were no earthquakes, holocausts or floods this time in which he could torture me. It was the script that was my nemesis. If I'd heard Charles say "Please, ma-demoiselle" or myself answer "Oui, Monsieur le Duc" once more I would have jumped out of my skin. Rachel Field had one belief about her great-aunt. I, in reading the Marquis de Sade's book on the same subject, felt that the governess and the Duc de Preslin must have been lovers. It was impossible for me to believe that they were not. Also, the casting of Barbara O'Neill, an extremely handsome woman, didn't help matters. As she was conceived for the film, the Duc's revulsion with her was not convincing. His wife was in actuality a sloven and a horror with none of the exterior beauty that was Miss O'Neill's in this film. An excellent actress, it was not her fault that she was not allowed to look the way she should. It was the director's fault. It was also par for the course when trans-ferring a character from a book to the screen. No matter what, look divine!

Boyer was a joy to work with. Intelligent and professional to the core—a truly fine actor! Tola planned every move be-forehand and the camera was his God. I thought of Willie Wyler who would get an inspiration and, on being informed that the camera was already in position, shout, "To hell with the cam-era. It's the slave, not me!" Tola had it all on paper. His method of directing was never to my taste. There was not the spontaneity or flexibility I found in Wyler.

As long as I live I will never forget the little boy in *All This and Heaven Too*. Little Richard was a beautiful child. Pale and sad with great dark eyes bordered in shadows, he was exquisite. That piqued little face topped by curly black hair was the embodiment of pathetic nonage. A face out of *Le Maternel*, it was designed to break your heart. He played neurotic, sickly types. He was about six or seven at the time.

Richard was supposed to cry in a particular scene and the poor child was having a hard time. Tola marched up to him and growled, "If you do not cry I am going to leave you here on the stage—*all* alone—*all* night." It was the cruelest bit of expediency I ever heard. He cried—but then was so terrified he couldn't stop. Long after the scene was finished, little Richard was still crying his eyes out.

But I could not really hold Tola responsible. The child had been sacrificed and thrown into the lion's den by others, nearer and dearer. His family were the culprits. He made more money with his pale neurotic appearance.

Since we had many children in the picture, I gave a large party on the last day of shooting. The restaurant was a fairyland of ice cream, cake and soda pop. The world of children captivates me and we were all having a wild time until I tried to find my little Richard. He was nowhere in sight. Getting his address, I drove to his house where, on a sunny day, I found him indoors in order to preserve his commercial pallor. I was furious and he was soon in the car and at the party. He had a ball!

Warners gave *All This and Heaven Too* a lavish premiere at the Cathay Circle Theatre. The last premiere I had attended was *Seed* at the same theatre. There's no question that the Hollywood premiere, so often satirized, is an exciting affair. If you are in the picture being premiered, it is difficult not to feel like a queen. Certainly it wasn't difficult for Ruthie to be the Dowager Empress. We giggled quietly at the change that had come over our lives since our arrival in Hollywood seven years before. Success is a joy for many reasons. Aside from the achievement itself, there is the opportunity to meet the great of the world. Doors open.

It is first class all the way. No more upper berths, sleazy curtains, dependence on others. No more of the indignities of impoverished anonymity. On the other hand I felt I was personally the same person I had always been. Success didn't mean that I had to lease Xanadu or entertain like William Randolph Hearst. I found the pomp and circumstance of some of my colleagues unsuitable. Their homes were mammoth sets for entertaining. I always wondered how they felt on those rare occasions when they were home alone. I would have felt like a lost lamb in a jungle!

Hollywood's social whirl is, for the most part, pretentious and politic. There were a few who gathered fascinating people together at a well-appointed board groaning under excellent food and wine. Certainly Basil Rathbone's wife, Ouida, was a magnificent hostess as was Joseph Cotten's wife, Lenore. The David Selznicks and the Jules Steins also entertained brilliantly. But most of Hollywood who decorated their homes like Scottish shooting boxes and sent the ladies off to the powder room while the gentlemen stayed at the table sipping brandy didn't know a credenza from an arpeggio.

And who wanted to be shipped off with the ladies anyway? I would have smoked a cigar to remain. A woman's world is not my cup of tea! At home, I would talk of the fall of the Lowlands and Paris; and Ruthie would insist that the chintz on the bedroom chair needed some doing. That's why I've always needed a man around the house.

There was more good acting at Hollywood parties than ever appeared on the screen. I was never equal to it. Small dinner parties, sitting around and exchanging ideas, is my most fun socially. Even during all the Hollywood years, I lived very casually. I also was too busy working to have much time for the social whirl.

Of course, I lived well and had servants. But this did not mean I didn't always contribute to the running of the house myself. If I have a hobby, my home has always been it. I remember being seen by fans putting out my garbage cans at Laguna Beach one day—and asked by one of them if Bette Davis was inside the house. The legend persists. A movie star is not quite a human being. While I deeply appreciate approbation of my work by fans, I always feel inadequate to the awe manifested by some. I want to say, I'm a human being just like you. Is it any wonder that many stars come to believe they are divinities? One night at a dinner party at Dwight Taylor's, he raised his glass in a toast, "To the greatest actress that ever lived." I blushed with self-deprecation as everyone rose. This was too much. It certainly was. My host finished the toast— "To my mother, Laurette!" My acceptance of the compliment was obvious to all present. It was truly my most embarrassing moment.

I adored swimming always, eventually had a pool. But my houses were no more impressive than hundreds here in the East. And always they were English or Colonial. Always it was as much like New England as possible. Four-posters, bull's-eye mirrors, Toby mugs, chintz curtains, fireplaces and everything in its place. San Simeon might have been a palace but there was no soap in the bathroom when I dined there once.

That summer I returned to Sugar Hill and started building the house at Butternut which was to be my favorite home for many years. Farney came to California again with his sister Barbara that next fall and they were my house guests. It was back and forth and I kept refusing his proposals of marriage.

I was not violently in love with Farney. I loved his loving me and our mutual love of the New England way of life was the tie that finally bound. He respected my career and was proud of my work. He was as removed from the theatre as anyone could be and had no interest in competing with me in any way. He was companionable, attractive and a divine host. Plus he was the most beautifully mannered man I've ever known.

Ruthie was cool about our eventual plans to marry. She had me back and I'm afraid didn't want to let me go again. Still, it was difficult to voice any respectable criticism of the Farnsworths in general or Farney in particular. He would someday inherit money, he was from a good family—important to Yankee mothers. I really think Ruthie found it hard not to like him.

Leslie Crosby in *The Letter* was my second chance at a Somerset Maugham character. The director was William Wyler. I was ecstatic at the prospect of being directed by him again. Leslie, after a prolonged clandestine affair that ends with her lover's marriage to a Eurasian, murders him claiming self-defense against the drunken, brutal advances of this "casual acquaintance." The affair is all prior to the film which starts dramatically with the shooting. Leslie's husband and lawyer are horrified by the crime but compassionate. After all, what woman wouldn't defend herself against such a man? The Eurasian widow has a letter of Leslie's to her husband. Through the payment of blackmail and the unhappy loyalty of the lawyer, Leslie is freed legally and even forgiven by her adoring husband, who eventually shares the secret of her guilt.

The husband, played by Herbert Marshall, offers her complete amnesty and she cannot accept it. She rejects this pitiable gift of love and charity with the famous line: "I still love the man I killed." It was such a cruel thing to say to the husband, I felt I could not say it to his face. I couldn't conceive of any woman looking into her husband's eyes and admitting such a thing. I felt it would come out of her unbeknownst to herself, and therefore she would not be looking at him. Willie disagreed with me—most definitely. I walked off the set! Something I had never done in my whole career. I might have been Hollywood's Maria Callas; but Willie Wyler was the male Bette Davis. I could not see it his way, nor he mine. I came back eventually—end result, I did it his way. It played validly, heaven knows, but to this day I think my way was the right way. I lost, but I lost to an artist. *The Letter* was a magnificent picture due to Willie. Again I was fascinated by the spontaneity and mood he created. There was a sultriness to the very air around us. The confrontation scene between Leslie and the Eurasian widow, played by Gale Sondergaard, in which the letter implicating her is bartered for cash, was played against the delicately ominous sound of a Japanese tinkler. Willie wanted silence at the moment the two women faced each other, except for the eerie tinkling in the background.

Yes, I lost a battle, but I lost it to a genius. So many directors were such weak sisters that I would have to take over. Uncreative, unsure of themselves, frightened to fight back, they offered me none of the security that this tyrant did. When working, Willie—like me—could be asked "Whom do you hate today?" There is always something to fight in this most imperfect of worlds. Creation is hell! It's all very well for everybody to adore each other but one inevitably has to take a stand. This inevitably has to make an enemy. There is a love fest that exists on some sets—all sweetness and light and everyone tipping his hat—the ice cream industry! Everything is charming and the picture turns out to be a dud. A good, honest fight never hurt anyone and if it means a better result, so be it. Or if it means a preservation of what is called spontaneity and honesty—go to it.

Being a Jeffersonian democrat, it was only logical that the Queen be constitutionally chosen. It was at this time that I was elected President of the Academy of Motion Pictures Arts and Sciences succeeding Walter Wanger. Having received two of its awards and countless nominations, I never imagined that I would hold its most exalted post. As the only woman so honored, I was frankly proud. But it was just this pride that shortened the tenure of my office. Evidently the position was meant to be a sinecure, on the face of their past experience with me— an unwise assumption.

At the first meeting I presided at as President, I arrived with full knowledge of my rights of office. I had studied the by-laws. It became clear to me that this was a surprise. I was not supposed to preside intelligently. Rather like an heiress at her deceased father's board of directors' meeting, I felt quite capable of holding a gavel.

There was much talk of not holding the Academy Awards dinner this 1941. Though we were weeks from being in it, the war was on and the usual dinner at the Biltmore might seem frivolous in the midst of national austerity.

I had arrived at the meeting intending to submit the proposal that we present the Oscars in a large theatre, charging at least $25 a seat and giving the proceeds to British War Relief. The members of the board were horrified. Such an evening would rob the Academy of all dignity.

I then went on to suggest that Rosalind Russell be the head of the committee running the affair. Mr. Mervyn LeRoy, who had previously been the chairman of Academy evenings, was insulted. Then I proposed that motion picture extras be denied the right to vote, since many of them didn't even speak English, let alone know anything about excellence of performance. A pall fell on the room. At this point Walter Wanger, the former President, wanted to know what I had against the Academy— I had won two Oscars.

All in all it was obvious that I had been put in as President merely as a figurehead. I sent in my resignation a few days later and Darryl Zanuck, who was my sponsor for the presidency, informed me that if I resigned, I would never work in Hollywood again. I took a chance and resigned anyway.

Jean Hersholt was the next President. During his term the Academy took the vote away from the extras—and the Academy dinner became a thing of the past. They have held the event in theatres ever since.

Since I spent my days in battle, directly after I finished *The Great Lie* I created a peaceful life for myself at home. Farney and I were married New Year's Eve of 1941 at Justin Dart's ranch in Rimrock, Arizona. Jane Bryan was now Mrs. Justin Dart. She had given up her career for marriage. I was still certain that I could have both.

Both in Hollywood and the now finished Butternut, Farney was a tremendous contributor to our home. His graciousness and energy, his omnipresence, were all a delight. Farney had been a flyer for many years. His knowledge of aviation won him a job with Minneapolis Honeywell Co., which had just invented a defroster for the wings of planes. Farney was in charge of the Disney training films of Minneapolis Honeywell made for the Air Force. His interest in his work was gratifying and his *laissez faire* concerning my working hours and my outside interests a marvelous change from my former marriage.

Ham, along with millions of others about this time, was drafted into the Army and came to the house to say good-bye. Completely irrationally, I was still fond of him. Life does such terrible things to people. How does one tell her children that men and women are not their superiors; that they are children too, grown big, grown desperate, grown dangerous but still as tender, still as vulnerable—strangled by their own dreams?

I told him to come back safely, to try and find someone who would make him happy. Farney and I were happy. Our light was a low one but steady. He didn't have an ounce of jealousy. He never questioned me about anything I did. He let me run my own life.

I was now on my first loan-out since *Bondage*. The same Sam Goldwyn who, ten years before, had wailed at the sight of my test and refused to hire me at three hundred a week, now paid me three hundred and eighty-five thousand dollars to star in Lillian Hellman's *The Little Foxes*. Like Harry Cohn at Columbia, Mr. Goldwyn had always been willing to pay for the artists he wanted. Mr. Warner, on my steely request, gave me Warners' share of the deal. Gregg Toland was the cameraman and Mr. Wyler was again my director. This was the first time we were not in accord with the concept of the character I played.

We fought bitterly. I had been forced to see Tallulah Bankhead's performance. I had not wanted to. A great admirer of hers, I wanted in no way to be influenced by her work. It was Willie's intention that I give a different interpretation of the part. I insisted that Tallulah had played it the only way it could be played. Miss Hellman's Regina was written with such definition that it could only be played one way. Our quarrels were endless. I was too young-looking for the forty-year-old woman and since the ladies of Regina's day had rice-powdered their faces, I covered mine with calcimine in order to look older. This Willie disagreed with. In fact, I ended up feeling I had given one of the worst performances of my life. This saddened me since Regina was a great part, and pleasing Willie Wyler was of such importance always to me. It took courage to play her the way I did, in the face of such opposition.

Archer Winston of the New York *Post* wrote of his visit to the Music Hall where he exited behind three matrons. After watching me, as Regina, rob her brothers and passively, coldly, murder her husband, one of the ladies remarked, "True to life, isn't it?"

Her friends agreed and, according to the reporter, they all went off to Schrafft's for a soda, supposedly to ponder the dullness of their husbands and the double indemnity clauses in their insurance policies.

Mr. Winston couldn't understand the abrasive Regina's appeal to the public. It frightened him and should have. Those Schrafft sodas were in celebration of their fantastic if momentary freedom.

The filming was torture, the film a smashing success both critically and popularly. But Willie and I never worked together again. It is too bad.

Farney and I returned to Butternut to vacation and work on our house. This was going to be my romantic dream of dreams. The little white cottage to end them all with woods and lawns and a barn and flowers everywhere for cutting, for sniffing, for just looking. Ruthie planted birch trees, rose bushes, and every variety of flower. It had all the peace of the English country homes I had adored so much. I was again safely ensconced in a picturebook life of respectable marriage. Ruth Elizabeth had rallied. She believed along with

Farney that my affection would flower into a complete life. Certainly both she and I were agreed about one thing. We both adored a man about the house; and Ruth Elizabeth was grateful that I had settled down once more. I've always been mad about a kitchen. It is the heart of the house and a place for creation and living. Playing house is a child's game I never put away.

Bobby was getting a divorce. The Davis girls were never happy at the same time. By virtue of her relationship to me, Bobby had many of the same problems my success was attracting. My solvency was a block for every man who entered our lives.

It was true to form that in order to get her divorce and have custody of her daughter, she had to give up her engagement ring and their automobile.

Uncle Paul and his family were now living with Ruthie. They had been most generous to us in the lean years. Certainly they would share in the time of plenty. I was more than a little irritated, however, when one of my cousins wrote me a few years before asking me for one day's salary to "put him through college." We have laughed about it since. He had done this behind his mother's and father's backs!

Next I made a picture with Jimmy Cagney. It was called a comedy. It had been decided that my work as a tragedian should be temporarily halted for a change of pace. Jimmy, who had made the gangster artistic—Jimmy, who was one of the fine actors on mine or any lot—Jimmy, with whom I'd always wanted to work in something fine, spent most of his time in the picture removing cactus quills from my behind. This was supposedly hilarious. We romped about the desert and I kept falling into cactus. We both reached bottom with this one. It was called *The Bride Came C.O.D.* It is amusing to note that some time later, I saw the film dubbed in French by French actors. I became convinced that the French critics were right when they said I belonged to them. Both Jimmy and I were suddenly fabulous in the picture. The language matched our naturally volatile gestures and gave the whole film a feeling of importance. We both emerged as great Gallic farceurs!

By this time I had become a favorite on the Continent as well as my beloved England. The French along with the rest of the Latin countries had accepted me as one of their own. Europeans and Latins are partial to tragediennes.

Temperament is something that is an integral part of the artist. Not temper, temperament. There is a vast difference. Temper is also of value to the artist. I lost mine violently about this time.

All contract players had a twelve-week layoff period each year without salary. I received my notice of layoff at the completion of *In This Our Life*. I had promised the publicity department that I would have stills taken, do interviews, etc., when I finished the picture. Early one morning, I arrived at the makeup department to get ready to be photographed. In burst Bernie Williams, the publicity man in charge of our film, saying as calmly as possible, "Take your makeup off. Go home—quickly." In answer to my amazed look he told me I was on layoff and the studio would have to pay me an extra day's salary if I did the work scheduled for the day.

Charging the studio for this one day would never have occurred to me. Publicizing a film was always as important to me as making the film itself. I had gone way beyond needing one day's salary. Like any professional, I knew I had to finish the job at hand. *Get her off the lot! How dare Mr. Warner think I would pressure them into one day's salary?*

Through my makeup, I saw my crimson face. I was throbbing with fury. *They always hang themselves, these men.* I whirled in the makeup chair and discovered that sheer frenzy had transported me to Mr. Warner's office. I had left a wake of secretaries and flying papers.

"How *dare* you," I hissed. "How dare you treat me like a chorus girl! How dare you order me off the lot! You should have known I had made dates to do publicity work for the film. You should know I would keep those dates—pay or no pay. Now I *am* getting off the lot and it is just possible that I may *never* come back!"

I left for a holiday in Mexico a week later and refused every communication from Warners for months. As far as I was concerned, I was through. *Fourth Warner Brother*—I feared if I saw my siblings again, I'd commit fratricide. I had indeed lost my temper! I had been insulted and made to feel cheap.

The Fourth Warner Brother returned eventually. Returned

to a contract tripling the amount of the old one. That is what one day's pay cost them. Ever "penny wise and pound foolish" were the movie moguls.

Through their stupidity, I received the contract I had been working for during all these years. Three pictures annually and a Queen's ransom for each.

CHAPTER
16

Under the new regime, I made one of my favorite pictures, *Now Voyager*. I was delighted with the result. I have not been satisfied with the finished product of many. It was typical that I had to fight for it. When I read in Louella Parsons' column that Irene Dunne was to be on loan-out to Warners for the leading role, I became apoplectic. The part was perfect for me and I was under contract to Warners. There wasn't one of my best pictures I didn't have to fight to get. And once I got this one, it was a constant vigil to preserve the quality of the book as written by Olive Higgins Prouty.

Claude Rains, Gladys Cooper and Paul Henreid were in this one with me. This was Paul's debut at Warner Brothers. His test for the film was shown to me for approval and I hated it. He was the wrong type for the part as seen on the screen. I felt like quoting Mr. Goldwyn, "Whom did this to me?" I asked to meet him. My bosses imagined they had another Boyer under contract. He wore a satin smoking jacket, his hair was brilliantined and he was covered in a pound of makeup.

"Do you like the way you look in the test, Mr. Henreid?"

"I hate it, Miss Davis. Completely wrong for the part!"

"I had a feeling you were not responsible. I might add, I thank God." We have to this day been the greatest of friends.

Another test was made and we were all delighted. Paul was

intelligent, sincere and charming in the part, and I must say to this day gives me the director's credit. I also used Miss Prouty's book and redid the screenplay in her words as we went along.

We were deep in war now and as part of the Stars Over America campaign, I went out on a bond-selling tour for the Government. It seemed outrageous to me that motion picture stars had to seduce people into buying bonds to help their country; but that's the way it was and always has been.

My territory was Missouri and Oklahoma and I think I was in every nook and cranny of these two states. I was delighted by the people I met and the beautiful rolling farmland.

Chief Jasper Sauntresh made me an honorary Indian Chief. In Oklahoma, I am officially known as Princess Laughing Eyes. A portrait of me as Jezebel was sold for a quarter of a million dollars' worth of bonds at Douglas Aircraft. In Tulsa, my autograph brought fifty thousand dollars.

With my usual tact, I informed workers in a factory in Oklahoma City that "Anyone who doesn't do what he can even if it's a twenty-five-cent stamp is not an American!"

I sold two million dollars' worth of bonds in two days. When I returned to Hollywood, John Garfield and I founded the Hollywood Canteen for servicemen. Hollywood had long needed one.

New York's Stage Door Canteen under Jane Cowl's supervision was serving a great purpose and we hoped to do the same. We started searching for committees and for the right people to head them. Jules Stein, the head of the Music Corporation of America, was a legend. Practically no one up to this time had ever seen him in person. I asked him to head our financial committee. Certainly there could be no one more helpful for this job. Mr. Stein accepted. When the canteen closed three years later, we had half a million dollars. The Hollywood Canteen Foundation under his leadership was formed—we now have close to a million in spite of the fact we have every year contributed enormous monies to worthy servicemen's causes.

The initial capital for the opening of the canteen was come by from a combination premiere of a Columbia Pictures film and a party at Ciro's afterwards. We charged twenty-five dollars a couple. We made $5,000 that night. The building we rented for our canteen was put in shape by volunteer help from all the guilds and unions of Hollywood who were represented on our board of directors.

On opening day, we had bleachers built and the public was charged one hundred dollars a seat to watch the servicemen walk across our threshold. This made $10,000 for the canteen.

As its president, I found the work exhilarating and rewarding. When one is working with volunteers, one's hands are full. I was taught that they must never be idle. They slapped many a shoulder and spanked many a bottom. But in the overall the Hollywood Canteen workers were marvelously cooperative and many of them truly dedicated. The whole idea of the canteen was to give the men fun, relaxation and the chance to meet personally and be served by the stars of Hollywood and not to be charged one cent. I will always be grateful for the loyalty of those who outlived the first flush of publicity and novelty and continued to work with us.

Some like Dietrich not only contributed glamour out front but backbreaking labor in the kitchen. John Ford's wife Mary ran the kitchen. Chef Milani planned the food, not a mean task when one is feeding thousands. It cost us three thousand dollars a week to operate the canteen. The entertainment was all voluntary. We had a name orchestra there every night. The contribution of the local chapter of the musicians union was probably the best all-out effort. I know of at least two marriages made at the canteen. Hedy LaMarr and John Loder met while waiting on table, and Betty Grable, then the GI's pinup girl, danced with one of the boys one night and later met the orchestra leader. Twenty years later she is still Mrs. Harry James.

Dinah Shore, Frank Loesser and Arthur Schwartz were all particularly giving and Frank Sinatra was the end of generosity. Christmas Eve was always a difficult night. Patriotism or no, this is a family night and we always worked on skeleton crew with a paucity of entertainment. I will never forget Bing Crosby and his four boys coming backstage one Christmas Eve and singing carols to the boys for hours. There wasn't a dry eye in the place. Actually a book could be written on the Hollywood Canteen alone.

Another film was made by Warners at this time, *Thank Your Lucky Stars*. I did a song in this, "They're Either Too Young or Too Old." I also, as part of the song, did the jitterbug with a boy who knew *how* to jitterbug. He was so nervous about

hurting me that I finally said, "Forget who I am and go to it."
I then said to everyone watching, "So long, everybody—it's
been swell working with you all."

The boy took me literally. I just put myself in his hands and
flying through the air was I. The fifty thousand dollars I received
for being in the picture went to the canteen. This was the idea
in the first place. During the second year of the Hollywood
Canteen, Farney died—very suddenly. He fell on Hollywood
Boulevard and lived only 24 hours, never regaining conscious-
ness.

I recalled that that morning he had been forgetful, disorgan-
ized, as he went off to work. He had seemed almost tipsy and
I joked about the possibility that he'd spiked his orange juice.
We'd laughed about it. Later on, he'd ordered me a leopard
stole at Magnin's. I heard later that while there he was dripping
with perspiration.

An autopsy revealed a blood clot. Farney had fallen down
the stairs at Butternut the previous summer. We thought nothing
of it at the time as he was not injured. It was unbelievable that
he was gone—just like that. And so young. It didn't seem fair.
It was my first actual experience with death. I was in a state
of shock.

Ruthie and I met Farney's mother at the airport. Her son
had died before she could get there. She told me upon arrival
the exact moment he had died. Farney had always said if anything happened to either of us, we would be buried at Butternut.
So we took him home. Mrs. Farnsworth, Ruthie, Bobby and
I took Farney back to the New Hampshire that he loved so
much.

His "quiet Birdmen" chums placed an airplane of carnations
over his coffin. After the funeral in Hollywood—before taking
him East—we all drank a toast in champagne and there was,
by their tradition, an extra glass filled for Farney. It took some
of the sting out of the awful business of blasting rocks and
uprooting trees to make way for the family cemetery after we
arrived at Butternut.

Mrs. Farnsworth's visits to the grave distressed me. "We
have to remove some trees, Bette. My boy can't see the mountains he loved so much!" She loved her son deeply—I wept
not only for myself but for her.

Bobby, who is more practical than I in many areas, cut

through all the nonsense one evening and said, "Ye gads, Bette! Are you really going to bury all the Farnsworths *and* us *and* everyone else who comes into your life *here?* I can see the funeral processions now." She, of course, was right.

When I returned to California, Ruthie stayed on and moved Farney to the family cemetery in Rutland, Vermont. She knew I couldn't have stood it. I couldn't have. My Ruthie.

Farney and I had a good life together. Classically European in tradition, I believed it would have gone on forever. We made few demands on one another and still he was always there. So was I. He filled the house with his sweetness and consideration of me. Now I was alone again. I will always miss him.

I went back to work to try and forget. *Mrs. Skeffington* was my next film. In the first place Fanny Skeffington was a famous beauty, which was a problem. I remember thinking when I made my first entrance (at the head of a flight of stairs, of course) with several swains waiting breathlessly for this divinity, *You are the creamiest thing that ever existed, Fanny. You're Venus and Mrs. Harrison Williams combined. You're just too beautiful to live.* This and Ernie Haller's photography got me by. Fanny's compulsion to remain young in the face of ruin was a desperate thing. I was both gratified and shocked when Dorothy di Frasso, a beauty herself, later asked me, "How in hell at your age do you know what it's like to lose beauty?" How did I know Mildred? How did Conrad know the South Seas? You just know it—that's all.

I was thirty-five, and a widow. I not only continued making films but also worked day and night at the Hollywood Canteen. These activities got me through the rough days, weeks and months after Farney's death.

In these years I made many enemies. I was a legendary terror; I had my fine Italian hand into everything. Thirty-five is *the* age for a woman, in my opinion. Oh—to stay thirty-five forever.

When I was my most unhappy I lashed out rather than whined. I was aggressive but curiously passive. I had to be in charge but I didn't want to be. I was hated, envied and feared and I was more vulnerable than anyone would care to believe. It wasn't difficult to discover that when people disliked me they really detested me. And they couldn't do any more about me than they could about death and taxes. I must have been a frustration to many.

I prefer to believe that on the set during *Skeffington,* my eyewash was filled with aceteyne by mistake. Aceteyne is a corrosive liquid that dissolves adhesives. It almost dissolved my eyes. I screamed in agony. Perc Westmore washed them out with castor oil. The series of accidents at work is too long for me to recount. I have played with danger all my life—and it, in turn, has flirted with me. My luck has always saved me from the elemental, Ruthie from the attacks of people. "It's the best fruit the birds pick at" she would often remind me. That phrase has helped me through many a painful moment.

Yes! I was thirty-five and Ruthie's possession still. I was at the zenith of my career and "earning more than the President of the United States" as the old chestnut went. Though widowed and alone, I was the father of a family. I was supporting three households since Mother and Bobby could never live together. And there was little Fay, whom I adored. My work went well and there was Butternut, an exquisite tombstone to my romantic dream. Evidently, despite what people thought, I couldn't have everything.

While I was visiting friends in Georgia during the war, I wanted desperately to meet the President. Roosevelt had just won his fourth term in the White House and I wrote for an appointment. Having adored him for years, I had openly supported his third re-election. One was not supposed to have political views as much then as now—certainly not out in the open. In those days actors were to subscribe to nothing more controversial than Lux soap.

Though the war had rallied many factors around the President, Roosevelt was still a dirty word in most of Bel Air's conservative Tudor mansions. To be respectable, one had to be anti-Roosevelt underneath all the red, white and blue. The very dynamism and compassionate legislature that drove these people mad made me worship him. This marvelous man was not only courageous, imaginative and progressive, he was my dream man as well. I arrived at the White House and found myself in line with hundreds of others.

At last I reached the great man. As I prepared to file past him, I felt like a little girl being given a diploma. I wanted to curtsy as he automatically extended his hand. When his eyes met mine, he threw back his head in that famous gesture of his and laughed.

"And how did *you* get into this mob, Miss Davis?"

"I wrote, Mr. President, asking to meet you and I received his invitation."

"This is ridiculous. What are you doing at a public tea? How long are you going to be in Washington?"

"I'm just here to see you. I'm vacationing with friends in Georgia."

"I'm leaving for Warm Springs for my first visit in a long time. Will you give me another chance to play host?"

A short time later, I received an official invitation to a dinner at Warm Springs, Georgia. A night to remember. I can only say that I feel the glow just writing about it. Haggard, nearer to death than we all knew, the President was still larger than life—all pluses. His inner vitality was astonishing.

I sat on the President's left at dinner. But for a few dignitaries, the great hall was filled only with the polio patients. I was suddenly covered with guilt, embarrassed because I was healthy, mortified that I could walk and run and dance at will. I felt my own wholeness was an affront to them. I've never been able to visit a hospital without becoming ill. My antennae quiver at the mere suggestion of physical suffering. And here they were, still gay, because their benefactor had made them that way. Nothing could beat this man down. Nothing had. I could tell that no horror he ever experienced ever brought a single whine—just anger and eventual triumph over it.

When five little girls, crippled, in braces—no more than five or six years old—hobbled out and attempting a bow sang "School Days," the President nudged me and whispered, "Do you think you can take it?"

I almost didn't. But Roosevelt kept that chin up. He had been carried in and placed at the table all smiles. Now he thanked each child personally. All the courage in the world was in that dining hall that night.

One of the President's favorite entertainers, Graham Jackson, then sang for him; but only after he placed an orchid on Roosevelt's plate saying, "Here, Boss, this is for you." He sang one folk song after another and then the President told him he wanted to hear his favorite of all. Graham Jackson smiled and opened those brown eyes wide and played a funny little ditty I had never heard. I was absolutely shattered when I recognized it a few months later as the song the Marine Band played following the President's cortege down Pennsylvania Avenue.

I think I doubted up to that point that giants could die. I know now that they really never do.

Before I returned to California I saw, at Mr. Wallis' request, *The Corn Is Green* in Chicago. The ovation I received in the audience that night took me by surprise. I heard a roar, and in turning around to see what was going on—I found out!

I feign no boredom with the public, who continued their greeting so long that Miss Ethel Barrymore was forced to look through the curtain to see what was wrong. I was gratified though my last desire was to upset the star of the play whose part I was going to do on the screen. Any actress who claims her fans are a bore is a liar. She also is impractical. They are the lifeline that continues the career. Watch out as an actor for only one thing—when they stop bothering you, you have had it.

The Corn Is Green was in every way a rewarding part to play. During the filming of it, I went with Ruthie to a cocktail party in Laguna Beach where Ruthie had her home. The moment I arrived, a very attractive man brought me a drink and never left my side.

Recently discharged from the Navy hospital at San Diego, William Grant Sherry was a painter, also a licensed physiotherapist. He was living at the time in Laguna very near Mother's house. I think now that no one ever paid court with the singularity of purpose that Sherry displayed.

Ruthie mistrusted him as did Bobby. She so continually criticized him, I realize now, that she drove me right into his arms. Her lofty appraisal of his work and his background put me on the defensive for him.

The more Ruthie went on, the more I saw of him. Sherry never wavered for a second. I know now that he had made up his mind to marry me the moment he set eyes on me—perhaps before. He took complete charge of things. I really believe I couldn't have avoided becoming his wife. This approach to a woman had seldom failed since the beginning of time.

This is it, I thought. *He is dedicated. He's a worker. He'll*

*ecome a fine painter and he worships me. It doesn't matter
hat he has no money. Sherry is an artist. These middle-class
oncepts mean as little to him as to me. What drive the man
as!*

Ruthie never gave up. When she met Sherry's mother, who
an an elevator in a hotel in San Diego, she was aghast. Sherry's
ather had been a head carpenter with the Theatre Guild. He
vas dead. I respected Mrs. Sherry for not sitting back and
etting her sons support her.

Ruthie was now "Bette Davis' mother." It was true that she
ad earned her comfortable position. It was true that I would
ever have made it without her. Her fear of losing me once
nore was not enough reason to become snobbish about Sherry
nd his family. But Sherry was a thorn in her side. She was
iolently against our marriage. It turned out she was right. But
or the wrong reasons.

Ruthie had met a man named Robert Palmer at Smoke Tree
Ranch in Palm Springs. A month before Sherry and I were
narried, Ruthie became Mrs. Palmer. Sherry and I became
nan and wife in the beautiful chapel at the Mission Inn in
Riverside, California. This time, all would be well. Sherry had
is work, I had mine. His adoration of me, quite naturally,
xcited me. I was no longer alone. Ruth Elizabeth was beside
erself. She was going to play house again.

We drove to Mexico on our honeymoon. En route my hus-
and threw me out of the car for some forgotten reason. This
vas only the beginning. Our first night in Mexico he threw a
teamer trunk clear across the hotel room. I never seemed to
ring out the best in men.

I cannot say that Sherry and I did not have a stimulating
elationship. He matched me in temperament all the way. I
vould say that I trailed him in this department. He wanted to
e indispensable to me and that, of course, was impossible.
Though industrious and pitiably contrite after his outbursts,
herry's dedication as an artist fell far short of mine and his
rustrations had a frenzy that terrorized me. I never either saw
r heard anyone when I was hard at work which seemed to be
lways. I was still a working actress first and now planning to
roduce my own picture. Sherry had his own atelier set up
ow. Each of us had his studio. Work came first and then—
ut we all are possessed in our own ways. What was, to me,

a necessary refreshment, a comma, a dash in my life sentence
of work, was otherwise to Sherry. I was possessed with my
career. Sherry was possessed with me.

I was a general in my field and doubtless I pulled rank at
home. Catherine was Great for a variety of reasons. I understood her and envied her Potemkin and Orlov. I was not so
lucky in this department.

Sherry wrought a great change in my life, however. If not
in my career, in my family. He did forbid Ruthie's arbitrary
presence in the house. He convinced me that I was now suf-
ficiently grown up to run my own life. I stopped confiding in
Mother at thirty-six. Her influence either direct or through sheer
resistance to it had dominated my private life up to this moment.

Her distrust and disapproval of Sherry now became loathing.
Having been alone and independent for so long, Mother could
not adjust to being a wife. She divorced Robert Palmer. It was
easier for me to see her mistakes than my own.

In the flush of the first year of my marriage to Sherry, I
encouraged Bobby to see more of a man we met at Laguna—
David Berry. I wanted Bobby to share the wonders of love.
Her health had improved enormously and she, too, was out-
growing Ruthie's influence. Bobby no longer felt that she had
to be a powerhouse. She was no longer guilty because she
wasn't I. The twenty-one hours of labor that she had inflicted
on Mother was an oft-repeated horror she was now growing
deaf to.

Bobby was emerging as herself. Mother had never really
understood her. Ruthie never had identification with Bobby.
Love, yes.

Like all happy brides, I had thrown my bouquet to my sister.
Now Sherry and I were a foursome with David Berry and Bobby
Davis. David was in love with Bobby and she, in no time,
with him. They were married and the Davis girls were now,
absurdly, Mrs. Sherry and Mrs. Berry! There was rhyme if no
reason to both our marriages.

I was still trying. Ruth Elizabeth was forcing me to. As for
Bette Davis, she was still working.

My first attempt at movie production was my last. I had a
contract to produce five films for Warners and I discovered that
with *A Stolen Life*, a remake of Elizabeth Bergner's European
film of twin sisters in love with the same man, I was no more

allowed to be a real producer than the man in the moon. As star in the dual role, I simply meddled as usual. If that was producing, I had been a mogul for years.

Glenn Ford, just out of the Marines, had a quality just right for the part of the leading man. The first day of the picture he arrived on the set with curly hair. My first executive order not unlike my unofficial ones was, "Give him a crew-cut immediately." When Curtis Bernhardt, the director, tried to change Glenn's way of speaking, I sighed before I stopped it. Since I always had a finger in every pot, it was not unusual that I fought other people's battles as well as my own. Not many novices know how to protect themselves.

"I want the natural way he speaks—his hesitancy is original. That's one reason I liked him for the part."

You don't hire someone and then change him. That was always the actor's biggest fight in Hollywood—to preserve his own identity as a performer. Today, everyone looks so alike that I can't tell them apart at all. I can barely distinguish the sexes.

Stolen Life turned out very well, in fact was a big hit.

Next Claude, Paul and I—the *Now Voyager* trio—made a picture called *Deception*. It was during the shooting of this film I found out I was pregnant. We changed the title from Deception to Conception! And Paul was the recipient of much kidding!

Sherry and I went to Butternut to await the arrival of the baby. Sherry was sure it would be a boy. An "infant Hercules." As for me, I naturally hoped for a girl. I was never the roseate madonna. I was happy I was having a baby, but there was no feeling I was doing something special. I didn't feel I was wearing a halo. Sherry analyzed:

"Creating a baby is the only creating for most women. You have been creating for years."

On Christmas night, I slipped on the ice returning from a dinner at a neighbor's. What a twenty-four hours that was. But B.D. survived. Sherry was wrong. This creation was unique.

In March we decided to return to Laguna for the birth of the baby. The winter was a severe one that year and the doctor, we felt, too far away in case of any emergency.

The new house in Laguna on Wood's Cove was by the sea. From every window there was a breathtaking view of sea and sky. I adore space. In the city, I want to push away the buildings with my own two hands and let the sky rush in. This house at Laguna was a dream filled with antiques, wood-paneled walls and all my beloved books. Keeping house does keep a woman busy and time flew. The last month of my pregnancy Dr. Carroll decided a Caesarean section was necessary. I chose the day in case it was a girl. May Day—a fun birthday for a girl. Sherry laughed. "It's a boy!"

Barbara Davis Sherry was born on May 1, 1947, at the Community Hospital, Santa Ana, California, a few weeks after my thirty-ninth birthday. The doctor informed me later that this was it. No more children.

Coming out of the ether I heard myself saying, "Poor Sherry. You married an old woman and I gave you a daughter—not a son."

But B.D. was a seductress from the beginning and her father forgave her. And for the first time in my life, I became a willing slave to another human being. I was thrilled that it was a girl. It seemed so right.

The night before leaving for the hospital we had discussed names—*if* it was a girl.

"She has to have 'Davis' somewhere, Bette," Ruthie insisted.

Bobby. Her love and loyalty were beyond reckoning. With tears in her eyes, she asked if I would name a girl after her.

"I think Barbara would be the perfect name. Barbara Davis Sherry." And so it was.

The first months of a child are spectacularly exciting. Jack Warner sent the baby three exquisite pearls on a gold chain— the start of a necklace he would complete, one pearl a year. The studio seemed in another world and I was satisfied to remain in Laguna which was suddenly dead center of the universe. I had bought so many enchanting tiny clothes for the baby. Dr. Carroll roared with laughter when he saw them.

"I hate to disillusion you, Bette, but she'll be wearing only diapers and nightshirts for quite a while."

I told him I was going to dress her up just for us. And I did. What a vision she was—already golden from the sun, which I exposed her to when she was eight days old. If there had been snow in California, she would have been bathed in it as I was at Crestalban. I wanted her on friendly terms with all the elements, healthy, strong, unsheltered. Sherry started her on gymnastics before she could walk. Fatherhood was good for Sherry. He worshiped B.D. and all was well for a while.

B.D. had made a drastic change in my life. I had no desire to give up my career but somehow it didn't matter as much. My life seemed full without it. I had won my battle. I had reached my peak—inside. I wondered what would have happened had Ham and I had children. I might have given up my work. I couldn't have things halfway. I had had my Matterhorn; now I was satisfied to be nestled in my little chalet. From Matterhorn to Jungfrau. The setting and the role suited me.

I took my time returning to work. Since *Deception* had been released very quickly, I had been off the screen for one year before I returned and made *Winter Meeting*. The director, Bretaigne Windust, had the idea that he would introduce a brand-new Bette Davis to the screen. He would have been smarter to leave the old one alone. The story of a New England poetess and a naval officer who plans to become a priest was a badly drawn triangle in which the church spire was the apex. It was a dreary film and hardly a triumphant return. Next I made a comedy called *June Bride* with Robert Montgomery. I had fun, as I seldom got a chance at a good comedy.

During all this, B.D. was my prime concern. I had turned my back to warm some milk and my defenses were down. My claws had been manicured for the nursery and now there was trouble on my left flank. I hated every minute away from her.

It was one of Mr. Warner's irritations that I never called him anything but *Mr*. Warner. My stormy visits to his office were a nuisance to him. As a further annoyance, I always wore sunglasses so he could not look into my eyes.

Actually weary of the whole business, I made, as it turned out, my last trip to his office to beg him not to make me play Rosa Moline in *Beyond the Forest*. The girl, Rosa Moline, was a version of Emma Bovary. I was at this point not young enough to play her. I also was not weak enough. *Bette Davis as a twelve-o'clock girl in a nine-o'clock town!* That is how it was advertised.

This set was the scene of my last battle with the studio. This "twelve-o'clock girl" asked for her release during this film.

My "brothers" let me go. I never heard from them again. B.D. was two years old and I had already added two pearls to the necklace myself. I finished *every* job the Warners ever gave me. I had to make a sound track for *Beyond the Forest*—the line "I can't stand it here anymore," these were the last words spoken by me on the Warner lot. They certainly hit the nail on the head!

It takes a lot of courage to voluntarily give up the financial security of a contract after 19 years. I still had many years ahead with Warner Brothers. It is like leaving home and going out in the world for the first time to seek your fortune. But I felt that if after all my fighting for the right scripts they were still giving me the wrong ones, there was no longer any point. Mother and Father had to go.

Whenever I drive down the Canyon Road toward Warner Brothers—that same road I traveled every morning starting way back when I was a kid—I look with pride at some of the roofs of those sound stages. I am responsible for a few of them being built. I also say here, I was one of the lucky ones—I had a Mother and Father for all those years, and they did well by me. I can't deny this. Those years were the greatest of my life.

Sherry and I continued to live in Laguna. I was now free to see much more of my daughter. We spent hours on the beach together—would call on Grandmother for tea. I was so thrilled to be a mother. Now I really did have everything.

Sherry's physical violence was a thing of terror to me. I began to worry about any signs of it with his daughter as the target. It is not unusual for the husband of a famous woman to be insulting to her in public. It is a sign, however, of weakness on the part of a man. It is also natural for a husband to want complete jursidiction over his wife. With me this is impossible. It is against my nature. I also felt that as a financial contributor to the family it should at least be 50–50 on the part of the husband. It was becoming apparent that our marriage would not go on forever. I'm afraid in Sherry's script he had decided he was the King. He crowned himself. I wanted to do the same thing many times—crown him.

Curtis Bernhardt and I started working together coincidentally enough on a film entitled *Story of a Divorce*. Our story was bought by RKO. B.D. played a tiny part in it. Barry Sullivan played opposite me. He told B.D. he was her first leading man. He even gave her a corsage to prove it! I worked with Jane Cowl in this one. It was the last part she played before she died. I was thrilled to be in the same scene with her. I had been an admirer since childhood. That is what so many people say to me now! Time and Tide wait for no man.

Story of a Divorce was released by Howard Hughes as *Payment on Demand*.

In the meantime, my story of a divorce turned into just that. "Payment on demand" is how, in the long run, I got mine. Alimony from a woman to a man was a new one to me. I am afraid my initial charm to Sherry was tied up in part with my earning capacities. There are words for women like this—there are words for men like this. Money is no object if it accomplishes what you want. By this time I wanted out, and money made it possible. I had the custody of B.D. Sherry soon afterwards married B.D.'s nurse. His heartbreak was obviously short-lived—no doubt the alimony softened the blow.

During the filming of *Payment on Demand*, Darryl Zanuck telephoned me to say he would send me a script if I would promise to read it right away. Since I had never seen or spoken to Mr. Zanuck since my resignation from the Academy when I was told I would never work again, I thought, as in the case of Mr. Arliss, some friend was ribbing me. "Right away, right away, Darryl dear," said I. It, however *was* Darryl and the script was *All About Eve*. He also told me that if I liked it, I'd have to be ready to start shooting in ten days, wardrobe finished and all! I had about five more days on the present film. It all sounded impossible and why worry? It probably was a lousy script anyway.

The problem was that Claudette Colbert was to have played Margo Channing but had seriously hurt her back, and they had to use the Curran Theatre in San Francisco, already contracted for, for the only two weeks available to them.

When I finished reading *All About Eve* I was on cloud nine. *Any* inconvenience was worth it. That night I met Joseph Mankiewicz for dinner to discuss wardrobe. He told me that Margo Channing was the kind of dame who would treat her mink coat like a poncho! I asked who would play Bill Sampson. He said he wanted Gary Merrill. Good, I said. He is a strong-enough personality to cope with Margo.

Edith Head designed my clothes. I went for fittings after work, and the following Sunday with my wardrobe complete, I tested them in front of the cameras at Fox. This was the first time I met Gary. They did photographic tests of us together. I was to look older than he as Margo. I did, and he was signed for the part of Bill Sampson.

When it was announced in the papers that I was to play Margo Channing, Mankiewicz received countless phone calls commiserating with him. He did receive two or three from fellow directors who congratulated him. Gary asked Joe who were the ones happy for him. He said one was Willie Wyler, who told him he would have a ball working with me.

I can think of no project that from the outset was as rewarding from the first day to the last. It is easy to understand why. It was a great script, had a great director, and was a cast of professionals all with parts they liked. It was a charmed production from the word go. After the picture was released, I told Joe "he had resurrected me from the dead." He had in more ways than one. He handed me the beginning of a new life professionally and personally. I also say a thank-you to Claudette Colbert for hurting her back. Claudette's loss was my gain. On what strange circumstances are whole lives changed. No broken back—no Gary Merrill.

I must confess, in the years that followed I felt less and less thankful.

CHAPTER
17

I had seen the film *Twelve O'Clock High* and the actor in it named Gary Merrill. I had never seen him before and I was greatly impressed by his performance and looks.

Bill Sampson was Margo's lover, her tower of strength who at last convinces her to marry him. As a fellow artist, Bill accepts her furies and eventually exorcises them through his love and his own equilibrium. His love of Margo as her professional security seems threatened by age, convinces her that, at forty, she should settle down and become a downright, upright foursquare married lady.

On the first day of shooting in San Francisco, as Gary and I rehearsed our first scene together I took a cigarette out of a cigarette case and waited for Bill Sampson to light it. He went on with his lines. I kept waiting for a light. When I realized he was ignoring the gesture, I asked if he were going to light my cigarette.

He looked me squarely in the eye and said: "I don't think Bill Sampson would light Margo's cigarettes."

I looked at him for a minute.

Of course Bill Sampson wouldn't. "You're quite right, Mr. Merrill. Of course he wouldn't."

I wondered at the time if that was Gary Merrill speaking to Bette Davis, to establish who was boss, or was it his opinion of what the character would do? I'm not quite sure to this day.

Margo Channing was a woman I understood thoroughly. Though we were totally unalike, there were also areas we shared. The scene in which—stuck in the car—Margo confesses to Celeste Holm that the whole business of fame and fortune isn't worth a thing without a man to come home to, was the story of my life. And here I was again—no man to go home to.

The unholy mess of my own life—another divorce, my permanent need for love, my aloneness. Hunched down in the front of that car in that luxurious mink, I had hard work to remember I was playing a part. My parallel bankruptcy kept blocking me, and keeping the tears back was not an easy job.

I found out Gary had spent all his summers in Maine. He had gone to Loomis in Windsor, Connecticut, where he was born and brought up. I had known the current headmaster, Frank Grubbs, years ago. Gary used to vacation as a child at Prout's Neck, Maine—just across the bay from Ocean Park, Maine, where I spent all my summers as a child.

I found him an excellent actor to work with—one with integrity. Our scenes went well together. By the time we played out our story and the actress had retired to be the little woman, I had fused the two men completely. Margo Channing and Bill Sampson were perfectly matched. They were the perfect couple. I was breaking every one of my rules. I always swore I'd never marry an actor. Gary told me that years before he had been inducted into the army directly behind Ham. Everyone had realized Ham had been married to me. Gary had said, "How the hell could a guy let himself get into a deal like that?" Now here he was. The cards were all reshuffled and we didn't either of us see the jokers in the pack.

Ruthie shook her head at the latest developments; but she was a cheer leader compared with my future mother-in-law. News of the impending marriage inspired her to eloquence.

"Have you gone crazy, Gary? Marrying a middle-aged actress who will throw all your antiques into the ocean!"

Merrill's defense of me was heroic.

"But, Mother—she *loves* lobsters."

I was no longer a free agent. I had a daughter to think of.

I sensed in Gary my last chance at love and marriage. I wanted these as desperately as ever. I had been an actress first and a woman second. I had proved what I wanted to prove about the actress part. Now I owed Ruth Elizabeth her due. It was an account that I wanted to settle.

When I accepted Gary's proposal, I made it contingent on our adopting more children. He was only too eager to. I was convinced that he would be a great father to B.D. and those to come. I knew Gary was a strong personality. For the first time, I took one on. I was no longer afraid of competition. There was no reason to be. Suddenly I was interested in *his* career. I was growing tired of mine.

To be married to an incompetent actor would have been impossible for me. This was not the case with Gary—he was good! Thoughts of the Lunts bemused me! An acting couple, productive, happy—in love.

We were married in Juarez, Mexico, on July 28, 1950, and I waved good-bye to all the statues of Paul Muni as we left for New England. B.D. spent half of our honeymoon with us— Gary's idea and a thoughtful one. She joined us at Robin Hood Island, north of Bath, Maine. Mother and Daddy had honeymooned at nearby Squirrel Island. Ruth Elizabeth had been conceived there. Now she was blooming. Her hopes were never higher. Her chance of a life, never surer. Bette Davis could rest on her laurels. Mrs. Gary Merrill would be a "downright, upright, etc.!" This was do or die for Ruth Elizabeth.

Gary was under contract to 20th Century-Fox. After our honeymoon he was sent off to the Virgin Islands to make a film about frogmen, co-starring with Dana Andrews and Richard Widmark. B.D. and I saw him off on the plane and then returned to Robin's house in Westport for a few days, we thought. We had called a doctor while on our honeymoon in Maine, telling him of our interest in adoption. While at Robin's, I was told our next child had been born and would I come to the hospital's nursing home the next day and see her? When Gary called that evening I told him we had a daughter and to think about a name. A few days later, after we each made lists, Gary suggested Margo. Of course. How perfect. We added the T—Margot was her name. The proper legal papers were drawn up and I took her home to B.D. When I walked in the house I told her to close her eyes, I had a present for her. I put a real live doll in her little arms. Her eyes when she opened them had all the wonders of the universe. She had a sister.

I had rented a house in Greens Farms, Conn., and now the three Merrills awaited Daddy's return from the Virgin Islands. The arrival date was put off and put off. There is no assurance ever of a finishing date on location. Until finally, the day came. Daddy was introduced to his new daughter, Margot. We all then were horrified to find that Daddy was being sent to Germany immediately, to make a film. We stayed in Connecticut until he once more flew out of our lives. I was wondering about being an actor's wife at this point. I felt more like a widow. After he soared off in the sky, we cried appropriately, girded our loins—and I, a nurse and the two children were off to California to find a house suitable to our growing family. We had a great incentive—to have it ready when Daddy returned from Germany.

We found a house near the one Gary had at Malibu—moved him out of his house—his antiques, and I did *not* pitch them in the ocean—moved all my belongings in, even found an intelligent woman to be B.D.'s governess. I worked like a beaver. This would be Gary's and my first home and I wanted it to be to his liking. He now had a household of women. Two daughters, Dell the cook, a baby nurse and a governess for B.D. He made lots of sly remarks about it, but I felt at the time, he really liked it.

The great day came. Daddy was coming home. How excited B.D. was. She loved him so. We went to the airport and practically broke our necks looking skyward for the first sight of the plane bringing Gary home to us. I was also nervous. I wanted him to like his new home. He arrived—so relieved to be back with B.D. and Margot and me—and did love his new house.

The walls that night rang with love, laughter and a closeness of two people who had found what they had always looked for. I had such respect for Gary and was so proud to be his wife. The next few months were the happiest we ever had. Storm signals every now and then of the tragedy to come— but soon forgotten in the overall compatibility. He loved Margot. It was his first own daughter. He took care of her often— diapers and all. God was in his heaven. Six months later we were asked to do a film in England. *Another Man's Poison*. The contract at our insistence provided for the whole family to travel with us. Gary and his harem—Dell, the two nurses, two daughters and a wife. Our departure from the Los Angeles airport was a sight indeed. Off to England were we. The following day we sailed on the *Queen Elizabeth* for England.

On our arrival there, Gary got his first taste of what it was like to be married to me. The English press was vile, as is always the case with actors from Hollywood. Next day one of the headlines referred to Gary Merrill as Mr. Davis. I was sick.

Gary skipped it with great grace. Underneath he must have hated it. He did not blame me however. He knew this was the last thing I ever wanted. I had had this kind of experience many times before. It seemed unavoidable. The press also referred to me as a middle-aged matron—plus a description of our *twenty* trunks. Oh Hollywood . . . Hollywood . . . how can one escape the tradition? Wealth galore! Normalcy impossible. No matter how simply one travels, and we did, they wanted us to be rich bitches—were most likely mad that we weren't.

Emlyn Williams was in *Another Man's Poison* with us. We became so fond of him. He has remained a real friend. We lived at Great Foster's in Egham during the filming of the picture. We went to Yorkshire on location. B.D. went with us. It was spring and how she cuddled all the little lambs on the hillsides.

It is very different making a film in England. There is a great contrast in technical equipment, wardrobe and all the amenities. Plus the lack of comforts the American actor has grown accustomed to.

Dell provided three very worthy remarks during our stay in England. She sat in a chair supposedly Ann Boleyn's—Great Foster was once a hunting lodge of my "pop," Henry VIII. Dell, sitting in this chair, said, "I am now part of history!" Coming over on the boat she was very seasick. Her shiny black skin was literally five shades lighter. She said, "Miss Bette, this ocean sends you over and brings you back." No greater description of seasickness was ever, in my opinion, given. The last remark was a result of a visit to Madame Tussaud's wax museum. A replica of me was there. I was discussing with her the fun it might be for B.D. to go there and see me, and yet I was afraid it might scare her—the resemblances were always so perfect. Dell said, to truly reassure me, "Don't worry, Miss Bette, Miss B.D. won't be frightened. She would never recognize you. It was done of you when you were young and beautiful!'' Out of the mouths of maids!

The other memorable event, which did add to the business of it all, and the concern, was the worst case of measles contracted by B.D. She was desperately ill. We hated to have to go off to work each day and leave her.

We sailed for home the 2nd of July, on the _Queen Mary_ this time. We sent all our henchmen home for a holiday. We brought with us an English nurse for Margot. The one from home had turned into a drunk and had been shipped back earlier.

The English nurse, B.D., Gary and I motored to Maine for a holiday, having rented a cottage at the Black Point Inn at Prout's Neck. Our beloved Maine where we hoped we would all live one day. Fate took a hand in this and it came about earlier than we had hoped.

After our holiday, we returned to California. Gary's mother and his Aunt Marion, she was the love of our life, came West and spent the fall with us. After they left, we decided to move into town from Malibu. I found a house in the old part of Hollywood—this time at the other side of Franklin Avenue on Camino Palmero. Into our lives then came Michael, at five days of age. B.D.'s baby nurse, Rose Suncox, was Michael's also. Michael was born on January 5, 1954. He was a blond bomber at birth and has stayed so ever since. Now we were five. We lived through an earthquake in this house, I might add. There were a few inside the house as well.

All was not going so well. Gary would often leave us for parts unknown. I worried about him. But, like the bad penny, he always came home. Gary's great desire was to be a free soul—no responsibility. The world to Gary is a jail he must break the bars of. To me the world is a coliseum. Merrill is like my father, cynical, bright, negative and earthbound. Our personality differences were getting in the way of our happiness together. My enthusiasm and belief in people were annoying to him. I was _not_ Margo Channing and he was not Bill Sampson. He is the eternal collegiate—his preferred mailing address a friend's couch. He adores rushing about, no strings, no ties. But ties and responsibilities he had assumed. Three small children and a wife. I knew this was my only true marriage. I had no intentions of its falling apart. For many years to come, I kept on hoping we could make it the marriage it had seemed to be in the beginning. There was no question that we loved and respected each other. How could we fail?

Gary was making films for Fox during this year. I was having a ball being a mother and running a house. I did make one film, *The Star*. I liked it but the public was lukewarm. I received another Academy nomination for my performance.

Out of the blue, I got an offer to do a musical in New York— a revue. I had had California after all these years. My career was in the doldrums. I wanted the children to be brought up in my beloved East. Gary couldn't have agreed more on all points. Also, I felt, if we got out of Hollywood our personal situation might change. I would have done anything for that. I was so in love. Mike was six months, Margot eighteen months and B.D. five by now. I agreed to do the show. We packed enough of our belongings to make the penthouse we had rented in New York on Beekman Place look like home. We loved being on the East River. The children were thrilled with the boats that went back and forth all day.

I was now embarking on my first stage venture since 1930, when I left for Hollywood. I was not a little apprehensive and a revue at that. Singing and dancing. I actually was embarking also on my black years, one tragedy after another. What you don't know won't hurt you. I didn't know.

CHAPTER
18

The Revue was called *Two's Company*—after the usual re-hearsal period we opened in Detroit. From the outset I felt the approach to the original intent of the show was all wrong, but because I was from Hollywood, it was very possible I didn't any longer know how things were done in the theatre. I only knew one thing—it was not going to be a good show material wise. The lyrics of the songs were by Ogden Nash, the music by Vernon Duke—the only good things about the show. The ballet became a far more important adjunct to the show than its star. In other words, they didn't "put their money where the dough was."

The night we opened in Detroit I received the traditional telegram from Ruthie—DON'T FORGET DARLING—I'M IN THE FRONT ROW. It was a frightening opening as it turned out. I had been kept up all the night before rehearsing and had gone through the complete show that afternoon. I was exhausted. The newness of theatre, plus being in a song-and-dance show for the first time, finished me off. I blacked out during my first number onstage.

Gary, who was in Detroit for the opening, thought I had dropped dead. As I came to, I only knew I had to finish the show somehow and say something to the audience to break the tension. As they raised the curtain, I came on saying, "Well,

ou can't say I didn't fall for you.'' The audience roared and
e went on with the show!

Our notices were not good in Detroit, Pittsburgh or Boston.
he critics couldn't have been more right. Finally in Boston,
ohn Murray Anderson was sent for. He agreed to do what he
ould for the show because he liked me in it. His ''little South-
n girl.'' What he did was miraculous.

I was not well when we returned to New York. I simply put
is down to fatigue. In fact, I felt I would never be able to
pen. A very good friend said, ''Bette, if you only play opening
ght, that's all I care about, the critics will never believe you're
l. They will say you're scared.'' With practically no rehears-
s, one preview and mostly new material, I did open and the
vation was, to say the least, heartwarming. The reviews were
loodcurdling. I lived on dexadrine and shots during the run,
ways exhausted. The houses were full—that was a comfort,
nyway. I had fun doing the show and most of the audience
ad fun seeing the tragedienne Bette Davis making fun of
erself. Puzzled by my permanent exhaustion, I went to many
octors that winter, all of whom agreed I couldn't have been
ealthier.

It had never occurred to anyone to examine me from the
eck up. One Saturday before the matinee, my face on one
de was swollen beyond recognition. Between shows I went
 a dentist, Dr. Carney, whom, strangely enough, I had met
ackstage after the show the night before. (Incidentally, he is
rt Carney's brother.) He gave me poultices to get me through
e show that night and said he would have a Dr. Stanley
ehrman look at me the next day, Sunday. After Dr. Behrman
xamined me, he said he wanted me to go with him immediately
 the hospital. He was head of Dental Surgery at New York
ospital.

''But I can't. I'm doing the Actors' Benefit show tonight! I
an hear them now. They'll say I was scared to do it. I have
 do the show tomorrow night.''

''Miss Davis, for this particular actor's benefit, I wish you'd
 to New York Hospital now. I've got to extract this tooth.''

I promised him I would the minute the curtain came down
at night.

That was my last performance of *Two's Company*. I did not
now it at the time. Bobby and I left the theatre after midnight

and took a taxi to the New York Hospital. After the usual X
rays, the tooth was extracted and I was given a hospital room
for the night. Gary was in California working. Bobby went
back to the apartment to see that all was well with the children.
Without her during these next weeks, I don't know what I
would have done.

Next morning Dr. Behrman came into my room and told me
I would not be leaving the hospital. I had osteomyelitis of the
jaw and he would operate on me in a week. I had never even
heard of such a disease.

Stanley Behrman's brilliance as a surgeon and his compassion as a human being have put me in his debt forever. It was
a long and difficult operation. Because I am an actress he felt
great obligation not to leave any scars, so he did the operation
from the inside of my mouth instead of making an incision and
operating from the outside.

Gary flew to New York and walked into my room with the
breakfast tray one morning before the operation. How desperately glad I was to see him. He was allowed to watch Dr.
Behrman operate.

After I left the hospital, Walter Winchell breathlessly informed me and the rest of the Nation "Coast to Coast," that
"Bette Davis had been operated on for cancer of the jaw."
Hardly a lovely thing to hear and just what the doctor ordered
for a patient right after an operation. Besides, it was a completely false statement.

A celebrity must and does expect and consequently hardens
himself to all sorts of erroneous coverage. If every time I was
misquoted or misunderstood I had worried about it, I wouldn't
have had time for a career. But this was hitting below the belt.
This meant that if the report were true, no one would have
dared to hire me again. This was unforgivable! Ruthie was
called immediately.

Gary was determined that an important retraction of Mr.
Winchell's story be written—not just an apology in his column
that would not possibly convince anyone. For years afterward
I was asked, "Just how serious *was* your operation?" It was
terribly serious but it wasn't cancer. Gary called Dorothy
Schiff, the publisher of the New York *Post*. He reached her
late at night. Miss Schiff heard him out and had a story written
that revealed the truth. We were always very grateful to her

It certainly helped, although no retraction ever completely does it. The rumors persisted.

There I was in the hospital for six weeks, out of the show, three children with the mumps they'd caught from the cook— all in all a dire period in my life. Recovering from this operation was a long haul and it was two years before I really felt myself again.

We now all had bandaged jaws at home except for Merrill, who still wanted to break Winchell's. We were quite a sight when Anna Magnani, replete with interpreter and agent, came to the apartment to visit me. I couldn't have been more thrilled. She was in New York and had always wanted to meet me. It was certainly mutual. I was a real fan of hers. From the first minute it was as if we'd known each other for years.

As vivid as her beautiful country, as explosive as a happy child, her eyes have known the tragic. But now, she was radiating excitement. "For Bette Davis—I wear my diamonds!"

Their sparkle was second to hers. We, through her interpreter, discussed acting, the world in general and children. Her own son is an invalid for whom she has always slaved and searched for a cure. B.D. was sitting beside me on the bed, her eyes glued to Anna. She had never heard Italian spoken before.

"Why, Bette Davis, do you not come to us in Italy—to Europe? You are for us. We are the same, you and I— Come to us!"

I thought of Cagney and me in that French dubbed picture I'd seen in Paris. It is true that Italian and French are the languages of the large emotion. It is true that often I have had the need to augment my speech with the passionate gesture. It is sometimes too much for our language. I was captivated as I listened to her.

When Anna left, she embraced me and said, "*Arriverderci,* Bette." Little B.D. called down the stairs to her, "*Arriverderci,* Anna."

"*Arriverderci, piccolina!*" she called back.

Gary wiped his brow and fell into a chair. He usually had just me to contend with.

"The two of you! There was enough electricity in this room to light all of New York City."

• • •

When I was well enough we said good-bye to New York, loaded the station wagon, Gary and I, a governess and the three children—plus Tinker Belle, B.D.'s poodle and a parakeet in a cage—and drove to Homewood Inn in Yarmouth, Maine, which Gary had found for us. We arrived there in April and stayed until September. During the summer there we started looking for a permanent home. We had decided to bring up the children in Maine. One day we drove down a lane lined with apple trees and turned a corner and there was a house— beside the sea—that we fell in love with. It was obviously occupied, so we backed up hurriedly so as not to be thought trespassers. We never stopped dreaming of that house! One day a real estate man called to say he had a house to show us. To our amazement and delight it was the same one!

We rented it for a year with an option to buy, sent for all our furniture from California and moved in in September of that year. B.D. was entered in the first grade at Waynflete, a well-established private day school in Portland about 15 miles away. A governess was found for Margot and Mike. Stokesy the children called her. Her name was Elsa Stokes. She was with us for three years. I felt finally like the downright, upright, four-square married lady—P.T.A. and all. Here we would live; the children would have all the permanency of a home that I never had—grow up with one group of friends. I even found the proper outdoor setting on the grounds for a wedding for B.D. The best-laid plans of mice and men.

We called our house "Witch-way" because we didn't know which way we were going and a witch lived there—guess who?

It was a three-storied white clapboard house with the open Atlantic all around us. Huge picture windows overlooked the water; and I never once threw any of our antiques out of them into the ocean. The porches, the stacked lobster pots, the open fires, the pond for skating in winter, the cove, the everything made it the perfect home for a family to be happy in. Its kitchen was my new amphitheatre; and I never wanted to get off the stage! Memories of our kitchen in Winchester and the recalled tastes and smells of Ruthie's cooking inspired me.

Maine was my greatest therapy. My illness and now my convalescence insulated me from the world. The little things at home kept me going, got me through the gradual dying out of the pain and the numbness of my jaw due to my operation.

I had always adored keeping house—had never had much time up to now. I had the world by the tail I *thought*.

For the first time, I stayed home while my husband worked. My Maine neighbors had expected Theda Bara, at least, in sequin sheaths. For three years I was solely a wife and mother and Gary fell out of love with me. This was certainly a switch. My crime had usually been the fact I was always working. Why couldn't I be just a wife?

"I don't want you in the kitchen all the time. How can you keep your sanity working around the house fourteen hours a day? How clean can a place be? You're not Mrs. Craig; you're Bette Davis."

I rather thought I was Mrs. Merrill. I was being what I had for so long wanted to be—a wife and mother—and as usual I approached all this with as much enthusiasm and perfection as I would approach playing a part.

There were schedules for the children to keep and schedules to be skipped if I thought it right. Michael's good-night kiss to the parakeet was charming until it became so necessary to him that without it he would let out a bloodcurdling scream. Margot's temper tantrums and curious lethargy demanded constant attention. And B.D.! I was not going to make the same mistakes with her that Mother had made with me. Here we were again. A spirited girl; quick, efficient and a potential manager. She had a will of iron and a daredevil streak in her inherited from her own father. All valuable assets if kept under control. Being a parent is truly one of the greatest responsibilities I know of. To be in charge of another human being is an awesome thing.

Margot's behavior finally so alarmed Gary and me that we decided to take her to the Presbyterian Hospital in New York for a thorough examination. What we had vaguely suspected now became a reality. She was a retarded child. She had a brain-injury. There would have been no way of knowing this when she was born. B.D. once said to a friend over the phone, "My sister has a broken head."

It was a bitter blow and an enormous heartbreak to Gary and me. We were advised to send her away to school. It was not fair to her to have to compete with normal children, and not fair to the normal children to have to cope daily with a retarded child who would often be violent in her frustrations to keep up with her brother and sister.

Although I understand the parents who share this problem, I cannot forgive any sentimentalization over the decision to send such a child away to a school if it can be afforded financially.

Margot, dressed in a sailor suit and hat, looking like the doll she is, left our home at three years old, eight years ago. Gary flew her to Geneva, New York, to the Lochland School. She has been a happy girl there under the guidance of its headmistress, Miss Florence Stewart. She has learned to cope with herself more and more each year. She loves her Christmas and summer holidays with us. The three Merrill children have a wonderful time when she is at home. With a sense of our loss, we send her back to Lochland each time. But we know it is the way it has to be.

In 1955, 20th Century-Fox asked me to play Elizabeth in *The Virgin Queen* with Richard Todd. B.D. and Stokes accompanied me to California. Gary stayed with Michael in Maine.

It had been three years since I'd been in front of a camera. I was sure of nothing. Least of all myself. The first day was a nightmare for me. I heard Henry Koster, the director, say, "O.K., let's try a take," and I heard my voice:

"Mistress Throckmorton, is this your pet swine? I see you cast pearls before him."

After the first take was printed, I relaxed. I really think this Elizabeth was finer than my first. I shaved my head and eyebrows as before. Raleigh's first entrance into my throne room panicked him so, that I was reminded of my own experience with Claude's Napoleon.

Young Mr. Todd, a serious actor and a charming boy, was so nervous he couldn't remember his lines. This had happened before to me with actors. I said to him, "Underneath all this get-up, I'm on your side, Mr. Todd."

One day during the filming, Daddy and Mike appeared on the set. They had flown out from Maine to surprise me.

It is a wonderment to me that Mike even recognized me. It also was the first time he had ever been on a motion-picture set—in itself an experience for a child. We were rehearsing a scene in which Elizabeth was giving Raleigh what for! Michael asked his father, "Why is Mommy mad at that man instead of you?" Michael had reason to make this remark. Our marriage had deteriorated into round four of the main event, and no doubt about it. I had high hopes that with my return to acting things would be once more as they had been.

The Academy that year asked me to present the award to the winning actor on the TV show of this event. My hair was still in its shaven state, so a very clever Elizabethan cap was designed to cover all this up plus an appropriate dress of the period. It was quite a moment, appearing in front of "my town" for the first time in three years. The welcome I received that night was truly one of the great moments of my life. I felt one and all wanted me to know I had been missed and they were glad to have me back. I also was thrilled that Marlon Brando was the winner. He and I had much in common. He too had made many enemies. He too is a perfectionist.

Here I was, back in the swing again. This time, not with as much enthusiasm. My real happiness was at home with the children. I felt that was where a mother ought to be. I didn't want to uproot them and move back to California. For the next few years Gary and I struggled to keep our home and somehow to keep each other. Although I closed my ears to the fact, it was all too apparent that it was a losing battle. When *All About Eve* was finished, Gary and I had asked Mankiewicz to write a sequel. Now we were writing it for him—and no happy ending was in sight.

CHAPTER
19

Shortly after my fabulous evening at the Academy Award show, B.D., Stokes and I returned to Maine. Summers there are, of course, Paradise. I was treasuring every moment, as I was returning to California in the fall to make *Storm Center* for Columbia—a story about a librarian who refused to ban a book. Julian Blaustein had approached me to play the part while I was working in *The Virgin Queen*. It was an exciting project to me and a subject I felt important to make a film about.

The film was not a success at the box office and *not*, in my opinion, because of its subject matter. I never felt it turned out to be a good picture.

I was then asked to play Aggie Hurley in Paddy Chayevsky's *Catered Affair* at M-G-M. Gary and the children came out for Thanksgiving and stayed on for the filming of the picture. We rented Fay Bainter's house at Malibu.

During our stay there Gary and I realized an ambition—we bought a Mercedes S.L. 190, black—red leather inside. When the picture was finished, Gary insisted I take a holiday with him. He said I had earned one. He chartered a schooner for two weeks in Florida and off we drove in our brand-new car to Florida. And then we would of course return to Maine. I hated leaving the children, but I felt Gary and I had not been together alone for a long time. This might cement our very enuous relations. The children flew home to Stokes and off we went to Florida. A month or so later we arrived in Maine farther apart than ever. There was no question we had had it. Stubbornly refusing to settle for a divorce, I suggested we all move to California that winter, since it was increasingly unfair that Gary had had to be so often away from his children during all those years.

We closed Witch-way, rented a California house, and hoped for the best. Gary was employed solidly that year. I was again able to be the wife and mother—the kitchen my domain. In April of that year Norman Corwin approached Gary and me to do an evening of *The World of Carl Sandburg* on a one-night-stand tour, starting rehearsals in August. After weeks of negotiating, the contracts were signed. We would rehearse in Maine, tryouts would be in Maine, the opening in our own Portland. Gary was most enthusiastic about the whole project. We planned our wardrobe before leaving California for home.

I felt the tour would be a great test of whether or not I really could enjoy the theatre. My experience with *Two's Company* had not been a real test. I had been so ill. I had to face it—I had been in California all winter with only one offer of a job. As I told everyone who asked me why I would take upon myself one-night stands, I said it was the best job offered me that season. And it was.

This was by now the tenth year of my marriage to Gary. He now had me under contract both ways, as a wife and as a co-star. Would this cement our waning marriage? Quite the reverse—security was always bad medicine for him. Once he had something, I'm afraid, he didn't want it any more. It then became a responsibility he resented. It tied him down. By the time we started rehearsals for the Sandburg show, Gary and I were living apart. It didn't make the tour an easier one, I might add—but a contract is a contract and there was no out.

B.D. and Michael went, that winter of our tour, to the Chadwick School in Rolling Hills, California. Bobby lived close by, and in case of any emergency as I was roaming the earth, she could take care of it for me. This relieved my mind enormously. How I always hated to leave my children. They have been my life from the day they were born. I, probably wrongly, felt only I could bring them up. Gary, the pied piper, the self-

styled headmaster who truly has magic for all children, love
his own freedom as well. This I feel true of many fathers. A
mother never thinks of herself first—she doesn't want to. And
if she did, she has no option. From the day your first child is
born, you are no longer a free agent. This in no way suggests
a man does not love his children. He just never assumes the
degree of responsibility the woman does. I might add that Gary
after a month of being "on duty" with his children, admitted
to me that women deserved the Croix de Guerre. He was exhausted by the time the sun had set each day.

One could be far less tired, come evening, if the answer
were "yes" to children all day. This is not fair to them. Actually, they grow to feel unloved. Discipline is a symbol of
caring to a child. He needs guidance. If there is love, there is
no such thing as being too tough with a child. A parent must
also not be afraid to hang himself. If you have never been hated
by your child, you have never been a parent. My children will
tell you I haven't made it easy. I believe, if home is not sometimes a jungle, they will eventually be unfit for the outside
world. The outside world is a jungle! Gary always called me
the "seven-ball juggler." He claimed I could study my lines,
polish the silver, prepare dinner, and still discover in a rage
that Michael had been wearing gym pants without knees when
he had assured me that he didn't need new ones. Mike's devastating little blond face may enchant me, and it does, but
evading the issue, no matter what the consequences, is not for
Mother Merrill. Younger than B.D. and a boy, his reactions
were all completely different.

I said to Mike one day, "A great part of your life will be
spent with women. Learn to cope now. You live in a household
of strong women. Speak up—or you won't be heard!" At ten
he speaks up loud and clear. And he is devastating. As B.D.
says, "Oh Mother, when Mike grows up—watch out! He'll
have to fight the women off." He will. But I think he'll enjoy
it, not run from it. Without the ability to cope with the opposite
sex, no one can lead a well-adjusted life. It's tough enough
adjusted! Impossible otherwise.

I remember when B.D. was about four years old, she came
home from school decrying the fact that "there are gangs in
school."

"You will run into gangs all your life, B.D. Get used to them now."

My children know that I love life and living. They also know that I believe that the world is a place for work as well as play.

I often think of the Chinese, who are blessedly free of juvenile delinquency in New York. It is unheard of that a Chinese child is dragged into court. Isn't it because he is almost immediately made a working member of the community? When a Chinese baby starts to crawl, it is given a task that makes him a contributing member of the household. He may simply carry the napkins to table; but with the happy gratitude and approbation of his elders, he is learning to relate to the family unit. He loves the approbation and looks forward to the job. This is the kind of safety and security a child needs. A mutual respect is added to the basic love. Love is not enough. It must be the foundation, the cornerstone—but not the complete structure. It is much too pliable, too yielding.

B.D. is now fourteen and is an adult emotionally. She is still living off President Kennedy's observation, when I introduced them, that she looked nineteen. Brimming over with joy and enthusiasm and a love for horses that is now centered in her very own mare, Stoney-brook, she is utterly trustworthy and responsible. She is a young woman of whom I am proud.

I knew little of Carl Sandburg's work at the time we signed the contract. I knew "Fog" and his fame for the Lincoln biographies. I became educated. I haven't words enough for this fabulous eighty-three-year-old genius. His head is carved out of Mount Rushmore and he still has a true virility. He always says to me, "I love all this kissing and hugging we do."

His words—"Let a joy kill you . . . Keep away from the little deaths . . ."—made me realize suddenly that had always been my failing or my salvation.

We opened *The World of Carl Sandburg* at the little theatre at Bowdoin College in Brunswick, Maine, in October 1959. The notices we received that night were glowing, and were repeated in every city, town and hamlet we played on the one-night-stand tour.

In New London, Connecticut—one of the thousands of towns we played—our triumph had tragic overtones. During the performance two elderly sisters, who had been staunch

admirers of mine for years, sat in the first row of the movie
theatre we were playing in that night. They had bought their
tickets months in advance, waited breathlessly for our arrival
and now sat enthralled. Before the curtain went up, one of
them died of a heart attack. I learned of this tragedy after the
performance. The other stayed to the end. We had a very small
audience that night—we always claimed "we killed them in
New London!"

Our opening night in Hollywood was the peak of our tour
and our trial by fire. The former Queen, in a little one-night-
stand show. Through in pictures obviously. It was a much more
lethal audience for Gary and me than any New York opening.

Hollywood perversely wants you to fail. And for Bette Davis,
the seven-ball juggler who once ran the town, the sound of
steel hitting the block would be the sweetest.

I was finally just where they wanted me—in a professional
valley, vulnerable. "Everybody"—but "everybody"—was
there. The Huntington Hartford Theatre was bursting with Ja-
cobins waiting for the deposed Queen. I could hear the knitting
needles as the houselights went down. I was terrified, but con-
fident our show was a good one. The chips would have to fall
where they might.

Ruthie was in the audience—her ritual telegram tacked up
in my dressing room: REMEMBER DARLING—I'M IN THE FRONT
ROW. This night, for the first time—and as it turned out the
last time—she actually was in the front row.

I was thrilled by the deafening applause that greeted my
entrance. However, it was the closing applause that would tell
the tale. Would it be as deafening?

It was. It was also Ruthie's night. Her girl was back in the
chips! Ruthie had missed my being in the limelight. Originally,
we were booked in the theatre for a week—we stayed four!

After the Hollywood engagement, we went to San Francisco.
It was the end of the tour. It was also the end of the Merrills
as husband and wife. Almost to the day, ten years later, in the
same city, in the same hotel, the same people gave up the
ghost. San Francisco is where we had fallen in love during
the filming there of *All About Eve*. The last explosion could
have been heard round the world. There was no longer any
point in even trying.

I am sure I have been uncompromising, peppery, untractable,

monomaniacal, tactless, volatile and ofttimes disagreeable. I stand accused of it all. But at forty I allowed the female to take over. It was too late. I admit that Gary broke my heart. He killed the dream forever. The little woman no longer exists.

Those years in Maine were too good to be true anyway. It was the wrong casting. Actors can't expect life to be this bucolic.

The World of Carl Sandburg opened in New York the next October with Leif Ericson taking over for Gary. We lasted only four weeks. It was a bitter blow. The children and I stayed on in New York for the winter.

B.D. was in the hands of an excellent tutor and a good riding academy. Mike went to the Allen Stevenson School. I spent the winter writing this book and hoping to find a play or a picture I wanted to do.

Alice Jane, a longhaired dachshund who is Mikey's love, Tinker, a French poodle whose left ear Alice will eventually devour, and Wendy, a Siamese cat, made up our household. In March I went to Hollywood to co-star with Glenn Ford in a remake of *Lady for a Day*, a Damon Runyon story that Frank Capra was going to direct for the second time.

Before I left for the Coast I was signed to play Maxine Faulk in the new Tennessee Williams play, *Night of the Iguana*.

While I was touring in Florida with *The World of Carl Sandburg* the year before, Mr. Williams came to our show and talked to me about being in his new play. Violla Rubber, our mutual friend and associate producer of the play, suggested that I play Maxine Faulk. It was certainly the tertiary part—but as I have said many times since, I would rather have the third part in a Tennessee Williams play than a lead in an ordinary play. Anyway, Tennessee and I had had a date for years.

Tennessee looks like a pleasant, middle-class Englishman, florid of face and casual of dress. His enthusiasm and humility, plus a feeling of loneliness, make you know why he is the genius he is. This is a man who soars!

I went off to Hollywood with the Williams deal set. Ruthie had been very ill since Christmas and Bobby was taking care of her. I saw her in Laguna as often as I could get away. Mother always planned everything. Her latest plan was to die. She was seventy-six and that bursting heart was exhausted.

"I'm tired, Bette! I want B.D. to have this and Fay that . . .

I'm tired, darling . . . tired of the fight—''

"Now just cut that out, Ruthie! I want no more of this nonsense.''

But it wasn't nonsense. Mother had had it. And one early morning she simply went to sleep. Mother was gone. Bobby and I were speechless. We wanted to hide in the bathroom as we used to do when we shared any grief. It seemed impossible. We felt like orphans. Her vitality, her joy, were gone forever. Her protection and her dependency, her wisdom and her little girlness and her guts. She was made up of so many things, my mother. Brutal honesty and silly deceits; self-indulgence and endless sacrifices; love and loyalty and that abundance of joy of living. She was so many things—a rounded woman, not a washed-out stereotype. Ruthie! Without whom.

My mother was gone. In a rush of guilt, I remembered my ambivalence. Without the exciting, ubiquitous Ruthie, I would have been nothing. How dared I expect perfection in so magnificent a creature? How dared I not understand that this cultivated, talented woman had given up everything for me; and then—only after my success was assured—exacted a price that could never nearly approximate her value?

Toward the end of her life, she had reversed herself and tried to make me stay with Gary. She didn't want me ever to be without a man as she had been. My triumphs were hers and so were my defeats.

Always I see her in the window in Norwalk, hunched over her negatives; marching into John Murray Anderson's; wandering through the five and dime for amusing knickknacks to decorate sleazy little apartments; rushing toward me at Grand Central Station and whisking me off to the hospital; installing a Franklin stove on a porch at Butternut and filling my houses with her beloved flowers. And her enthusiasm.

I'm afraid that nothing mattered to me—the movie, the play, anything. Ruthie was gone. As Cousin John said, "What she was, she was to the end.''

When she invited guests to her house in Laguna, she would say, "Do what you like—it's Freedom Hall!'' *Freedom Hall. Do as I say* was more like it! How we all used to laugh.

She was prepared to leave us all. Her affairs were in perfect order. In a drawer in her desk was a list of instructions.

". . . I intend to die as extravagantly as I have lived. I want my casket to be one of those silver things.''

Mother could have asked for gold. She had earned it. On her tombstone is written:

RUTHIE—*You will always be in the front row.*

CHAPTER

20

If the battle of the sexes has become a war unto death, then I have been through it all. From drummer girl to Five-Star General— Retired, if you please.

I was handed the responsibilities of a man at twenty. Being little girl, sister, aunt and daughter to a mother was difficult. It was impossible to put my foot down. She had done so much for me.

Once the pattern is set, that's it. Bobby's daughter—no luckier than Ruthie, Bobby or I in marriage—has recently made me a grandfather. At this moment of writing, my obligations include three generations. Papa now has seven children and a horse. The only future marriage I would even remotely consider would be with Paul Getty.

I know now that my marriages—all of them—were a farce. What always started out in rehearsal to be a dream romance always ended in tuppenny melodrama. Each was different and all were the same. Variations on the same theme. As usual, the trouble started with those major considerations—the script and the casting.

Most men came to me with muscles flexed. It is a role as popular as Hamlet and just as rarely well played. All my marriages were charades. And I was equally responsible. The role of little woman was just as synthetic for me. I suppose I came pre-shrunk. The posture was absurdly belittling and brought further diminishing returns. But I always fell in love. That was the original sin.

Certainly modern woman in her agonized freedom has not lost the need of mastering. The female has gained more strength than the male. He, it seems, has lost his. When a man is challenged by an equal, he seems to retreat.

I have needed taming and I always looked for a Petrucchio. But I never let one take me on. I made it difficult, all right. But so did Kate. There wouldn't be much of a contest if the end were predetermined. Yes. I confess I found one man in my life. But he never tamed me because I flew like a bat out of hell.

It is impossible to know what would have happened had I allowed a husband to hold the purse strings. Early events made it impossible. My pride and independence precluded the chance later. I never learned to take. It has been a great fault not shared by some of my mates. I could never ask a man for anything. A man wants to be needed. But I couldn't be dependent in any way. That above all, I think, was my classic crime.

Without financial dependence on her husband, a woman loses patience more quickly, the areas of boredom loom larger. Unlike her mother and grandmother, she doesn't shrug her shoulders and make the best of things. She sets about to make them better. Today, more and more women are saying, "I've had it."

I do not say they are happier than their mothers or wiser; but facts are facts. A successful workingwoman cannot have the same set of values and reactions as her sheltered nineteenth-century grandmother. Power is new to women. We undoubtedly misuse it. I have been in the front ranks. Many who have lost the feminine thing and been forced to, aggress in order to survive. The swing toward a matriarchal society is here again.

If it is true that I was strengthened by my father, most men today are weakened by their mothers.

In all of my marriages there was no equality in incomes. This never bothered me until the inequity was taken for granted. I was old-fashioned enough to believe that a mate shared everything. Who ever heard of one partner prospering, the other languishing? What was mine was his. But I am lured to paraphrase the famous "but what's his is his." I discovered that

when a husband made one hundred dollars a week, he never
so much as offered to pay the gas and electric bills. He simply
bought himself some more clothes. The thought would have
been enough. It would have replaced the deed with me. But it
was never offered.

Perhaps I wanted to run the show; but if that is so, then they
all allowed it. Men usually balk at being the male while ac-
cusing you of robbing them of their virility.

It is said that it is virtually impossible to rape a woman. I
contend that it is equally impossible to emasculate a man. It
has taken all these years for me to realize that men and women
must come to each other whole. It is only then that one and
one make a unit. The fractions add up to nothing.

Each in a marriage must make a contribution. Of course.
What was that old song? "You're the cream in my coffee . . .
you're the salt in my stew"? How great and how true. One
has a right to expect such a complement. I was always eager
to salt a good stew. The trouble was that I was expected to
supply the meat and potatoes as well. This is the farce of our
epoch and most wives know it. Now the celebrated woman,
the rich woman, the strong woman, finds everything compounded.

Many men, like me, have been rejected by their fathers. I
became my own years ago; but now, in the maze that is the
modern emotional relationship, men find their fathers in
women. Now, with the solitary exception of General Eisen-
hower, I am the least likely father symbol extant. I have been
screaming this into the wind all my adult life. But the fates
decreed otherwise.

The high-powered male wants peace when he gets home.
The man of action wants a place to lick his wounds, a tender
mate to soothe his fevers. He deserves these ministrations.
Classically, the man is the soldier, the woman his nurse. But
there are high-powered females today who need the same solace
after dark.

She spends her days in the same arena fighting just as hard.
She is strung to her highest pitch when she returns home. But
if she reasonably expects the same considerations, she becomes
a monster. Man or woman, a human being cannot discard the
habit of authority and station for naked slavery. But miracles
are expected of a woman. She is expected to be a quick-change

artist. If she loves her home, she takes care of it. Nothing could ever stop me from running my house. It is second nature for me to clean and cook. But on my terms. I cannot be a servant but the keeper of the house.

Well, I tried. I tried everything. I attempted to be all things to all men and found that it was simply an extension of my daily struggle—one more strain. I found I was now acting twenty-four hours a day, seven days a week. Marriage is the toughest contract of them all.

Like Julie in *Jezebel* I had to remain in charge and when the man allowed it, I lost all respect for him. I certainly made it impossible. The "Whats" matter in this world, not the "Whys." No matter the reasons. I was a hellion and I made my bed. It has taken me all these campaigns to realize that if my husbands were weaklings, it was I who attracted them. The one man—that one Petrucchio—I was petrified of. Ruth Elizabeth had one goal all her life—to find a real man. Bette Davis ran interference all the way.

I am that new race of women. But there is a new species of man as well. Unlike the leaners, he is sufficient unto himself. Our era has given him frozen foods and a thousand and one available services that make a woman around the house expendable.

Some of the happiest hosts I know are bachelors. The whole point of marriage has been blunted. If a woman doesn't need a provider and a man doesn't need her homemaking, then half the reason for their alliance is gone. If either ever reveals a talent for auto-reproduction, there will never be another marriage ceremony.

The act of sex, gratifying as it may be, is God's joke on humanity. It is man's last desperate stand at superintendency. The whole ritual is a grotesque anachronism, an outdated testament to man's waning power. It's all we've got and so we make the best of it. It is not, however, sufficient reason for matrimony.

It has been my experience that one cannot, in any shape or form, depend on human relations for lasting reward. It is only work that truly satisfies. I think I've known this all my life. No one could ever share my drive or my vision. No one has ever understood the sweetness of my joy at the end of a good day's work. I guess I threw everything else down the drain.

But they all settled, my husbands, and enjoyed the fruit while they tried to cut down the tree. Every last one of them resented his position without trying to change it. A better way to say it—the responsibility always shifted to me. Since they were all bigger than I physically, there was a way of punishing me.

My father unfortunately balked at beating me. My husbands did not. I have always been terrorized by physical violence. The indignity of it humiliates me. This was their ammunition. And I evidently drove them to use it.

Their inadequacies, their feeling of secondary position in the household, always led to resentment, bitterness and jealousy. When they yelled for Daddy and I answered, they lashed out at me in fury.

Why did they always stay to the bitter end? Why didn't they leave as they so often threatened to? I suppose, like children, they were afraid to leave home.

I am not a chameleon. All my life I fought dishonesty and misrepresentation. I remember my battle to keep Warners from displaying *The Corn Is Green* with ads consisting of a picture of me (playing the Welsh schoolmistress) in black satin décolletage. Well, I found my husbands' advance publicity fraudulent. The weak are the most treacherous of us all. They come to the strong and drain them. They are bottomless. They are insatiable. They are always parched and always bitter. They are everyone's concern and like vampires they suck our life's blood.

It is the strong who need care. It is they who need constant replenishment. It is the strong who are vulnerable. But "Don't worry about her. She can take care of herself!" is what you hear from the beginning. It is the strong for whom I will do anything. It is they who need consideration.

Like Gulliver, I have been used as the Lilliputians' landscape. I have been walked over always. I have survived it because I survive everything; so far—anyway.

Of course, I replaced my father. It was my Pyrrhic victory. I am responsible. Every spark grows to consume itself. It is true. I became my own father and everyone else's. Ruthie knew this. I think she saw it start very early. And this is why she eventually handled me as she had her first husband. She was every inch the wife that Harlow Morrell Davis reckoned with and eventually abandoned. I never could.

This is all true but there is another strata beneath this one. It is hell to dislike a parent. I longed to love my father. I respected his intellect, his power. I wanted this in a man beyond my fear of it.

In Rome a couple of years ago, I met Magnani once more. That brilliant, lonely woman. She fixed her gaze on me one day.

"Ah, Bette Davis! How I envy you. You have everything—a career and a husband!"

I couldn't tell her then we were in the same boat. Now she knows.

If I ever hear that marriage ceremony again I will scream with laughter. And I would wear black. That ceremony for me is interred with the corpse of Ruth Elizabeth. This is not to say that I will not fall in love again. Love I cannot escape. But one is soon enough released from its bondage. No more of Thoreau's quiet desperation.

No more long-term contracts. I am free and we all know what solitude that brings. But I have always been alone, really. I should have known enough to travel light; because no one could really come with me on my trip. I fought this knowledge for years and now I face it squarely.

My children however are the dividends I miraculously earned with all my wildcat schemes. But how strange that the circle has come full round. I am exactly where Mother was at the beginning. Alone with my children—alone against the world. But I have had my fulfillment in my career. Ruthie never did—either in love or work. She sacrificed everything for me.

"I don't like it that you're going to be alone in the house, Mommy. Who's going to be with you when B.D. and I are away at school?"

Ten-year-old Mike. I felt my face begin to crumble. And that's exactly why I sent him off to school. I do not intend to use my children as crutches. At this moment, the world of children is the only sane and gratifying one to me. The silence of the house is painful. These occasional weekends are nothing. I cannot wait until Christmas. We'll all be together again. This will be the second Christmas without Ruthie. Without our "weeping gifts." But I have my work and I'll be fine.

My children will never see vulnerability and sacrifice. This is the tie that binds as no other—and forever. I want them bound to no one, not even to me. And I am all right. I'll be fine! I keep saying over and over!

The Williams play was my first without Ruthie. There are going to be so many firsts from now on.

Our out-of-town tryout of *Iguana* opened in Rochester. Rochester! It's almost too pat. A flood of memories carried me from my dressing room to that stage on opening night. Cukor and *Broadway*, Ruthie and the striped wallpaper, the beginning, the prelude to all this. How ironic that I should return to Rochester. I recalled my train trip with the cast—my first separation from her.

"Remember, darling. Study the part of Pearl . . . she's going to have an accident."

I stood waiting for the curtain to go up. All the old nerves were there. Then I felt my spine stiffen.

Western Union never sent it; but it was telegraphed all the same. No one can ever convince me it wasn't.

"Remember, darling—I'm in the front row."

Mother was there. I saw her, back at Cushing when I graduated, smiling gaily in that old flowered hat that was supposed to hide her developer-poisoned face. I saw her sitting there spunky and proud. I could never let her down. My cue came. "Curtain up, light the lights, we've got nothing to hit but the heights."

I made my entrance. Maxine Faulk said, "Shannon! Hi Baby—I've been expecting you here."

Everything did come up roses.

CHAPTER
21

Catching Up: 1962—1989

G. P. Putnam's Sons first published my autobiography *The Lonely Life* in 1962. Over the years, *The Lonely Life* has become a sort of textbook of what a successful film career necessarily involves. Many readers have misunderstood the title: it is not *A Lonely Life*. I most certainly have not had a lonely life. The title *THE Lonely Life* refers not to me but to all artists. Artists certainly are not the boys and girls next door. They take a different approach to things and are often considered peculiar in their ways—in what they say, and do.

I've received more fan letters than you can imagine asking where one can find a copy of *The Lonely Life*. These letters were a large factor in my decision to allow the book to be republished with an update of the highlights and happenings in my life from 1962 until now.

One of the most important events of my life during these years was meeting Kathryn Sermak in 1979. She is my assistant and collaborated with me during the writing of *This 'N That*. The second most important event was the addition to my life of Harold Schiff, who through these years has been my lawyer and a great friend.

Books seem to have been a great occupation for me in the years since 1962. In 1974 I worked with Whitney Stine on a book titled *Mother Goddamn*. This book is solely about my career and is still very popular today.

In 1987, G. P. Putnam's Sons published *This 'N That*, a book written with the high hopes that the story of how I overcame a stroke and mastectomy and continued successfully with my life and my career could inspire others. It did just that. I received many letters from stroke victims thanking me for my encouragement.

This 'N That was on the *New York Times* bestseller list for months, and the planning of the publicity for it was in the capable hands of Kathryn. The publicity tour took us to many places and countries. The first stop, here at home, was the enormously successful book signing at B. Dalton's on Hollywood Boulevard. Traffic was stopped in all directions. There were hundreds of people, the lines to get in went for blocks, and the boulevard was jammed. We were told the people came from all over. Some were even there the night before, waiting to be one of the first to have their book signed. It was an impressive sight and the success of all this was due to Kathryn's expert planning. The signing took place on Valentine's Day, which gave it an added glamour.

Our next stop for publicizing the book was New York City, and the high point there was my appearance on *The David Letterman Show*. To be sure, Mr. Letterman and I were an odd couple to do a show together, but I thoroughly enjoyed working with him. I wore a dress Kathryn had brought back from Paris. It was black with a beaded heart, made for me by the American designer Patrick Kelly. Mr. Letterman told me he was flattered by my appearance on the show and he thoroughly approved of Patrick Kelly's dress. The audience roared with laughter much of the time, and this appearance was a great success.

Our next stop was England. A publishing house there bought the rights to our book, so we spent much time in London publicizing it. The most memorable event in London was the book signing at Hatchard's Book Store in Piccadilly Circus. Kath had handled all the previous arrangements with the manager of the store. The only item she disagreed with him on was the number of London bobbies needed to ensure complete security for me while at the bookstore. The manager kept insisting that with all their store security, they would need no more than three London bobbies. Since Prince Andrew had only had two, we couldn't possibly need more. Kathryn insisted that we have at least eight or ten. She was very knowledgeable about the crowds I usually attracted. She was right and won her point. I will never forget leaving the bookstore after two hours of signing books to find the streets jammed with people. Buses had to be rerouted, and the headlines in the paper the next day read BETTE DAVIS STOPS TRAFFIC IN PICCADILLY. Needless to say, our book was again very successful and made number one on the bestseller list in England.

The third launching of *This 'N That* took us to France after a French publishing house bought the rights to it. We spent much time in Paris talking about our book and I appeared on practically every talk show. The highlight of these interviews was the one with Frederic Mitterrand, the nephew of the President, on his show "Au Cote de Chez Fred." It turned out to be more of a tribute than an interview. I was overcome by his research of my career, his ability to speak in English as well as French. He had made a tape of the French actress Jean Moreau talking about me and of a superb pianist playing many of Max Steiner's scores from my films. Kathryn was one of my guests on the show, as well as the designer Patrick Kelly. There was a most touching ending to the show. Mr. Mitterand asked Kathryn to read aloud a letter she had written about me, which was a chapter in our book. She, of course, read it in French. I was totally impressed not only with her French but also the way she read it, with such sincerity it brought tears to many eyes.

While we were in Paris, I was given a luncheon in my honor by the President of France, Francois Mitterrand. Kath and I were thrilled to meet the President, feeling this was an unusual invitation to be extended to an American actress. President Mitterrand made me very proud when he said in his speech that I was an exemplary ambassador from Hollywood. A homey touch was the presence of President Mitterrand's rather large dog. Like President Roosevelt, who always had his Scottie, Falla was with him wherever he went.

Unfortunately, books can give one more joy and less heartache than children. During the writing of *This 'N That*, my daughter B.D. published a book about me, co-authored with her husband, Jeremy. It was far from a nice book. It broke my heart! B.D.'s adopted father, Gary Merrill, always criticized

me for spoiling B.D. As it turned out, I guess he was right.
The shock of her book, as I have already stated in *This 'N
That*, was more catastrophic than the mastectomy and stroke.
To publish such a book during the time I was fighting for my
life made it doubly a crime. To the many who constantly ask
me if my daughter and I have reconciled, the answer is No,
never!

Looking back on the highlights of my life from 1962 until
now, there certainly have been many. These were momentous
years, professionally and personally. I have been involved in
many projects and have received many wonderful accolades in
the years since this book was first published.

I ended the first edition of *The Lonely Life* with the words
"everything's coming up roses." I was overly optimistic. The
first film I made after writing the book was *Pocketful of Miracles*. Everything did not come up roses during the making of
this film. It was the first time the great director Frank Capra
had consented to have an associate producer, Glenn Ford (who
was also my co-star). It was Ann-Margret's first film, and she
proved to be a very good actress and most certainly terrific to
work with.

Originally, I was given the dressing room next to Mr. Ford,
but after about a week of shooting, he asked the assistant
director to inform me that he would like Miss Hope Lange to
have my dressing room. The assistant seemed very uncomfortable telling me this. To make it easier on him I said, "Dressing rooms do not make good performances, put me anywhere
you like."

I have never given my performance as Apple Annie in *Pocketful of Miracles* enough consideration. It has turned out to be
one of my more popular performances with the public, much
to my surprise.

A major accomplishment during these years was playing Jane
in the film *Whatever Happened to Baby Jane?* Joan Crawford
and I got along famously much to the huge disappointment of
the Hollywood press. The director-producer, Robert Aldrich,
fought hard to have this picture made. All the major studios
turned him down because the banks felt Crawford and I were
unbankable. There was interest from some if he would recast
the "two old broads," Davis and Crawford. But Aldrich re-

fused. As a last resort, he went to the Seven Arts Production
Company. Eliot Hyman, the head man, felt it would make a
fabulous film and said he would "back" it.

Baby Jane was completed with one week of readings, three
weeks of filming, and two weeks of post-production to film
the scenes showing the early lives of our characters. As we
were wrapping up, I took out a want ad in *The Hollywood
Reporter*. Even today, this ad is remembered by many people
worldwide. It read:

> Mother of three—10, 11, and 15. Divorcee. American.
> Thirty years experience as an actress in motion pictures.
> Mobile still and more affable than rumor would have it.
> Wants steady employment in Hollywood (has had Broad-
> way). BETTE DAVIS, c/o Martin Baum, GAC. Refer-
> ences upon request.

There was great objection by one and all to my ad. Those
who were part of my professional life felt this a very foolish
thing to do. It was also misunderstood. If I had not been employed at the time, I never would have done this. I did it to
poke fun at the bankers and their list of who was not bankable.
If we were not allowed to make films, how would they know
whether or not we were bankable?

As it turned out, the film was a sensation. *Whatever Happened to Baby Jane?* proved how wrong the bankers were. All
costs were covered in the first weekend it was released and the
movie made film history. *Baby Jane* was such a huge success
it proved there was no reason for me or Miss Crawford to ever
be on their unbankable list.

After the film was out, Jack Warner gave a luncheon honoring Miss Crawford and me. Since Warner Bros. was one of
the major studios that had turned us down, and since they were
my studio for many years, I guess the luncheon was an apology
of sorts. It was the first time I had been on the Warner lot in
fourteen years. It was a most nostalgic experience. I remember
toasting Mr. Warner, thanking him for the luncheon, and calling him "my father," which heads of studios often were to
their stars. I admitted that I had often been a difficult daughter
to bring up. There was much laughter and camaraderie at the

luncheon, which was rewarding after all the years. Father had obviously forgiven me.

Aldrich decided to show the film at the Cannes Film Festival that year. My daughter B.D. and I were invited to go with him. B.D. had played the daughter of the next-door neighbor, but her decision to be in *Baby Jane* had nothing to do with a future film career. This she never wanted. I thought she was very good and showed signs of talent as an actress. Deciding to have B.D. go with me to Cannes, however, turned out to be one of the greatest mistakes in my life. It was there she met Eliot Hyman's nephew who she fell in love with and eventually married. I believe it was this union that, years later, produced B.D.'s book about me.

Of course, some of my most memorable difficulties have been caused by directors. In the summer of 1967 during the making of *The Anniversary*, which was filmed in England, the director, Alvin Rakoff, and I did not see eye to eye. One example of his direction was when he told me to "count to five while looking in the mirror, pause two beats, turn and walk away." One hardly gives performances while counting! I was in a state of shock. I couldn't believe what I had heard. That was not my idea of direction. I persuaded the head of Hammer Productions to fire Mr. Rakoff, who was obviously not meant to direct me, and replace him with Roy Baker, who directed the film brilliantly. My character, Mrs. Taggart, wore an eye patch. I had them made in New York before I left for London. The eye patches were made of the same material as each costume I wore. Very chic indeed. Twentieth Century-Fox was the producer in America. I guess our film *The Anniversary* was too much for them as it was never released here. There's no doubt about it, the mother which I played, was a wicked woman.

I've always been sad Fox did not bring this film to America. Having been famous for many years for playing bitches, this one definitely topped them all.

An enormous departure for me was playing a Eurasian woman in the film *Madame Sin*, filmed on the Isle of Mull in Scotland. To look the part, I spent two and a half hours each morning in makeup. All my dresses were black and were designed by Edith Head, who sent them over to Scotland. Robert Wagner was my co-star and producer for this television pilot, which was financed by Sir Lew Grade. I adore R.J., which made up in great part for having to endure the freezing weather, the long distances to location for filming, and the director—a wee bit of a monster.

When we arrived in Glasgow to take the boat to the Isle of Mull, the station was crowded with white-haired ladies, each holding a bouquet of white heather (a flower the Scots consider very lucky) to give to me. R.J. turned his back and walked away from me, shaking with laughter. Later, when I asked him what was so funny he said, "Now we know how old you are."

Shortly afterward, I was stung twice by a wasp. There was no one in the hotel at the time. The doctor for the island was in a medical unit some sixty miles away, and the whole cast and crew were off shooting. The arm where I was stung was so hard it felt like a piece of wood, and my mouth was swollen to twice its normal size. I was petrified until the doctor finally came and gave me some very powerful shots. He told me that wasp venom is so poisonous that a sting can be fatal, particularly if one is stung in the vein where I was. Who knows? Maybe the white heather saved me. At the end of the film R.J. gave me a beautiful wasp-shaped charm on a chain with another charm saying "To Madame Sin, With Love."

During these "catch-up" years I also made two films in Italy. *The Empty Canvas* was produced by Carlo Ponti and co-starred Horst Buchholz, who played a Nazilike character. Mr. Buchholz was very disappointed to find out that I did not look like Baby Jane, which amused me very much. The film never came to America, but with good reason.

The other film, *Lo Scopone Scientifico* (The Scientific Card-player), co-starred Joseph Cotten and Alberto Sordi. Very soon after we started filming, I changed Mr. Sordi's name to "sordid." He could speak perfect English but refused to do so, saying he couldn't be funny in English. English, Italian—it didn't matter. He was all slapstick in any language. I was truly disappointed that this film was never shown in the United States, probably due to the fact that "Mr. Sordid" added about forty pages to his part of the film, and it was very dull footage. So Joseph and I lost out. It's a pity, because Joseph's and my scenes were very interesting indeed. Fabiani, the great Italian couturier, had designed my clothes for the film, and they were beautiful!

CHAPTER
22

After finishing *Lo Scopone Scientifico* I went back to my beloved home, Twinbridges, in Westport, Connecticut. My son, Michael, announced his engagement to Chou-Chou Raum. I had always promised him that when the time came, I would give him one of my rings to give to his girl, so I did. Of course, I tried to persuade him to finish law school first, but Michael is strong-willed and I think he was tired of driving 600 miles every weekend to visit Chou.

Michael always had a mind of his own. I'll never forget the incident I call "While the Cat's Away, the Mice Will Play." I was going to make a film in Switzerland, and ten minutes before I left for the airport in New York, Harold Schiff called to tell me I couldn't leave the country just yet. He had not received the money for the film. I had told Michael he was not to come back to Westport every weekend while I was away. Michael thought, "How would Mother ever find out?," and decided to go to Westport to spend the weekend with Chou. Upon arriving home, he was horrified to see all the lights in the house on, which meant one thing: Mother had not gone to Switzerland. In a panic, he decided the best thing to do was to hide out at his sister's home, also in Westport. The next day B.D. decided she had better tell me that Michael was at her house, which she did. You can imagine the stormy session that ensued.

And so on May 19, 1973, Michael Woodman Merrill and Chou-Chou Raum were married at the Westport Unitarian Church. Michael's father, Gary Merrill, came to the wedding. It was sort of a reunion for Gary and me because we had not seen each other for quite a few years. We both felt it important, no matter what our personal situation was, to both be at Michael's wedding.

The wedding day was full of emotion. Michael's fraternity brothers all drove from North Carolina to Westport to be at his wedding. I felt this was a great compliment to Michael. He was surprised and thrilled to see his great college friends . . . to say nothing of the surprise it was to Chou's mother to find about two dozen hungry college boys at the reception. Not ones to pass up the chance for a free meal, the boys quickly forgot their manners, and in they dove. The delicious refreshments quickly disappeared, much to the embarrassment of the hostess.

I was very proud of the way Michael looked as a bridegroom, and his bride, Chou, is a very pretty girl. Happily, their marriage has been a huge success. They've been married for seventeen years and have two beautiful sons, Mathew Davis Merrill and Cameron Snow Merrill. They now live in Chestnut Hill, Massachusetts, and Michael has a very successful law practice nearby in Boston.

During the years I was under contract to Warner Bros., I had gone many times to see the head of the studio, Jack Warner, to ask him about the rights to a book about Aimee Semple McPherson, the most famous and notorious evangelist of her day. The Hays office, which was the censorship group in those days, refused to give us permission to do any film about her. They felt Aimee McPherson's morals did not befit someone who claimed to be religious. Probably her most morally outrageous behavior was her claim that she was on a religious pilgrimage in the desert, when in fact she and a man from her church had spent the time hiding out and living together as man and wife. The Hays office claimed Aimee Semple McPherson, who was called Sister Aimee, was a religious whore, and under no conditions would they allow any film to be made about her, to my great disappointment.

In 1975, the censors finally allowed a film to be made about
Sister Aimee. I was in the film, not as Sister Aimee, but as
her mother. Faye Dunaway was cast in the leading role. There
were many days on the set when I would have given anything
to have been playing Aimee. Miss Dunaway was without doubt
the most impossible co-star I've worked with. She was never
on time and never knew her lines.

Many of the scenes were filmed in a 5,000-seat tabernacle
in Denver, Colorado. We needed the tabernacle full for several
of the scenes, so there was an open invitation to any citizen of
Denver to come to the tabernacle and watch the filming. Their
payment was a box lunch. The first day there was a packed
house. Miss Dunaway was supposed to be in the first scene,
but the minutes rolled by and there was no Miss Dunaway.
Our voluntary audience started leaving. Something had to be
done, so I decided to stop this unfortunate exodus. I began to
sing, "I've Written a Letter to Daddy" from the film *Whatever
Happened to Baby Jane?* The audience gradually drifted back
into their seats, and the day's filming was saved.

In all my years as an actress, I have only criticized two
actresses with whom I have worked. The first is Miriam Hopkins and the second is Faye Dunaway, whose name is most
appropriate. Several times I wished I could have "Dun-away"
with her. Any race for witchery featuring Miss Hopkins and
Miss Dunaway would most definitely end up in a tie.

The one good thing that came from playing the mother in
The Disappearance of Aimee was working with James Woods,
whose hobby was photography. One day on the set he took
some photographs of me, and a few years later one proved to
be perfect for the cover of *This 'N That*.

In 1977, I was honored with The American Film Institute
Life Achievement Award. The American Film Institute was
founded for the preservation of films past, present, and future,
although it has other functions. It helps advance the art of film
and awards scholarships to talented newcomers in the industry.
Also, each year it gives a life achievement award to some
member of the industry for his or her work over a lifetime,
work which has "stood the test of time." Mine was the fifth
of these awards and I was the first woman recipient. The first

four were John Ford, James Cagney, Orson Welles, and William Wyler.

Jane Fonda was the mistress of ceremonies, and she helped make the evening a very smooth-running affair. The most spectacular film footage of the evening was a series called "The Faces of Bette Davis." There were many speeches made about me, for the most part by people I had worked with: Henry Fonda, Paul Henreid, Geraldine Fitzgerald, Natalie Wood, Olivia de Havilland, Joseph Mankiewicz and, best of all, my favorite director, William Wyler. I was particularly proud of a line from the speech of George Stevens, Jr., when he presented me with my award. He said, "Tonight we are here to celebrate a woman of uncommon originality and distinction who, throughout a bold career, dared to be different." I felt this was probably the best description of my career.

In my acceptance speech for the A.F.I. Award, I said the award was like the frosting on the cake of my career. In former years, I had won two Oscars, the top honor any actor in Hollywood can receive. I most certainly felt that way when receiving mine, and this prestigious award is one I will always treasure.

In one of my leaner professional periods, with no script to my liking in sight, I was—to my great surprise—offered a Disney film, *Return From Witch Mountain*. I was rather intrigued with the idea of finding out how Disney's special effects were created. My young grandson, Ashley, was thrilled when he heard that his grandmother was to be in a Disney film, and for the first time was very impressed with the fact that I was a movie star. From then on he treated me with infinitely more respect. I found all this to be great fun.

Another high point in my career, in Ashley's opinion, was a song which became number one in the U.S., "Bette Davis Eyes," sung by Kim Carnes. Having his grandmother sung about in a rock 'n' roll hit was even more wondrous to Ashley and to me. The lyrics, written by Jackie DeShannon and Donna Weiss, are amazingly close to the truth about me. Also, Kim's low, husky voice is not unlike my voice. I was delighted for them all, especially Kim. This was her first big single record success. She won a gold and a platinum record, copies of which she gave to me. They proudly hang in my home.

Some years later I was offered another Disney film, *Watcher in the Woods*. The character I was asked to play in this one was a reasonably good part, as opposed to the role in *Return From Witch Mountain*. *Watcher in the Woods* was directed by John Hough, produced by Ron Miller, and co-starred David McCallum, Carroll Baker, and, in the leading role of the young girl, Lynn-Holly Johnson, whom I felt was seriously miscast.

We filmed in England at an old manor house. My hairdresser, Peggy Shannon, who always went with me on films—especially if they were shot on location—was not able to accompany me on this one. That left me in a very serious situation. I had to have someone to go with me, so I asked my friend Wes Carlson if he knew of anyone. A few days later he called to tell me he had found someone whom he thought would be perfect for the job, so I agreed to interview her.

The next day, Miss Kathryn Sermak arrived at my house at 11:00. She was an extremely attractive young girl with beautiful brown eyes, and she was impeccably dressed, which is important in an assistant of mine. Kathryn's credentials were very impressive: she had graduated from U.S.C. with honors, traveled extensively, lived abroad, and worked as an assistant to a royal family residing in the United States. I explained to Kathryn what her job would be and asked if she was available to accompany me to England where I was scheduled to make a film. I was delighted when she accepted because I had a hunch about this girl.

While we were there I learned that I had been nominated for an Emmy for Best Actress for my role in *Strangers*. It was a particularly worthy script: the story of a mother, played by me, and her daughter. The daughter, wonderfully acted by Gena Rowlands, tries to regain the love of her mother after a separation of twenty years. Finally the daughter reveals that she is dying of cancer. Michael DeGuzman was the writer of this brilliant script, giving us speeches that amounted to full-page monologues.

I did win the Emmy, and felt I deserved it, not only for the character I portrayed, but for the difficulty of the part and the hardships of filming. We worked in the bitter winter cold of Montecito in Northern California.

A year later, Kath and I were in New York on her birthday and much to my surprise, when I wished her a happy twenty-ninth birthday she looked at me in horror and said, "This is only my twenty-fourth birthday." Laughing, I said, "Good thing the agency lied." Otherwise you might not have gotten the job. My hunch turned out to be right, however, because she has been a wonderful assistant.

That following year my sister, Bobby, died. I was visiting the Hymans at their farm in Pennsylvania when Bobby's daughter, Faye, called me with the sad news of her mother's death. What a loss to us all. How we would all miss her and always will. I had named my daughter B.D. after her (Barbara Davis, like my sister, but we called her B.D. so we wouldn't have two Bobbies in the family).

Bobby had stayed with the children so many times when I was away working, seeing to it that all was well. The feeling of security that my children were well taken care of was her great present to me. In all these years since her death, I often think how wonderful it would be if she were still alive, and we could be living together.

In 1981, I filmed a television special called *Family Reunion*. It was very "special" because my grandson, Ashley, played a major part in the film. Of course, he had never been in a film before, so I took an enormous chance when I asked the producer, Lucy Jarvis, if she would agree to Ashley playing the part of the eleven-year-old boy in the script.

The idea was not totally out of the blue. Ashley had often come home from a film he had seen and imitated the characters. He was quite good at it, which made his mother, B.D., feel he might have some potential as an actor.

The film was made in the wintertime, with snow and below-zero temperatures in the charming little town of Locust Valley on Long Island. To say that Kath and I were nervous as we drove to the location that first day of shooting is the understatement of the year. We both realized that if for any reason Ashley was unable to do what the director required, it would not only be heart-breaking to Ashley but it would mean he would probably have to be recast. Such a failure for one so young would leave its mark for many years to come. As it turned out, he was unbelievably cool, poised, and gave a very good performance. As we drove back that night there was joy in all our hearts, and I found myself humming Ashley's favorite song of the time—"Celebration." The relief Kath and I felt was humongous.

During the making of the film Ashley and I became close friends. Yet I felt a lot of animosity from his mother while Ashley and I were working together. I have often wondered whether this, along with her other jealousies, could have given her the idea for the awful book she wrote about me. Not only was the book a terrible blow to me, it was also a heartbreak to lose Ashley's friendship and never be able to watch him grow up.

After *Family Reunion*, I was sent a script for *A Piano for Mrs. Cimino*. I agreed to make it when I learned the director was to be George Schaefer, who for many years had been responsible for the television drama series *The Hallmark Hall of Fame*. I chose Keenan Wynn as my male co-star. George Schaefer was a delight to work with and Keenan proved to be the perfect choice. I felt I gave one of my better performances and was delighted to receive the Monte Carlo Award for it.

Another particularly worthy script was *Right of Way*. The subject of the film was an individual's right to choose to die. The topic has been a major controversy in medical circles for many years. None of the major networks would make the film, so the cable network H.B.O. produced it. We filmed *Right of Way* in Los Angeles and worked on sound stages. No locations, which was an award in itself, because most films today are made on location. I was fortunate and thrilled to have Jimmy Stewart as my co-star and to once again be directed by George Schaefer. Jimmy was terrific to work with—always prepared and enthusiastic. I told him one day that I wished I had met him when I was younger, because I would never have let him escape me. In the film he gives my character, Mini, this tiny little wave, which I adored. I often use this tiny little wave myself now in remembrance of the movie with Jimmy.

CHAPTER

23

One of the most terrific evenings in my honor during these "catch-up" years was an occasion called The Army Ball. I was awarded the Distinguished Civilian Service medal, the nation's highest honor for a civilian, and I have been told that only very few people have ever received this award. Mr. Roy Thorsen had been in touch with the U.S. Defense Department in Washington for months and had received the unanimous decision by the departments of Armed Forces—the Army, Navy, Air Force, and Marines—that I should receive this award and be invited to an Army Ball in my honor. Of course, I said yes. This wonderful award was bestowed on me because of my work with the Hollywood Canteen during the war years. I was the founder of the Canteen, an organization which insured that when servicemen came through Hollywood before going off to fight the war, they would have a chance to meet Hollywood stars. The Hollywood Canteen also provided free entertainment to military people during World War II, hosting up to 3,000 service men and women a night. After the war, the Hollywood Canteen closed, and I helped organize the Hollywood Canteen Foundation, which raised funds for veterans' activities.

Mr. Marsh, Secretary of the Army, flew from Washington to personally present me with this medal. There were Scottish bagpipes, magnificent flowers, and all the high-ranking officials of the four military branches in their full regalia. It was a thrilling sight. The evening featured a skit of a night at the Hollywood Canteen, and the skit was accurate in every detail. I was quite impressed. And when I was presented with my medal by Mr. Marsh, about twenty to twenty-five people, all of whom had worked at the original Canteen, were lined up behind me on stage. It was a particular thrill for me to see all my great Canteen helpers again: Roddy McDowall, Paul Henreid, Mrs. John Ford, Van Johnson, Jane Withers, Martha Raye, Bob Hope, Virginia Mayo, Joan Leslie, Gloria De-Haven, Margaret O'Brien, etc. To have our Hollywood Canteen be so honored by the United States government after all these years was a most rewarding experience. It was an awesome feeling for that little girl from Lowell, Massachusetts to be honored by her country.

I did not make another film until 1985, a year and a half after suffering from my mastectomy and stroke. I went to England to start filming the television film *Murder With Mirrors*. Murder it was, but I was happy to begin acting again. My co-stars were the very talented Sir John Mills and Helen Hayes, first lady of the American theatre. She flattered me often, asking me to help her understand how to work for a camera because it was such a different technique from acting on a stage.

On the last day of shooting, I received a phone call telling me that B.D. had written a nasty book about me. Her book left a deep scar and an emptiness in my life. At the time her book was published, I was told B.D. had become a very active member of a religious group which I had never heard of. She even went as far as to write me and tell me that God had told her to write the book. "What kind of God?" I said to myself. Again, I am proud to say, I have weathered this storm as well as I did others.

The first theatrical film I made in ten years was *The Whales of August*. My co-stars were Lillian Gish, Vincent Price, and Ann Sothern. It was late fall of 1986 and we were filming on Cliff Island in Casco Bay, not far from Portland, Maine, where I had once lived for many years. *Whales of August* was originally an off-Broadway play written by David Berry, who also adapted it for the film. Mr. Berry was on the set almost every day, keeping a watchful eye on his script. In my view, our very opinionated, disagreeable, macho director, Lindsay Anderson, eliminated and changed what we all thought were important lines. My character, Libby, was a blind and extremely cantankerous person. Often I felt the sharpness of Mr. Anderson's invisible knife as he cut lines I felt were necessary to my character. I felt he was not good at listening to other people's opinions. Certainly, he never listened to me, Mr. Berry, or Vincent Price, who often beefed about Lindsay's direction of him. Mr. Anderson was infuriating to us all.

I felt *Whales of August* was a very courageous film to make in this day. No sex. No violence. It was just a simple story of two aging sisters. But I suppose the biggest reason I accepted the offer to be in this film was that I could spend some time once more in my beloved state of Maine.

Oddly enough, on my flight to Maine I discovered that my ex-husband, Gary Merrill, was on the plane. We had not seen each other for many years, so it was a rather odd coincidence. Whenever I tell this story to my friends, they ask, "What did you do? Did you talk to each other?" Of course we did. I went and sat down in the seat beside him. It was a very one-sided conversation, however, as he was reading a book and continued to do so. So I gradually faded away and went back to my seat. We managed to avoid the press at the Portland airport.

The premier showing of *Whales of August* was, interestingly enough, in Paris during the same time Kathryn and I went to the Deauville Film Festival where they were honoring my film career. I had been invited to the festival other times, but since Kath also lived in Paris and was working with a group of people from Nelson Entertainment on the promotion of the film, I agreed, knowing she would be there months ahead organizing all the events I would be a part of. They had set up the press to include interviewers from about twenty-five countries. Kathryn planned a more than successful press conference, unlike anything Deauville had seen before.

In preparation for my arrival at the festival, my suite had been completely re-decorated in my favorite, American Beauty red. An extravagant gesture. When I departed from Deauville, the suite was dedicated to me by Monsieur and Madame Barrier, the owners of the Hotel Royal in a very charming ceremony. There was the customary ribbon for me to cut and a plaque on the suite door with my name on it. I have been told a huge photograph of me taken at this dedication now hangs on the wall of the suite. Some of my friends now jokingly call me "suite Bette Davis."

At the former Strassburger mansion, there was a cocktail party given in my honor by the mayor of Deauville, Anne D'Ornano. I was presented with La Croix De Chevalier de la Legion d'Honneur medal, regarded as one of the highest civilian medals the French government can bestow. Monsieur Francois Leotard, the French Minister of Culture and Communications, flew from Paris to present me with this medal. His presentation speech was most flattering. He spoke about my contributions to audiences during my career, even naming some of my films. Somehow, one is doubly flattered when praise for one's work comes from another country.

The closing event of the festival was a tribute dinner in my honor, which Kathryn had been working on for many weeks. It was the most impressive gala affair that Deauville and I had ever seen. The dinner took place in the ballroom of The Hotel Royal instead of the nearby casino, the usual site for such occasions. The black-tie, sit-down, five-course dinner for 150 guests was another first for the festival, as was the dais where all the actors at the festival were invited to sit. There was a champagne waterfall, and the waiters were all in sixteenth-century costumes and powdered wigs. And at one point, about six waiters entered the ballroom with a six-tier, seven-foot-high cake. The names of many of my films were written on the cake in icing. It was an absolutely magnificent sight.

The music included some of the Max Steiner scores from my films. Kath talked me into singing the song from *Baby Jane*, "I've Written a Letter to Daddy," feeling it would make the atmosphere less formal so the dinner guests would be less intimidated meeting me. Later that evening I went to each and every table to say hello to the guests and thank them for coming.

Topping off the dinner at the end of the evening was a wonderful surprise. Through the long glass doors of the ball room I saw a sudden burst of the most magnificent fireworks coming down like a beautiful waterfall, followed by the spelling of my name in lights.

I have never been so overcome. The fireworks received a standing ovation from the dinner guests. I was so proud of Kathryn's success in planning and executing this entire evening

hat I gave her a big hug. I think there were even a few tears
n my eyes. I was particularly proud because at every turn she
had run into obstacles. It was an evening never to be forgotten
by any guest who was there.

When we were leaving Deauville, the staff of The Hotel
Royal all lined up at the door, some with roses to give me. It
was a most rewarding and flattering moment.

CHAPTER
24

During the winter of 1987, I was sent a script by the writer
producer/director Larry Cohen, titled *The Wicked Stepmother*
There was something very familiar about this script that made
me feel I had read it before. My agent told me I had, and that
I had turned it down. How I wish I had turned it down the
second time! I had a meeting with Mr. Cohen, who seemed to
be a very pleasant gentleman. Again, how wrong I was. Special
effects were very popular in films at the time, and *The Wicked
Stepmother* was full of them. Partly for this reason and partly
because Mr. Cohen suggested that Kathryn be the associate
producer on the film, I accepted the part. I was thrilled for
Kathryn. Certainly by now she was very knowledgeable about
the industry and capable of doing the job.

We started the film on my eightieth birthday. I felt the timing
was one of Mr. Cohen's friendlier gestures. But as to Kathryn's
being made an associate producer, it was a complete farce.
Mr. Cohen would not listen to any of her ideas. Kathryn and
I both fought to make this a good, quality picture. But it was
not to be.

Mr. Cohen's direction of me in the role of Miranda was even
more of a farce. I was not allowed to express any opinion about
my performance. I believe this was the first time in my career
that a director refused to listen to anything I suggested. I had

THE LONELY LIFE   269

met my waterloo. Every step we took in a scene was planned for where he wanted the camera to go.

After four days of shooting, I had to go to my dentist so Kathryn and I went to New York, supposedly just for the weekend. Before we left we saw all the film that had been shot that first week, both with and without me. Kathryn and I were in a state of shock. The film without me was full of tasteless, vulgar moments that had nothing to do with the original script at all. The photography was appalling. At my age, it could have been very damaging to any future offers for a film if these scenes were shown. The more I thought about it, the more I realized there was no way I could return to finish the film without causing serious damage to my career. As each day went by, the dread of finishing the film became worse and worse, until I finally realized I had to have the courage to walk. And I did.

After many dental appointments and some dental surgery, my dentist informed me that he had done all he could, so Kath and I returned to California. The producer was informed that I was not finishing the picture, nor was Kathryn. We later heard that Mr. Cohen was going to finish the film without me.

Over a year later, Kath and I saw the finished product. If ever I had any doubt about my decision to walk from the film it was put to rest. I felt my decision was justified, and I was glad that Kathryn, as always, had been a terrific backup, telling me to stick to my guns. I always felt I owed my audience honesty, and I didn't want to make a film unless I believed in it.

Prior to leaving *The Wicked Stepmother* I had been invited to receive yet another award, this time from the Italians. The Campoine d'Italia Merit of Achievement Award was presented to seven other recipients: Gene Kelly, Robert Mitchum, Joseph Cotten, Ali MacGraw, June Allyson, Samantha Eggar, and Glenn Ford. Now with *The Wicked Stepmother* out of the way Kathryn and I were free to go. We all stayed at the beautiful Villa D'Este Hotel at Lake Como, where we laughed with relief that we were not on the set.

In 1987, I received yet another award, which was one of the most exciting events in these years. The Kennedy Center Award is given each year to artists in many different fields. I had wanted for so long to win this prestigious award, and finally I had. Each year when the Kennedy Center Committee in Washington sent out a brochure asking for suggestions as to who should receive the award for that year, I would write in large letters ME! It often crossed my mind that perhaps I had never been chosen because I was a Democrat and the White House was Republican.

Ronald Reagan being the President the year I won made it a double joy, because we had both been contract players at Warner Bros. It was interesting to see him in the capacity of President. He was a most charming host and most flattering in his remarks about all of us. In the east room of the White House, prior to the main ceremony in the theatre, President Reagan said in his speech, "Bette Davis, if I'd gotten roles as good as yours and been able to do them as good as you, I might never have left Hollywood."

Kathryn, sitting in the President's anteroom adjacent to his box, was most impressed and proud of me when he told her the story of our working together on the film *Dark Victory*. He said that my constant fighting for the best of everything in the films I made inspired him to fight for some of the best decisions he had made.

I was thrilled to hear Angela Lansbury's speech about me and my career. Her brilliant delivery was inspiring to watch and listen to. Walter Cronkite, Hume Cronyn, Jessica Tandy and Jimmy Stewart also honored me by appearing on stage. I was overcome by the praise from one and all.

The other winners included another Davis—Sammy by name—as well as Perry Como, Alwin Nikolais, and Nathan Milstein. I always like being the only woman surrounded by a group of men and in this case, such talented men.

A dinner for the honorees was given by the Secretary of State and Mrs. George Shultz. Dining in the elegant State Department room was like dining in a king's palace.

Standing in the receiving line along with the Secretary of State and Mrs. Shultz was Senator Edward Kennedy. I was thrilled to see him once again, and even more thrilled when he gave a speech that evening at the dinner, especially since it was, I am told, the first time in seven years that he had spoken from a podium. In his speech he talked about the founding of the Kennedy Center and thanked me for my loyalty and friendship to the Kennedys throughout the years.

I was also honored by a most incredible speech by David Hartman, a man I so enormously had admired for so many years. It was wonderful to see so many talented people from so many different professions all in one room. The Kennedy Center Award now holds a very prominent place in my home.

The Film Society of Lincoln Center also gives a most coveted and prestigious award each year to one person from the arts, featuring a tribute evening in the recipient's honor at Lincoln Center in New York City. Year after year I was disappointed not to be chosen, but finally in 1988 I was.

Kathryn had moved back from Paris and was very instrumental in planning the publicity for my evening at Lincoln Center. There was not a day that went by in the week preceding the award ceremony that I did not do some major newspaper interview or talk show.

It is hard to describe the enormity of the fantastic event that took place in my honor. There was not an empty seat in the 2,700-seat Avery Fisher Hall. I was told this was the only time they had a sold-out house for The Film Society's awards ceremony. The film footage shown covered my sixty-year career in films, starting with scenes from my first film, *Bad Sister*, and extending to my most recent, *The Whales of August*. It truly was a work of art in both the editing and the choice of films.

Jimmy Stewart, Ann-Margret, Geraldine Fitzgerald, and Joseph Mankiewicz all made speeches about me. What they said and the sincerity with which they said it made me burst with pride.

The members of the audience were from many countries, and the love and admiration I felt in the theatre that night was overwhelming. The cheers and applause as I rose to make my acceptance speech was overpowering. I felt very chic in my Patrick Kelly evening dress, designed especially for this occasion. I had been given a beautiful set of pearl earrings and a bracelet for my birthday, and I wore them along with my black mink hoop headdress—a most attractive finishing touch to Patrick's dress.

All those I loved the most were at Lincoln Center that night to help me celebrate. Kathryn, Harold Schiff, my escort, my long-time friend Robert Osborne, and my son, Michael, and his wife, Chou. The festivities ended with a charming buffet dinner at Tavern on the Green.

CHAPTER
25

The last gala event in this catch-up of *The Lonely Life* is another award evening in my honor. For this event, Kath and I traveled to San Sebastían, Spain. The San Sebastían International Film Festival each year gives a special award called The Donostia, the city's name in the Basque language. It is presented to an actor or actress for lifetime achievement in the motion picture industry—a most prestigious award. I felt doubly honored when I was told I would be the first woman to ever receive it.

Kath and I had less than three weeks to make all the necessary preparations—a very short notice for all the work that goes into planning my appearances, interviews, and press conferences, not to mention clothes, makeup and the award evening itself. I decided to telephone Gregory Peck who was a past recipient of this distinguished award. He assured me the festival was superbly organized.

On September 13, 1989, Kath and I left California for Spain on M.G.M. Grand Air with our first destination New York. Making the headline news that day was whether or not the Senate would pass a bill to ban smoking on all domestic flights. Needless to say, the outcome had not yet been decided and I was overjoyed and relieved. Kath and I couldn't help but wonder, Would this be the last time time I'd be allowed to smoke on a U.S. flight? We laughed as I took out my cigarettes and thoroughly enjoyed our five-hour flight.

We stayed over in New York at the charming Plaza Athene Hotel. The next day, we were leaving for Paris when it started to rain. I adore the rain and have always felt it brings me good luck. "We're off to a good start," I told Kath. It was an evening flight and since I've never been able to sleep on planes, we spent the night going over final details. Two weary travelers arrived at Paris' Residence Maxim's knowing that makeup sessions would begin at six the next morning.

From Paris, we boarded yet another plane and flew to Biarritz. There are easier ways to travel to Spain; however, the festival insisted my first appearance in their country be in San Sebastían. The only way to get there is either via England or France and then drive over the border. We chose France.

When we arrived at the tiny airport in Biarritz, to my utter amazement I was greeted by a small marching band from the Basque region. They all wore their traditional Basque costumes. A small gathering of town folk greeted me, and some of the children and mothers presented me with flowers. I was deeply touched. I went over to thank each and every band member before leaving to embark on a beautiful hour drive through the Basque countryside into the stunning seaport of San Sebastían.

After three days of traveling we had finally reached our destination: the lovely Victorian-style Hotel Maria Christina. I was overcome by the mobs of people and press waiting in ninety-degree weather to greet me. I was later told they had waited more than two hours as there seemed to be a confusion about my arrival time. I felt horrified they had waited so long. I am proud of the fact I have a reputation for not being late— usually I'm always a few minutes early. It's partly from my Yankee upbringing—showing good manners—and from my theatre training. You could never be more than five minutes late, or you were fired.

For three days I was not seen by the press. They were puzzled as to what I was doing up in my room. Although Kath had prepared everything in California, it was important now to see the actual setup and make the necessary changes—which she did. We also had to meet with the director of the festival, Diego Galan, the stage director for the award evenings, my translator,

my makeup man, and the Secretary General, Pilar Olascoaga,
a most efficient woman.

The press conference was held at the Hotel Maria Christina
in their grand salon "excelsion" for 200 members of the international press. I was asked some unusual, interesting, and,
at times, stimulating questions from the press. Here are some
excerpts from my free-for-all press conference:

> "Miss Davis, rumor had it that a few years ago, you
> were offered a part where you had to be naked on the
> screen."

> I replied, "A few years ago, Mon Dieu! I am now in
> my eighties, a few years ago, I was in my seventies. I
> don't think anybody would want to see me naked at sev-
> enty years old. [The audience laughed] No. Never in the
> 40s, 50s, or 60s were we asked to be naked on the screen.
> Today's actresses are often asked and I think it's horri-
> ble."

> "Miss Davis, where have you been naughtier: on the
> screen or in real life?"

> "Na-ugh-tier?" I replied. After taking a long pause, I
> said, "fifty-fifty," and the audience roared.

> "Miss Davis, you've given a good part of your life to
> the cinema. What do you expect from the cinema?"

> "Well, on the practical side," I said, "to make a good
> living is very good. And I expect and hope for good
> scripts. I hope also that I may always be acting. I love
> my work. That's what I get from the cinema, always the
> love of it."

> "What is your opinion about the director William Wy-
> ler?"

> "William Wyler, in my opinion, was, will be for all
> time, the greatest director Hollywood ever had. I owe my
> career in great part to his direction of me in *Jezebel*, *The
> Little Foxes* and *The Letter*. I would have had a much less
> career without having been directed by Mr. Wyler. No
> question about it. I also think his film *The Best Years of
> Our Lives* is truly one of the greatest films ever made."

> "What was the atmosphere like on the set of *All About
> Eve?*"

"It was a completely joyous film to make. Everybody in the cast was 'so right' for their characters. We all had a great feeling that we were doing something 'special.' I was very fortunate to play Margot. Originally, Claudette Colbert was cast to play Margot Channing. I was sorry for her that she hurt her back. I was most fortunate to be her replacement. It was a marvelous experience."

"What effect did the blacklist have on Hollywood in the fifties?"

"They were the most horrible and tragic years. It was a disgrace. All our talented writers were gone. We had no scripts. They [the writers] were all in prison and not all of them were party members. It was like Hitler, Germany. You could not believe it was America. The Hollywood Ten. It was a disastrous thing. After they came out of prison, they all took new names. Some of them even won Oscars and nobody knew who they were because they could not use their own names. They weren't allowed to. It was just a terrible disgrace."

"What advice would you give today to someone who wants to become an actor or actress?"

"Well, I think the first step is to be so sure themselves that this is what they want to do. Know that it is not an easy profession—one of the most difficult there is—and to not ask for advice. Just decide that is what they want to do. That is the first advice I always give to anyone who asks me this question."

The next question was asked to the director of the festival

"Why has it taken the festival so long to give Miss Davis this award?" the reporter asked.

"Big dreams take a long time in coming true and this year we've reached the tops," the director replied, flattering me.

"*Muchas gracias*," I said. "Time was getting short and I'm glad they invited me when they did, otherwise I might never have been around to come."

"Miss Davis, out of all the famous people, which one would you like to accompany you on stage when you receive your Donostia Award?"

"Well, regarding famous actors—I have to be very blunt and say I am very honored to be going on that stage alone. Yes. Very honored."

The audience then screamed with laughter shouting, "Bravo, Bravo!"

"Miss Davis, in your career, have you been in a similar situation as Margo Channing? And in all the characters you have played, which character is most like you personally? And which character was the hardest for you to play?"

"Three questions. Tres preguntas. Well, as for Margot Channing, no," I responded. "She was a totally different kind of actress than I. Her frenzy about her age—I have never gone through this at all. I would have liked to stay young but even at a young age I played old parts. Queen Elizabeth, for example. I was thirty playing a character of sixty. No, Margot and I were totally different types of actresses. The character I feel that is most like me in real life was Kit Marlowe in *Old Acquaintance*. No question about it. We were definitely the same kind of woman. The character I feel which was the hardest to play—Aggie Hurley in *The Catered Affair*. She was a housewife from the Bronx. Without doubt, she was one of the most against-type characters I ever attempted. *The Catered Affair* will always be one of my proudest efforts as an actress."

"Miss Davis, out of all the films you've made, who was your favorite actor to work with?"

"I never really had a favorite actor. In the early pictures, I made many with Leslie Howard, George Brent. Both very fine actors. I always felt privileged to work with Claude Rains. He was truly a great actor. I wish I could have also made a great film with Spencer Tracy, but he was Metro Goldwyn Mayer, and I was Warner Bros. The studios at that time never really let us work with actors from the other studios. I think he was our greatest American actor for variety. I feel Hollywood's greatest American personality actors were, of course, John Wayne, Clark Gable, Gary Cooper. Mag-ni-fic, all of them, wonderful personalities but Tracy, the greatest American actor, I think."

"Miss Davis, a great many people feel the most important thing in life is love or the absence of love.''

"What kind of love?'' I asked. ''There are many kinds of love—love of family, marriage, friends.''

"Love between a man and a woman,'' the reporter clarified.

"Well, I have to admit, that was not my most successful area in life, not at all. But I have to add to that, it is not easy for a famous woman to have a successful marriage. A man may think beforehand that being married to a famous woman would not be difficult and he would not mind. But he does, and it cannot be helped. In my case my marriages were not successful.''

"Miss Davis, because you have won two Oscars and were nominated for eleven, what is your opinion on giving prizes and what are their purposes?''

"I call my awards my blood, sweat, and tears. If you are admired enough in your work to receive an award and to be given a lifetime achievement award, it is, of course, a great honor. One never does get over that. Never. I am very grateful and have been very fortunate to have received many during my long years.''

"Miss Davis, what do you think of the colorization of films today?''

"Colorization is breaking the hearts of many of us today. I saw *Dark Victory* with colorization. All the good taste in clothes, the good taste of the set decorator, are all gone. It just breaks your heart. I don't know if it will ever be stopped. One could really cry to have the modern generation see a film colorized like *Dark Victory*. Some films are made only to be in black and white. You can change the whole story, the impact it might have, the scoring of the music might have been different if we knew it was going to be colorized. I think it's terrible that we have no protection from this. Truly breaks your heart.''

On Friday, September 22, I was presented with the Donostia Award by the mayor of San Sebastían, Xavier Albistur. The evening started at 9:00 P.M. There were heavy thunder showers all day. I felt sorry for the people who had worked so hard on this festival. They had planned an enormous screen to be set up in the plaza square for the public, who could not get into

the theatre, to watch the evening's event. I started to feel that
maybe no one would show up. Kath reassured me they would.
I have always felt this way before any public appearance of
mine because the responsibility to draw a crowd is virtually on
me.

When Kath and I left the hotel for the Victoria Eugenia
Theatre, I was in disbelief at the many hundreds of people
waiting in the pouring rain to see me. The crowds went for
blocks on all sides of the streets, even the plaza square was
filled with people. I was overwhelmed. I had them stop our
car so that I could get out and shake hands with people along
the route. Pouring rain be damned. If they could take it, so
could I. A Basque marching band started to play as Kath and
I entered the gorgeous old theatre. There was a line of Basque
guards on both sides with their touching swords forming an
arch for us to walk through.

Many of the people threw flowers at my feet. Never have I
seen or had this happen to me. It truly was incredible. We were
then greeted by the city's mayor, Senor Albistur. We stood as
they had an excellent Basque dancer perform for me.

The ceremonies began with the director of the festival saying
a few words, followed by the famous Spanish actor Fernando
Rey, and then the mayor. The curtain rose to my standing at
the podium smoking a cigarette and saying, *"Buenas noches."*
The audience went wild and gave me a long standing ovation
before the mayor presented me with the Donostia Award. I
must say, it is a very handsome award, crafted in silver and it
looks very old-world European.

The next night, the closing evening of the festival, took place
at the same gorgeous theatre. La Concha de Oro, the best
picture award, is the last one presented. As I opened the envelope to name the winner, it was a tie between the film from
Bolivia, *La Nación Clandestina*, and from the United States
of America, *Homer and Eddie*.

Receiving the award from Bolivia was Jorge Sanjines and
from America was Andrej Konchalovski. When Mr. Konchalovski came up to receive his award, he got down on both
knees and knelt in front of me. I was flabbergasted, and the
audience went crazy with applause. It truly brought the house
down and was a fabulous way to end this incredible festival.

• • •

As Kath and I close this chapter now, we are looking out of our window from the Hotel Maria Christina on to the Bay of Biscay. And so ends an account of the happenings and highlights in my life since the writing of my autobiography *The Lonely Life* in 1962, until now. I will now voyage forth. Having the stars, no need to ask for the moon.

EPILOGUE:
by KATHRYN SERMAK
1990

For Miss Davis' fans, whom she always acknowledged and loved—I wanted to let you know she worked hard to finish this book and to leave you with something from her. It is for this reason, I will try and shed some light on "what happened."

She was in good spirits, excited about her book, the overwhelming adulation she had just been given in Spain, and looking forward to appearing on *The Joan Rivers Show*. She was thrilled about a new film she was to make the following year and for the first time in ages, life was running too smoothly. She even said it: "Kath, this is all too perfect."

Miss D. purposely planned an extra week in Spain following the festival to put the finishing touches on this book. The schedule of the festival at San Sebastián had been terribly demanding. On the closing night, I could see she was tiring. She had held up like the trooper she was for all her public appearances but, very unusual for her, she canceled out on the gala dinner following the award show and scheduled at one in the morning. Instead, she returned to the hotel at about eleven.

During the next few days, time so carefully set aside to complete this book was interrupted by television interviews and dinners with local dignitaries. But then she began having chills and fatigue. One local doctor pronounced it a flu bug, but actually seemed more enchanted about Miss D. and her films than concerned about her health. When we spoke long distance with Harold Schiff ("the father of the family," as she always referred to him), she told him not to worry, she would see him in a few days in New York. During this time we continued with the work on her book.

A few days later, Miss D. awakened with a fever, too weak to get out of bed. It seemed quite possible she had fully developed the flu. Due to her recent radiation treatment for cancer, we were very concerned. There were consultations with other doctors, her medical team in California, and Mr. Schiff. It was becoming more and more obvious she could not make that long journey back to the United States, and that she should be hospitalized as soon as possible. The decision was made to go to the American hospital in Paris, because it was the closest hospital equipped to care for her specific needs. Being too ill to board a commercial airline, we had to use an air ambulance and hired a Lear jet for the trip.

We left Spain on Tuesday, October 3. Impeccably dressed and groomed as always, Miss D., despite the illness, was excited about her first flight on a private Lear jet. The crew stepped off the plane, somewhat amazed to see Bette Davis. Very few people knew our plans. Also, they were expecting someone in a far worse condition. They brought out a stretcher which Miss D. had no intention of using, nor did she. Once airborne, she was curious about the plane, its next destination, surprised they had come from Switzerland and quipped, "Don't tell me what this is costing."

Although we had never been in the American hospital, such places were not new to us. As soon as the doctors completed their first round of tests, we set about trying to make the room as homey as possible. The hospital brought in a cot and it was like we were back in New York Hospital.

Tests continued on Wednesday, and we were told Miss D. was making progress and that if it kept up we could expect to be going home in about four days. She spoke to her son, Michael, who wanted to come visit her, but Miss D. told him she preferred to see him when she got back to the United States. That evening, Miss D. grew very weak, and the tests results that came in the following day were shocking. From thinking we were headed home in a few days, suddenly the situation was grave. The doctors confirmed the worst—the cancer was out of control.

On Friday morning, October 6, we woke to a beautiful autumn day. Miss D. said she preferred we have this day alone, which the nurses respected. We spoke about life, the unbelievable situation we were in, the years we had spent together, and all the great fun we've had. She spoke of those she loved dearly, of her son, Michael, and her great friend, Harold Schiff, who was always there for both of us, through thick and thin, no matter what hour of the day or night; he was our rock. It was late afternoon when I mentioned that dark clouds were gathering. Miss D. smiled.

During one of the doctor's visits that day, she actually apologized for having been a burden to him, for arriving so ill and then dying in his hospital. It took all her energy to say the things she so badly wanted to say. The doctors administered morphine to get rid of the pain and hoped this would induce sleeping. They were amazed that in spite of heavy doses she remained totally conscious and cognizant.

Around eleven P.M., it started to rain in earnest. Miss D. dismissed even the private night duty nurse, asking that we be alone. She had me sit on her bed, holding her hand, and said a few things to me, and I to her. Shortly after that, she passed away.

The next four days were consumed with the normal complications that surround the death of a celebrity in a foreign country. It was decided by transatlantic conference that there was too much to be done stateside. Mr. Schiff would have to remain in New York to handle the legal and political red tape and I would manage the Paris end. With the help of a friend, I managed to get through the overpowering task of dealing with hospitals, embassies, mortuaries, the press, transportation etc.

On Wednesday, October 11, I brought Miss D. back on an Air France flight direct to Los Angeles. I had chosen the most elegant casket in Paris. Its title was most appropriate, "The Empress." It was long, rectangular, mahogany—heavily carved with gold scrolling on the sides. She was dressed in a black evening gown similar to the one she wore at The Lincoln Center gala in April. I would like you to know she was beautiful, her face serene and at peace. As the plane was taking off, it started to rain again. I have never had a great affinity for rain, but this time I found it to be a great comfort.

Back in Los Angeles Mr. Schiff was at the airport to meet me, along with Mike and his wife, Chou, and Miss D.'s long-time friend Robin Brown. Mr. Schiff had completed all the private funeral arrangements for the following morning. Miss D. had long-ago arranged her burial site, a family crypt. It is at Forest Lawn Memorial Park, high on a hill, overlooking Warner Bros. Studio. There is a classic roman statue of a woman, standing about six-feet tall, on the marble sarcophagus. Miss D. had always specified a very private funeral with only family members who loved her and a few designated friends. She wanted no press media, photographers, or reporters. This she was given. At the service, her son, Michael, spoke tenderly of his mother and his words touched each and everyone there. Her casket was covered with a blanket of white roses and gardenias, her favorites. On October 12, 1989, at 11:00 A.M., Miss D. was buried next to her beloved mother and sister. As per her wishes, on the crypt it says, "Bette Davis. She did it the hard way."

There have been many false rumors and stories printed pertaining to her last days. I feel it is important to set the record straight. Miss Davis left for Spain feeling fine and with the full approval of her doctors. In the summer of 1989 she underwent radiation treatment for cancer. Only her doctors and those closest to her knew this, not even the nurses were informed. Word that she had given up and was starving herself are totally false, and hurt her deeply. For the many who asked about her daughter, B.D.—no, they never spoke after the publication of B.D.'s book, nor did Miss D. mention her during those last days. As to her retarded daughter, Margot—much earlier Miss Davis and Gary Merrill had made legal and financial arrangements for Margot's permanent care. Her son, Michael, and his family were always in close touch. The deep love and mutual respect were ever present and brought her great joy.

MEMORIAL

"The great power of Bette Davis was that she always knew who she was. She always knew that man or woman, she had an obligation, a power, and a responsibility to herself and her audiences."

—James Woods

"An extraordinary legacy of acting in the twentieth century by a real master of her craft, Miss Bette Davis."

—Angela Lansbury

"Real Bette Davis—five feet two inches of dynamite. She was a New England Yankee: disciplined, honest, hardworker, never puts on airs, tells it like it is, always gives you one hundred percent. Especially these last few years she has shown, it seems, extra strength, courage and dignity, and she can always laugh at herself."

—David Hartman

Miss D.'s memorial tribute was by invitation for her friends and co-workers in the industry. The hungry requests by fans for more information concerning the memorial is why the following paragraphs will be in detail. I would like to give you a bit of the background as to why things were done the way they were, and feel the article from *The Hollywood Reporter* states the rest.

285

• • •

The Bette Davis Memorial Tribute was held November 2, 7:00 P.M. at Warner Bros. Studios, Sound Stage 18. Miss D. liked to be "the first," and her memorial was the first to be held on a sound stage. It seemed most appropriate to have it at Warner Bros., the studio she was under contract to for eighteen years, and Sound Stage 18 was where she had made such films as *Kid Galahad*, *The Letter*, *Now Voyager*, *Old Acquaintance*, *A Stolen Life*, and *Winter Meeting*.

Miss D. had often told me one of the things she liked about Warner Bros. was it being a "workers" studio, unlike the others at that time who pampered their stars with diamonds and jewels. She only preferred a good script. She had also stated definitively, after attending other Hollywood memorials, that she didn't want a circus. No flashing cameras, no endless streams of flowery personal tributes.

The atmosphere would be that of a working film set and that was the look we tried to achieve for her. The set was decorated with old film props. From lights, cameras, to the original clock that was used in the film, *Mr. Skeffington*. A platform was built, and in the center of it stood an old podium. It was outlined by a garland of gardenias, Miss D.'s favorite flower. Above the podium hung a giant screen for projecting the film clips from the Lincoln Center tribute and the A.F.I. montage "Faces of Bette Davis." To either side of this screen, suspended in midair, hung enormous blow-up–size photographs of Miss D. from her films *Jezebel*, *Now Voyager*, *What Ever Happened to Baby Jane*, and two from *All This and Heaven Too*. The guests sat on standard folding wooden chairs, typical of what the crews use, and entered to background music scored by Max Steiner from some of Miss D.'s films. Projected on the huge screen was a black and white still photograph of Miss D. from *All About Eve*. The following is a reprint of *The Hollywood Reporter* article by Paula Parisi [on November 6, 1989]. It is to give you an essence of the evening, and the outstanding warmth, humor and dignity which David Hartman, as emcee, James Woods, and Angela Lansbury brought to the 400 friends and co-workers who came to pay their respects. They gave us both great good laughs and tears.

TEARS AND LAUGHTER ABOUND
AS INDUSTRY REMEMBERS DAVIS

The stars twinkled above and onscreen at Warner Bros.'
Stage 18 on Thursday night as 500 friends and fans of the
late Bette Davis gathered to pay tribute to the legendary
performer, who died Oct. 6 in Paris. She was eighty-one.

Clint Eastwood, Ann-Margret, Linda Gray, and Robert
Wagner were among those who attended the touching
ceremony.

Tears streamed and laughter tinkled through the cav-
ernous stage as clips from Davis' most scintillating performances unspooled in a half-hour film presentation,
which included scenes from *All About Eve, Jezebel, Bordertown, It's Love I'm After*, and many more of her films.

Large photos of Davis were ethereally suspended in
midair on visible wires—the only decorations on the outsized stage, where the actress shot six films, including
Now Voyager and *Old Acquaintance*.

The memorial tribute, themed "I Wish You Love,"
was hosted by David Hartman, James Woods, and Angela
Lansbury.

Attendees also included Lindsay Wagner, George Ham-
ilton, Jill St. John, Roddy McDowall, Vincent Price, Ste-
fanie Powers, Kim Carnes, Glenn Ford, Julius Epstein,
Vincent Sherman, Rudi Fehr, Joan Leslie, Janis Paige,
Anna Lee, Lionel Stander, Carol Kane, Natalie Schafer,
Ralph Edwards, Lisa Hartman, Diane Baker, Charles
Pierce, Betty Lynn, Sidney Guiluroff, and Teresa Wright.

Woods delivered a powerful tribute to the actress,
whose moving performances he said, "had the power to
rip the screen apart." Woods, who worked with Davis in
The Disappearance of Amy and took the portrait that graces
her book *This 'n That*, said seeing the actress in *Now
Voyager* as a youngster influenced his own decision to
pursue acting.

He lauded Davis' portrayal of the emotionally distraught
heroine of that 1940's film, calling it "poetry on the screen
like Yeats might write," asking, "What kind of courage
does it take to open the soul so deeply?"

"There are two kinds of people, those of us who write poetry, and those of us who read it," Woods observed.

"Even those of us who couldn't read poetry, read her work with some amount of genius, simply because of the beauty with which she'd written it."

He praised the indomitable Davis' early fight for women's rights as she struggled for roles she wanted in the male-dominated studio system.

"Thank God she worked as hard as she did in her prime," said Lansbury, who bashfully admitted that when she started out, people referred to her as "a young Bette Davis."

"She has bequeathed to us all an astonishing legacy," Lansbury said, "bravura acting of the first order."

Hartman, who had emcee duties throughout the ninety-minute event, read a laudatory telegram sent by President and Mrs. Bush. "America loved her," the Bushes acknowledged. "How fortunate our nation is to have her contribution to the art of film making."

On screen, Davis often played characters as sharp-tongued and uncompromising as she was known to be offscreen. Her talent as a performer was matched by her temper; her wit was sharp and her patience short.

The ceremony came to a solemn close as the silvery images onscreen faded to gray for a few brief moments.

Then, a blazing beautiful color still of the actress froze onscreen, accompanied by the bittersweet lyrics to "I Wish You Love," sung by the actress herself, from the record album "Bette Davis Sings." Woods summed up the sadness and awe of the evening when he said, "For those of us who are going to be there, and those of us who are there now—up in heaven they're saying, 'Buckle your seat belts, it's going to be a bumpy eternity.'"

It was her wish that the song "I Wish You Love" be played as her last farewell to those she loved:

> Goodbye,
> No use leading with our chins,
> This is where our story ends,
> Never lovers, ever friends,

Goodbye,
Let our hearts call it a day,
But before you walk away,
I sincerely want to say:

I wish you bluebirds in the spring
To give your heart a song to sing
And then a kiss, but more than this
I wish you love.

And in July, a lemonade,
To cool you in some leafy glade;
I wish you health and more than wealth,
I wish you love.

My breaking heart and I agree
That you and I could never be,
So with my best, my very best,
I set you free.

I wish you shelter from the storm,
A cozy fire to keep you warm;
But most of all, when snowflakes fall
I wish you love.

As the song finished, Robert Wagner got up and turned on a
work light, which is how a film set is left at the end of a day's
shooting. Each guest was handed one white rose as they left,
in memory of an irreplaceable woman.

K.S., 1990

ACKNOWLEDGMENTS
by K.S.

Once again, I would like to thank all those people who worked on Miss D.'s memorial. Harold Schiff, who had final approval on all the arrangements, and for his tireless support. Michael Black, Miss D.'s agent, who originated the concept of having it at Warner Bros. and for immediately putting the wheels in motion. Warner Bros. and Burbank Studios for graciously freeing Sound Stage 18, and for making available over one hundred of their very skilled and professional staff. They also most generously assumed all expenses. George Schaefer, who assisted me and gave of his time and expertise in bringing all the elements together. My thanks to our invaluable first assistant director, John Pore. To David Hartman and Robert Wagner, who not only participated in the evening but were supportive in its production. Also, to Angela Lansbury and James Woods for their brilliant and touching speeches.

Thank you to Wendy Keyes for her superb job on the film clips from Lincoln Center and to the A.F.I. for giving me permission to use the montage "Faces of Bette Davis" from their 1977 tribute evening. To Don Ovens, for the many hours he spent editing and compiling the perfect arrangement of Miss D.'s film music. Arturo's flowers for donating, out of love to Miss D., 500 beautiful white roses. Michael Anderson, for providing the memorial cards on such a short notice. Roddy

McDowall, Robert Osborne, Jose Eber, Marvin Paige, Jill St. John, Michael Black, the Sermak family and Helen de Werd for their enormous support. And thank you to my helpers: Matt Hanover, Jim Lichnerwez, Roger Martin, John Smith and Ralph Zeek who found no task too menial, and for the hundreds of letters, phone calls and messages of appreciation after the memorial.

May 21, 1990.

Dear Mother,

As I write this letter it seems as if you are still here to talk to me, help me and guide me through life. But you are not, and I miss you terribly.

You will always be with me. My life was shaped by you. You were tough yet fair, honest, a perfectionist. Your desire to excel in your profession was unmatched. At home we had our different moments — what family doesn't? But the warm and loving times are those that stand out in my memory. You always wanted me to be the best and you always wanted the best for me.

Thank you for everything. My love forever.

Mike